The
Treasure Hunter
of Santiago

'WHERE IN the whole cycle of romance shall we find anything more wild, grotesque, and sad, than the easily-authenticated history of Benedict Mol, the treasure-digger of Saint James?'

— George Borrow, *The Bible in Spain*, 1843

The
Treasure Hunter
of
Santiago

Peter Missler

DURRANT PUBLISHING

Gabicóte Publication nº 2

Published in 2010 by Durrant Publishing, Norfolk

Paperback ISBN 978-1-905946-22–8
Hardback ISBN 978-1-905946-23–5
ePub ISBN 978-1-905946-24–2

Cover illustration: *The Silver of Saint James* by Francisca Shilova
For further paintings and illustrations by Ms Shilova,
see D-Art Francisca on http://www.xs4all.nl/~privet/

The text of this book is revision 2010.01

**This study was published with the generous backing
and support of the George Borrow Trust.**

∞ The paper used in this publication meets the minimum
requirements of the American National Standard for Information
Sciences—Permanence of Paper for Printed Library Materials,
ANSI Z39.48–1992. The paper is acid-free and lignin-free.

Printed and bound by Lightning Source.

This is a 'Print-On-Demand' book by Durrant Publishing
http://www.durrantpublishing.co.uk/
It may be ordered on-line at Amazon, or obtained through special
order at most bookshops.

For Ann Ridler

A Borrovian Treasure in her own right

Contents

Prologue 1

I The Vagrant

1 The Carlist Civil War 7
2 George Borrow: the Genius in a Nutshell 11
3 Benedict Mol 15
4 Of Truth, Mistrust and Treasure Hunts 19

II The Looters

5 The Storm of Andoche Junot 29
6 Lies and Looters 39
7 The French Connection 46
8 Soult in Oporto 50
9 The Silver of Saint James 63
10 Red Herring, *Rara Avis* 73

III The Search

11 Narrative Fraud 91
12 The City of Santiago 93
13 The Pauper from the Machine 101
14 Canon and Blunderbuss 108
15 A *Zahori* in the *Cárcel de Corte* 115
16 His Excellency Alejandro Mon 122
17 A Farewell in Madrid 128
18 The Chapel of San Roque 131
19 The Opulent Cesspool 136

IV The Aftermath

  20 The Fall of Mon 147

  21 The Spanish Twilight 156

  22 The Treasure of Ney 163

  23 The Grim Reaper 173

Epilogue 177

Appendices

  1 From George Borrow's *The Bible in Spain*, chapter 42 185

  2 Press reports and other primary sources 189

Bibliography 197

Index 219

Acknowledgements 223

Illustrations *(pp 77–88)*

1. George Borrow
2. Manuel Godoy
3. Andoche Junot
4. Nicolas Soult
5. Michel Ney
6. Sir John Moore
7. Memorial plaque to Moore
8. The tomb of Moore in Coruña
9. Oporto: the place of the bridge of boats over the Douro
10. The *Altar to the Martyrs of 1809* on the Douro quay
11. Santiago: the spot of the Inquisition Palace
12. Santiago seen from the Santa Susana mountain
13. Borrow's Oviedo *posada*
14. The Alameda of Santiago
15. Ground plan of the San Roque complex
16. The San Roque chapel from the north
17. The San Roque procession of August 16th
18. The San Roque statue above the chapel door
19. Cosme and Damian above the hospital entrance
20. The *Hospitalillo de San Roque* from the south
21. The patio of the *Hospitalillo de San Roque*
22. 'Dig Here!'
23. The inside of a Spanish prison
24. Front page of the *Eco del Comercio* n° 1,584
25. Baldomero Espartero
26. Jeronimo Valdés
27. The church of San Martiño of Laraño
28. The chapel of Santa Susana at Santiago
29. Alejandro Mon

Maps

Map 1. Galicia and Northern Portugal 38
Map 2. Oporto in 1809 59
Map 3. Santiago in the 1830s. 94

Map 1 is from the 1838 map of Spain and Portugal produced by the Society for the Diffusion of Useful Knowledge. Our thanks to David Rumsey for permission to use his digital copy of the map in the illustration. http://www.davidrumsey.com/

Prologue

I N EARLY August of 1838, right in the middle of the First Carlist Civil War, an outlandish figure arrived with the weekly mail coach at Santiago de Compostela, the ancient pilgrimage town in the far north-western corner of Spain. He was a corpulent, burly old man of some sixty or seventy years of age, with hectic, livid blue eyes and the ruddy complexion of a blond Middle European. His dress, though expensive and well-made, was the oddest of possible outfits. It was entirely cut from bright green cloth, and topped by a large-brimmed, high-coned hat, while he wielded in his hand, as symbol of office, a long bamboo staff adorned with the stone image of a savage animal. In short: he looked much more like a clown or a cabaret magician than the thing he really was: a government agent on a highly delicate mission.

It would not be easy to classify this man correctly. Until only a few months earlier, one would simply have called him a tramp, since he used to beg his bread in the streets of Madrid and the hamlets of Castile. Yet it would be a little unfair to brush him aside so roughly, for his poverty was only recent, the plight that callous times visit upon the ageing poor who have outlived their utility. He had known better times in the past. Throughout a long and eventful life, he plied many a trade and earned his keep in a remarkable variety of ways. He had been a soap-boiler and a tailor, a cobbler and a horse-farrier; and before all that, he had been a soldier: a mercenary who had come to Spain many decades ago to fight for pay.

His roots were Swiss. He had been born in one of Switzerland's German cantons as the son of the local hangman, and when still in his teens had joined, like many of his compatriots, the Papal Guard in Rome. Around the turn of the century he drifted to Spain, either to serve in the Spanish Royal Bodyguard or as a soldier in Napoleon's invading armies. When the French war ended, he was demobilised, but he stayed on in the country, married to a Minorcan woman, doing odd jobs, raising some children, slowly growing old. His life had neither been remarkable nor particularly gratifying. But now, after so many decades of scraping the barrel of penury, good fortune had finally come his way. He had found himself a patron and a protector and was doing well for himself. It showed in his fabulous, extravagant costume. It showed also in his lavish manner of living. He travelled by the most expensive mail coach. He boarded in the best hotels. His pockets were filled with public money; and in his wallet he carried an official recommendation to the authorities of Santiago, which lent him considerable privileges. He had come to dig up a treasure, hidden thirty years previously by men now dead, in one of Santiago's monumental buildings. And he came to do so on behalf of no one less than the Minister of Finance himself.

The Swiss was, in short, the only official government *Zahori* who was ever employed.

I

The Vagrant

1

The Carlist Civil War

T HE DECADE of the 1830s – when the Santiago treasure hunt took
place – was not a happy time for Spain. Fernando VII, easily the
most unfit and foolish king ever to occupy the Spanish throne, had
died in late September 1833. He left as his heir a three-year old daughter,
Queen Isabel II, to whom he bequeathed a country on the brink of civil
war and a people who hated one another with the ferocity of carnivores.

Fernando had wasted his life and his reign in a foolhardy attempt to
continue the Middle Ages deep into the Age of Industry. For twenty-five
years his sole ambition had been to maintain a primitive monarchy of
absolute kingship, in which the Catholic Church was dominant and
almighty, and most political decisions were taken by a tiny clique of
royal favourites, who loitered around the king's bedchamber and in the
shadier corridors of the palace. It was a mission doomed to failure from
the start. What might still have worked a hundred years before, was
definitely out of date in the early decades of the 19th century, even in a
country as backward as Spain.

The new political ideals of the Enlightenment, already blossoming
in France, were simply irrepressible. Not even the Inquisition, now
reinvented as an instrument of censorship which specialised in smok-
ing out dangerous, forbidden books of French philosophy, was able to
stop these modern 'Liberal' ideas from filtering into the budding middle
classes. These, the moneyed merchants, the academics and the literate
artisans, dreamed of the separation of Church and State, of a unitary
system of taxes, of access by all men of merit to the seats of power, and
most of all, of a constitutional king under constant control by an elected
parliament. The *ancien régime* would hear none of it. Instead of reforms
it offered persecution. And so the Liberals could only bide their time,
and speak, in whispered tones so as not to end up in the dungeons of the
Holy Tribunal, of the glorious day that soon would dawn.

The Peninsular War, which ravaged the land between 1808 and 1814,
brought the turning point. Known to Spanish history as the 'War of

Independence', it was also to be the war of innovation. Initially, when Napoleon ordered his armies over the border, the Spanish Liberals let patriotism prevail over political programme. They fought loyally for Fernando alongside their Conservative countrymen, battling, paradoxically, against the very French armies who had come to carry in the much-desired constitutional reforms on the point of their bayonets. Yet even as they opposed the French armies, the Liberals never shed their ardent French ideals; and this led them to make a lethal miscalculation. In 1812, taking advantage of the absence of the young king – who was enjoying a pleasant exile in Talleyrand's Valençay palace – they gathered together in Cadiz, the last bastion of unoccupied Spain. There, to the jolly drumbeat of French siege-guns bombarding the town, they pushed through, blatantly against the time-honoured rules of the realm, their own radical Constitution[1]. When Fernando returned after Napoleon's defeat, he found his kingdom changed into a Constitutional democracy, which ruthlessly curbed his powers and prerogatives. To accept it was unthinkable to a man of his temperament, and, prodded by the Church and Conservative politicians, he solved the dilemma in the easiest way. During a nocturnal raid, he arrested most of the parliament and the whole Liberal leadership, locked them up in the prisons of Madrid, and declared the hated charter void.

This was the start of an ceaseless and bitter struggle between the Liberals and the Conservatives which would last for more than a century. Within a year, the first of a long succession of military uprisings took place, staged by frustrated and infuriated Liberal officers in provincial garrison towns. Most of these *pronunciamentos*, as they came to be called, were quickly suppressed and their leaders hanged or shot. But one of them, led by Rafael Riego in 1820 near Cadiz, succeeded, and a three year Liberal regime was put in place, whose leaders did everything in their power to make this experiment at democracy fail dismally. Cronyism and corruption, party infighting, arbitrary expropriations and blatant

---

1 How very paradoxical the Liberals' position really was, becomes clear when one compares this 1812 *Constitución de Cádiz* with the one which King Joseph Bonaparte granted the country as soon as the Emperor crowned him King of Spain. Except for the second article – which in the French version granted freedom of worship, and in the Cádiz Constitution imposed Roman Catholicism as the state religion – the two charters are virtually identical!

sins against the liberties of their own charter, were rampant. The ensuing anarchy gave the Conservative powers of Europe the perfect excuse to intervene. In the summer of 1823 France sent an army, which was quick to liberate the king from Liberalism and reinstate the absolute monarchy. Fernando, spiteful for having been forced to swear the constitution, installed a regime of torture, exile, incarceration and firing squads which lasted another ten years. It was to buy him neither peace in his realm nor hope of a continuation of this style of government. From abroad, the Liberals staged countless landings on the coast, in vain attempts to overthrow his tyranny by *guerrilla* warfare. Inside the realm, they took to insurrection, sabotage and letter bombs. Blood was always answered with blood; hatred generated hatred, revenge sired revenge. The country was rent asunder in irreconcilable factions which fought each other with the mindless disgust which is only found where brother turns in anger against brother.

Then Fernando fell mortally ill, and the country began to slither towards civil war. The Conservatives, eager to make the best of a bad situation, turned to the King's younger brother, the blindly pious Don Carlos Isidro, and proclaimed that under the rules of the old Salic Law, no woman could ever become Queen of the Realm as long as there was a single male heir alive in the royal family. Queen Mother Maria Cristina thereupon sought the support of the Liberals, who were waiting in the wings, impatient to regain power. They in their turn ruled that the Salic Law was no longer in force, because it had been partly, but secretly, abolished by Fernando's father in 1789. Consequently they declared three-year old Isabel the legitimate Queen of Spain, under the wings of a Liberal, constitutional government.

Within days of Fernando's death, Conservative revolts broke out all through the land. The Liberals managed to hold on to power in Madrid and to smother most of the local rebellions. But up north, in Navarra and the Basque provinces, the brilliant Coronel Zumalacarregui brought together an improvised fighting force, and his Carlist irregulars managed to keep the Liberal army busy and at bay in the deep, inaccessible valleys of the Pyrenees and the ravines of the Cantabrian mountains. The actual area of operations was only a tiny triangle in a very big land, and perhaps the war might have been contained. But soon, in the rest of the Peninsula, the rowdy Conservatives did what they had done with such zeal and success during the French war and the three years of Liberal rule of the 1820s: they formed small mounted *guerrilla* bands that roamed the countryside, robbing and killing wherever they could. Since their numbers were too small to take on the regular army, they concentrated their attacks on stage coaches, wagon trains and lone travellers instead. In their fighting style, their targets, and their mindless cruelty they were indistinguishable from common bandits. Yet they called it a Holy War in legitimate defence of Altar and Throne. A Sacrificial Bleeding of the Nation describes the carnage better; for this, the First Carlist Civil War, was to last seven long and catastrophic years; years of famine, death and pillage, a calamity that was only to end when both sides had practically bled to death and the country lay in ruins.

And into this mayhem rode George Henry Borrow, polyglot, adventurer and future author of extravagant best sellers. He rode in on a magnificent Andalusian steed, with a cranky Greek manservant at his side, and a mule charged with bags full of Gospels in his wake. Borrow had come with a high-minded Mission. He had travelled all the way from England to convert Spain to Protestantism and to steer her away from her backward, Popish ways. Modesty – need it be said? – was never George Borrow's greatest virtue.

2

George Borrow: the Genius in a Nutshell

W<small>E WOULD</small> not know half of what we do about the Treasure Hunter of Santiago had it not been for George Borrow and his 1843 missionary memoirs: *The Bible in Spain*. Born in 1803 in Norfolk, Borrow was one of those eccentric, cocksure travelling Englishmen who swarmed through the 19th century like jolly honey-bees away from the hive. Yet unlike most of his fellow travellers, George Borrow was no idle aristocrat on some ennui-inspired *Grand Tour*, nor an aesthete looking for artistic thrills. Borrow was only a working boy, whose origins were about as humble as his talents were great. His father, an army sergeant, had worked his way up to the rank of recruiting officer through sheer discipline and dedication. In the turbulent days of the Napoleonic wars, such a task involved frequent moving from one garrison town to the next. This rambling lifestyle left little room for formal education of children and was quick to plant a vagrant trait in the boy which would remain with him all his life. Young George spent as much time, if not more, roving out on the heath as he did in classrooms; and he soon fell in with the tribes of nomadic travellers who everywhere roamed the English countryside, particularly with the English Gypsies. With one of these – a young man called Ambrose Smith whom he later immortalised in his writings as Jasper Petulengo – he struck up a close and life-long friendship. Borrow was accepted in Ambrose's family, the two youngsters spent days on end riding through the countryside, boxing, lying in the grass, and talking of the million things that young men talk about. Borrow even learned the gypsy language Romany from his friend, as much of a rarity then as it is now, and a tell-tale sign of things to come.

Young George, for all his rowdiness, was anything but a fool. His school attendance might be erratic, but he visited some of the finest grammar schools in Britain, and at one time in his life he was tutored by no less a scholar than William Taylor, the brilliant Norwich linguist. All that teaching fell on very fertile ground. Borrow possessed an unusually bright mind, a near photographic memory, and a more than remarkable gift for languages. In the course of his life, he managed to master some sixty altogether: easy ones such as Danish and Spanish next to difficult ones like Hebrew, Arabic, and Russian. It took him remarkably little trouble. Like Richard Burton and Heinrich Schliemann after him, he was able to learn a complicated foreign tongue in a matter of months; an ability which, when combined with the paralysing neurotic depressions which haunted him all his life, shows clearly that he was one of those 'mad geniuses' whom capricious nature sometimes tosses upon the stage to mock the notion that intelligence belongs to the mentally sane. One of his most impressive feats he pulled off when in 1833 he applied for a job with the British and Foreign Bible Society, a Protestant organisation set up to spread Holy Scripture in vernacular translation to all the corners of the globe where it was not yet available. At the time, the Bible Society was looking for someone who could see a Manchu-Tartar translation of the gospel through the press in Saint Petersburg. Borrow applied, and was asked to return six months later for a competitive examination in this most exotic language. He did so, won the contest, and was hired – which took him to Russia for the next two years.

Having successfully performed his task, Borrow was next dispatched to Spain. The task which faced him there was, to put it mildly, a delicate one. He arrived in early 1836, and landed straight in the middle of the Carlist Civil War and the political uproar over the new Constitution. Since the freedom of the press and the authority of the Church over its flock were the two hottest controversies in that struggle, the plan to print a vernacular, Protestant Bible and distribute it liberally among the Catholic populace, was not so much a religious act as a political provocation; one which certainly would carry repercussions and make the Bible salesman many redoubtable enemies. But Borrow was a man of strong convictions, which only grew stronger on meeting opposition. So he set to the task with all the energy and dedication which he could derive from his excessive anti-Papism; and to the consternation of his employers, he soon turned his uneventful, almost dreary job into a personal crusade of his considerable ego against Popery in all it forms.

It would perhaps be unfair to say that Borrow *sought* conflict with the Catholic Church, but he certainly never shunned it. At every step of the way, he made sure to attract the greatest possible attention. He published articles in local newspapers, printed brightly coloured posters to notify the public that vernacular Bibles were for sale, carried Gospels in Spanish to distant towns and villages, and at one point even engaged a sandwich-man to walk the streets of Madrid with advertisements for his books. Not yet satisfied with the iconoclastic impact of his Spanish New Testaments, he next printed the Gospel of Luke in Basque – the native tongue of the Carlist rebels! – and another one in Romany-Caló – the language of the Spanish Gypsies, widely believed by the priesthood and the superstitious to be the 'jargon of witches', in which the devil himself addressed his followers.

Unwisely, the ecclesiastical authorities balked and sought redress, but Borrow was a martyr and a crusader rolled into one, and faced up to them with all the deliberate defiance of a self-styled zealot. When a hard-pressed government, loath to alienate the Church any further, put obstacles in his path, he engaged the services of Sir George Villiers, the British Minister to Madrid, to bully them back into permission. When at long last they passed a law forbidding him to sell his books, he con-tinued to do so on the sly, peddling them to the peasants of the Spanish countryside. In short, Borrow made sure to be martyred, trusting in the protection of the Lord and the British Legation. He got what he wanted. In May 1838, he was jailed for a few days on a trumped-up charge; that same summer the sale of his vernacular Bibles was definitely forbidden and he was ordered to remove them from the kingdom. A year later the good vicars of the Bible Society, whose drawing-room ideals did not include a revival of the Thirty Years' War, quietly summoned him back to Britain.

Never, during these busy times, did Borrow's self-adopted Gypsy nature leave him. He remained restless throughout, and since his assign-ment gave him an excellent excuse to move about, he travelled widely through Portugal and Spain, roaming the cities, plains and mountains of the Peninsula and consorting with its shepherds, its beggars and banditti, its smugglers, soldiers of fortune and other assorted curiosities of com-mon humanity. Part missionary, part explorer, a Livingstone *avant la lettre*, he observed, he studied, he inquired into everything; and he wrote it all down in long florid letters, meant as much for posterity as for the addressee. The characters that he met and described include some of the giants of the age: men like Mendizábal, the Jewish general and financial genius, who was one of Spain's most flamboyant prime ministers; George Dawson Flinter, an officer of Irish stock who celebrated as many triumphs as he suffered catastrophes throughout the Carlist War; and the hard-pressed, delicately-placed archbishop-elect of Spain, whom the Vatican would not recognise but the Liberal regime refused to replace. But there are also the less famous and more picturesque: Antonio da Traba, a bulky fisherman and smuggler from Finisterra, who claimed to have sailed on the *Victory* during the battle of Trafalgar and to have seen Nelson die with his own eyes; Antonio Buchino, a formidable, sarcastic Greek manservant, so quarrelsome that he rarely stayed longer than a few days – and sometimes only a few hours! – with any one master, and yet served ambassadors, prime ministers and dictators of Spain in the course of a long and turbulent career. There was Balseiro, the famous cutthroat; Luis Usoz, the brilliant Hebraist; Francisca Diaz-Carralero, the blind Manchegan Poetess, perhaps the greatest poetical *Wunderkind* ever born. And last but not least, there was the Treasure Hunter of Santiago, a 'man from Lucerne' called Benedict Mol, who begged his bread in the streets of Madrid, and dreamed of a chance to dig up a fabulous fortune in diamonds and gold.

3

Benedict Mol

T HROUGHOUT HIS life, George Borrow was a great outdoors man. He was given to swimming and horseback riding, and long walks through the countryside at a pace with which few people could keep up. Big cities quickly smothered him with their dirt and dust and filthy air; and Madrid, a city so sweltering with the 'flaming vapours' of summer that even the Spaniards 'lie gasping and naked upon their brick floors', still more than others. So when living there in the mid 1830s, Borrow did the only feasible thing to escape the oppressive heat: he went for long daily strolls on the western outskirts of town, in the valley of the Manzanares river, a pleasant, idyllic spot, almost like a city park, where *tout Madrid* came for their afternoon constitutionals, to linger and meet their friends, and sleep their siestas under one of the many shady trees.

It was here, in the spring of 1836, that the English missionary was first introduced to the Treasure Hunter of Santiago by a mutual acquaint-ance, an Asturian orange salesman who plied his trade on the bank of a nearby canal. A lusty gossip, this Asturian made it his habit to point out remarkable folk to Borrow, adding comments and stories about each; stories which Borrow, always ravenous for the anecdotes of Romantic Spain, listened to with keen attention. One afternoon, the orange sales-man drew his attention to a shabbily dressed person whom Borrow later described as

> a bulky old man, somewhat above the middle height, with white hair and ruddy features; his eyes were large and blue, and whenever he fixed them on any one's countenance, were full of an expression of great eagerness, as if he were expecting the communication of some important tidings. He was dressed commonly enough, in a jacket and trousers of coarse cloth of a russet colour, on his head was an immense sombrero, the brim of which had been much cut and mutilated, so as in some places to resemble the jags or denticles of a saw.

The Asturian greeted this man as 'Don Benito Mol', and explained to his English friend in a quickly whispered aside that the gentleman had once been a soldier of the Royal Bodyguard. Borrow's appetite was immediately whetted. He engaged the old man in conversation, and six years later gave a meticulous account of their exchange. Don Benito, he wrote,

> returned the salutation of the orange-man, and bowing to me, forthwith produced two scented wash-balls which he offered for sale in a rough dissonant jargon, intended for Spanish, but which seemed more like the Valencian or Catalan. Upon my asking him who he was, the following conversation ensued between us:
>
> 'I am a Swiss of Lucerne, Benedict Mol by name, once a soldier in the Walloon guard, and now a soap-boiler, at your service.'
>
> 'You speak the language of Spain very imperfectly,' said I; 'how long have you been in the country?'
>
> 'Forty-five years,' replied Benedict; 'but when the guard was broken up, I went to Minorca, where I lost the Spanish language without acquiring the Catalan.'
>
> 'You have been a soldier of the king of Spain,' said I; 'how did you like the service?'
>
> 'Not so well, but that I should have been glad to leave it forty years ago; the pay was bad, and the treatment worse. (...) I should soon have deserted from the service of Spain, as I did from that of the Pope, whose soldier I was in my early youth before I came here; but I had married a woman of Minorca, by whom I had two children; it was this that detained me in those parts so long; before, however, I left Minorca, my wife died, and as for my children, one went east, the other west, and I know not what became of them; I intend shortly to return to Lucerne, and live there like a duke.'
>
> 'Have you, then, realized a large capital in Spain?' said I, glancing at his hat and the rest of his apparel.
>
> 'Not a cuart, not a cuart; these two wash-balls are all that I possess.'

'Perhaps you are the son of good parents, and have lands and money in your own country wherewith to support yourself.'

'Not a heller, not a heller; my father was hangman of Lucerne, and when he died, his body was seized to pay his debts.'

'Then doubtless,' said I, 'you intend to ply your trade of soap-boiling at Lucerne; you are quite right, my friend, I know of no occupation more honourable or useful.'

'I have no thoughts of plying my trade at Lucerne,' replied Bennet; 'and now, as I see you are a German man, Lieber Herr, and as I like your countenance and your manner of speaking, I will tell you in confidence that I know very little of my trade, and have already been turned out of several fabriques as an evil workman; the two wash-balls that I carry in my pocket are not of my own making. *In kurtzen*, I know little more of soap-boiling than I do of tailoring, horse-farriery, or shoe-making, all of which I have practised.'

'Then I know not how you can hope to live like a hertzog in your native canton, unless you expect that the men of Lucerne, in consideration of your services to the Pope and to the king of Spain, will maintain you in splendour at the public expense.'

'Lieber Herr,' said Benedict, 'the men of Lucerne are by no means fond of maintaining the soldiers of the Pope and the king of Spain at their own expense; many of the guard who have returned thither beg their bread in the streets, but when I go, it shall be in a coach drawn by six mules, with a treasure, a mighty schatz which lies in the church of Saint James of Compostella, in Galicia.'

'I hope you do not intend to rob the church,' said I; 'if you do, however, I believe you will be disappointed. Mendizabal and the liberals have been beforehand with you. I am informed that at present no other treasure is to be found in the cathedrals of Spain than a few paltry ornaments and plated utensils.'

'My good German Herr,' said Benedict, 'it is no church schatz, and no person living, save myself, knows of its existence: nearly thirty years ago, amongst the sick soldiers who were brought to Madrid, was one of my comrades of the Walloon Guard, who had accompanied the French to Portugal; he was very sick and shortly died. Before, however, he breathed his last, he sent for me, and upon his deathbed told me that himself and two other soldiers, both of whom had since been killed, had buried in a certain church at Compostella a great booty which they had made in Portugal: it consisted of gold moidores and of a packet of huge diamonds from the Brazils; the whole was contained in a large copper kettle. I listened with greedy ears, and from that moment, I may say, I have known no rest, neither by day nor night, thinking of the schatz. It is very easy to find, for the dying man was so exact in his description of the place where it lies, that were I once at Compostella, I should have no difficulty in putting my hand upon it; several times I have been on the point of setting out on the journey, but something has always happened to stop me. When my wife died, I left Minorca with a determination to go to Saint James, but on reaching Madrid, I fell into the hands of a Basque woman, who persuaded me to live with her, which I have done for several years; she is a great hax, and says that if I desert her she will breathe a spell which shall cling to me for ever. *Dem Got sey dank,* – she is now in the hospital, and daily expected to die. This is my history, Lieber Herr.'

In this somewhat impromptu manner, the Treasure Hunter of Santiago made his debut on the stage of burlesque Spanish history.

4

Of Truth, Mistrust and Treasure Hunts

ALL TALES of hidden treasures must be thoroughly mistrusted; especially those that speak of treasures still waiting in the earth; and nowhere more so than in Spain. With the exception of Muslim Egypt, there has never been a land which spawned so many Golden Fables, and so many simple-minded folk who lend them credence. Here every town and hamlet has its legend of a fabulous buried hoard; every century its stunning harvest of poor dupes, who climbed up the mountainside or scrambled into some infernal cave with a shovel and a pickaxe, to dig, day in, day out, for years on end, ruining their health and their patrimony, chasing madly after phantom gold. In the course of twenty centuries a veritable industry of treasure hunting has sprung up. Psychics and soothsayers offered their services to help peasants and townsfolk locate the proper spot to dig. Magic books taught recipes to make demons reveal the burial places of treasure and ways to free them of their protective spells. Town and countryside were flooded by a corpus of mysterious manuscript booklets, which contained the secret annotations of wealthy Romans or Visigoths or Moors, who – fearful of carrying their wealth over dangerous roads when driven from the land – had buried their gold and jewels in the earth with an eye to their future return. All these efforts certainly generated fabulous wealth; but not for peasants digging under rocks and fountains, not for the citizen who tore down the walls of his house in search of treasure trove. It made the fortunes of the trickster, the con man, the charlatan and the fraud, that breed of leeches which invariably follows in the wake of need and wishful thinking. One ought to be extremely careful before one lends credence to tales of hidden gold in a land so very addicted to make-believe.

Benedict Mol's fantastic tale of the Santiago treasure is no exception. Mol has all the looks of a small-time swindler. He was a vagrant, a penniless veteran of the Peninsular War, a man arrived at old age in penury who was obviously looking for a lucky break. He had nothing to lose and everything to gain from people's gullibility, first and foremost an interested sponsor who might provide his daily bread for as long as hope or greed or misplaced trust continued. A man like that cannot be taken at his word. Even his most innocent statements are highly suspect – let alone his promises of buried riches.

And yet, Mol's story was somehow sufficiently convincing for the very government of Spain to get involved in the murky business of gold-digging – and not just once, but twice within a decade. How could this be? These men, a political clique as wicked and self-serving as any pack of Latin rulers in the robber baron age, may have been venal and may have been silly, but they certainly were no fools. They would never have engaged upon anything so absurd and risky as a treasure hunt without a minimum of reason. Consequently there may have been more to Mol's tale than appears at first sight, and it only makes good sense to scrutinise the story well, to sift truth from falsehood, and the likely from the improbable.

Of course, that is easier said than done. For a start, we do not *have* the story that convinced the government. It was not recorded; or if it was, the record has not survived. We only have the version which George Borrow says Mol told him; a version which is probably not the one Mol offered the authorities, and which is certainly not the full and honest truth. As cover stories go, that tale certainly had its merits. It was a small masterpiece of deceit, an intricate composition in which truth and falsehood, historical fact and outright lies, were blended in a clever fashion. But no matter how beautifully done, such a thing does not make Truth, and it cannot be trusted out of hand.

George Borrow himself never seems to have entertained the thought that Mol was deliberately spinning him yarns. He dismissed the tale of hidden treasure out of hand, then almost sheepishly echoed everything else the Swiss dished him up. He should have known better. For one thing, he ought to have been put on the alert by the eagerness with which Benedict Mol revealed his dearest secrets to a perfect stranger. Mol, he writes somewhere, was 'at all times remarkably communicative with respect to his affairs and prospects'. That is putting it mildly. Rather than 'remarkably communicative', Mol's liberal disclosures deserve to be called 'recklessly garrulous' in a treasure hunter who had been waiting thirty years for his one great opportunity in life. Any man with half the information that Borrow received from the Swiss in the course of a few meetings, might easily have gone to Santiago and taken a shot at gold-digging himself.

The clue lies, of course, in the eye of the beholder. Borrow – the brilliant linguist with a photographic memory and an outsized ego – was smugly aware of being the brightest boy on the block. Self-confidence breeds conceit. Borrow made the classic mistake of highly intelligent people – and particularly of those urban Rousseaus craving for their Noble Savages in distant lands – of thinking all common folk to be simple, truthful and – most devastating of all – transparent. Mol was none of those. He was, on the contrary, a consummate impostor. He lied about his past, lied about the provenance of his treasure and the burial place where it now lay, lied perhaps about that 'looter friend' of his who supposedly had hidden the hoard three decades earlier. And all through his merry chatter he only gave away enough of his secrets to whet the appetite of his audience and invite 'gratuities'. This he clearly did well enough, for even George Borrow – who through his own wayward youth among vagrants and gypsies was perfectly inured to the tricks of con men – readily admits to giving the man money on various occasions. So anyone who thinks that Benedict Mol was a dupe better look again. There can be no question he was something of a charlatan. But a dupe? For that the vagrant Swiss was far too cunning!

And then there is George Borrow and the question in how far *he* may be trusted to tell the truth. The matter is of some importance, since Borrow is our only source for the early history of Mol, so that any small chicanery of his automatically magnifies into a major distortion of the record.

Borrow's reliability is – to put it mildly – a moot point. The trustworthiness of his writings has been called into question ever since he first began to publish, and today, a century and a half later, that war still rages on in all its bookish bloodshed. Borrow is a tricky author for philology to tackle. At heart, his works belong to non-fiction and even to autobiography, yet the stories he tells are often too good to be true, too weird to be real. His books are crowded with extravagant characters whom none of us ordinary mortals ever seems to meet, and they abound in unlikely coincidences, the truth of which few sensible people are willing to accept offhand.

To some extent, such scepticism is simply the price any author pays for pretending to tell his own personal adventures rather than stories labelled as fiction from the start. Nobody would dream of subjecting, say, Charles Dickens or Victor Hugo to the sort of scrutiny that Borrow's very own admirers – a tiny clan of the devout who proudly style themselves 'Borrovians' – have unleashed upon their most beloved author. With the slogan that 'there are few delights to compare with shooting at one's heroes', these men and women have treated Borrow like the suspect of an artful crime, whose every word and action must be verified and checked. The baptismal records of his characters have been traced in parish registers the world over. Old, yellowed newspapers have been closely examined from cover to cover in quest of dates and confirmation of events. The diaries of acquaintances and the memoirs of distant relatives have been combed through in search of small, nay, insignificant details. The results are stunning in their thoroughness. To give but a few examples, there is a minute, pound-and-penny study of his wife's household account book for a few holiday weeks in 1854; there are comprehensive biographies of pugilists whose fights he possibly witnessed; and there is even a small essay on a Welsh settle in which he once may have rested for all of half an hour! In short: had George Borrow been bullion and his disciples gold-diggers, the lot of them would have struck it richer than King Croesus himself.

And what conclusion may be drawn from all that drudgery and toil? The conclusion is that Borrow can rarely be trusted to tell the pure truth in any of his writings; but, at the same time, that he almost never made things up from scratch. What he did was to embellish. If the occasion so demanded (and it rather often did…) he *improved* the raw material of his memories, so as to create a more exciting narrative and to produce the kind of thrilling, sensational adventure which his audience of amusement-starved Victorians demanded from books of travel in distant and exotic lands. As one expert investigator once wrote, Borrow 'never let the facts get in the way of a good story' and 'was quite prepared to tell things as they ought to have been, rather than the way they were.' To him the technique made perfect sense. He was far too earnest and egotist an author to dabble in outright fiction, yet he also had to keep his sales figures in mind and please his readers. So whenever his prime material failed him, he often added a pinch of the picturesque or a handful of *picardias* to the brew.

One minor episode from his journey to Galicia will make a good enough example. In late August 1837, Borrow visited the village of Finisterre, a cluster of miserable shacks built beneath the famous Cape at the farthest north-western corner of the Iberian Peninsula. Finisterre means 'End of the earth', and rarely was a name more deserved. Today it is still a remote spot; in those days it was barely a part of the inhabited world. As it was nearly impossible to reach over land, few if any outsiders – let alone foreigners! – ever came here. A stranger was quickly eyed with suspicion by the local fishermen; and what is more, the Carlist Civil War added an ample dose of wartime paranoia to the distrust already in place. If, therefore, a traveller wished to stay out of trouble, he needed a good, legitimate reason to explain his presence. Borrow had none. He went to the Cape because of a romantic whim: to see a remarkable place with his own eyes, and to stare upon the slice of ocean where some twenty months before, while travelling to Lisbon in a rickety steamboat, he had nearly been shipwrecked. Inevitably, he got arrested on suspicion of being a Carlist spy, and was dragged before the town's mayor, who proposed to have him shot before the door – not at all an empty threat in these wayward days of few questions and quick bloodshed. But just as he was to be marched to his death, a sturdy, barefoot, musket-carrying mariner called Antonio da Traba intervened. Traba had served with the British Navy for a time during the Napoleonic Wars. He recognized Borrow as an Englishman, and for old time's sake, saved him from a useless death and a nameless grave. We know that all this truly happened, from Borrow's letters home and from the later investigations of a local schoolteacher.

So far so good. But then, five years later, Borrow included this adventure in *The Bible in Spain*; and the whole of it got thoroughly upgraded. He gets arrested, Borrow says, not for being a run-of-the-mill Carlist spy, but because the fishermen mistake him for the Pretender Don Carlos himself, changed in height and stature by a magic cloak! His guide, a little hunchbacked fellow from a nearby town, is thought to be Don Carlos's crown prince Don Sebastian. And old Antonio da Traba did not simply serve in the British Navy as a mercenary, but claims to have fought at Trafalgar on an English battleship (i.e. *against* the navy of his own fatherland, which at the time was allied with the French) and even pretends that he stood next to Nelson when the Admiral was killed aboard the *Victory*! All that is obviously make-believe, stuff that Borrow tagged on to the basic tale to make it even juicier than it was already. Yet in all such cases, it takes close scrutiny to sift the true bits from the false, the fabrication from what really happened; and even then one can never be completely sure what bit is fact, what bit embellishment.

In one case only can we trust George Borrow blindly; trust him, that is, to tell a brazen lie. That case is the Catholic Church. Borrow was a fierce, almost pathological anti-Papist, an incorrigible church-basher, whose loathing of Rome and her priesthood bordered on the obsessive. In later years, looking back on his career, he was to boast that he had 'written against Rome with all his heart, with all his mind, with all his soul, and with all his strength'. And one ought to add: with all his imagination. For when it comes to his personal Crusade against priests, friars, bishops and popes, Borrow's tendency to rig things becomes extreme. He felt no scruples whatsoever in larding his texts with the most preposterous, fabricated slanders. A rare village priest of honest faith may escape his censure; but other than that no catholic dignitary ever comes away un-scathed. All of them are venal, scheming, stupid and corrupt. All of them harbour devilish plans, reason like Hottentots, surpass Judas Iscariot in duplicity, and spit on the holiest tenets of their very own faith. In short: whenever Borrow writes about the Church of Rome, he can be trusted to talk rubbish.

With things in such a state, to use George Borrow's works as an *historical* source is risky business. So much of it is true, that one is easily tempted to give the benefit of the doubt to tall tales which by earnest standards ought to be disqualified. Yet so much of it is fable that, unless one has an outside source to verify his claims, one should categori-cally refuse to trust him. But outside sources are few and far between. There rarely is another eye-witness report, and most of Borrow's trivial adventures never made it to the papers. This then leaves us only with Borrow's own letters home, written and sent at the time of his travels. Even though they are penned by the very same man, these letters make outstanding comparative material and an excellent touchstone for the truth. They cover the exact same ground as *The Bible in Spain*, yet they are more sincere and less sensationalist, because they were addressed to the General Committee of the Bible Society, a body of domesticated parsons already so stunned by their employee's adventures among horse-thieves, gypsies, vagrants and smugglers that they really needed no more dazzling. If anything, Borrow played down his wild adventures in his correspondence, so the same event told in a letter is usually the more reliable version of the two.

Unfortunately, Benedict Mol never appears in the letters. He is in fact so conspicuously absent there that one might easily think Borrow never met the man at all, but merely assembled him out of material pillaged from hearsay and press reports. That, however, is not the case. A letter from a friend of his, the Santiago bookseller Rey Romero, which in due time we will see, gives independent and irrefutable proof, not only that the treasure hunter himself existed and came to Compostela in search of his hoard, but also that Borrow and the Swiss knew each other personally. It is a pity that it proves no more, and that we therefore have no choice but to take Borrow at his word for most other aspects of the tale. A word which, as we've seen, is not always as good as gold.

In conclusion we may say that both Mol and Borrow are unreliable. The Swiss was an impostor and a charlatan, who told a rosy-coloured fable to his English friend. In his turn, Borrow adapted the treasure hunter's tale to his own narrative needs. Where Mol lied, Borrow may innocently have passed on the falsehood. Where Mol spoke the truth, Borrow may have 'enhanced' things for literary reasons[2]. Each man probably stuck sufficiently close to the truth to maintain the credibility of his tale. But each also bent essential fragments to his will, whenever fabrication was

---

2 One thing which almost certainly is a Borrovian embellishment is Mol's allusion to '*gold moidores*'. The *moidore* (the English corruption of the Portuguese expression '*moeda de ouro*', i.e. 'coin of gold') was an old Portuguese coin of high value, minted from 1640 to 1732, and mainly used for transatlantic colonial trade in the Caribbean, continental Europe and the British Isles. Because of its intrinsic value, it may still have circulated here and there in 19th century Portugal, but the fact is that we never find it mentioned in any contemporary source except in the writings of... George Borrow! Even Borrow, however, never uses the word in his Portuguese letters, but only in the dramatised text of *The Bible in Spain*. Might it be that it was somehow a darling currency of his? It certainly seems so – and if this is the case, we even know where he got the idea. For the coin plays a prominent role in many 18th century storybooks about Caribbean pirates, foremost among them Borrow's own favourite childhood novel, the very book from which he learned to read: Defoe's *Robinson Crusoe*.

more convenient than truth. We therefore find ourselves in a most perplexing hall of mirrors, in which one looking-glass of falsehoods reflects another one of half-truths, whose own image is already a distortion of the facts. This makes for a very blotted picture. So it will take a very close look at the historical context before we may hope to unravel the tangle and answer the questions: was there a treasure, who could have hidden it, and how come intelligent men believed in its existence?

II

The Looters

5

The Storm of Andoche Junot

THE TIME Mol had in mind when he mentioned that his treasure was buried '*nearly thirty years ago*' was the time of the Peninsular War, the gruesome conflict which broke out in 1807 when Napoleon decided to occupy Portugal and Spain. This decision has often been regarded as one of the Emperor's worst mistakes, second only to his invasion of Russia five years later. And a grave mistake it certainly was; for in the long run, this Peninsular adventure, undertaken so light-heartedly, was to turn into Napoleon's own private little Vietnam: an interminable, unwinnable war of attrition against volatile *guerrilla* bands and undercover city *saboteurs*, which gobbled up ever more resources, ran thousands of troops through the meat-mincer each month, and pinned down innumerable divisions urgently needed elsewhere in the European theatre. Impossible to bring to a close one way or another, it was to lose Napoleon the military momentum, the war in the north, and ultimately his throne. He himself admitted as much in hindsight, when many years later, exiled on frosty, wind-swept Saint Helena, he looked back upon his whole astonishing career and bitterly concluded that 'the Spanish ulcer destroyed me'.

Yet none of this could really be foreseen in the summer of 1807. On the contrary: at that particular time, to capture Portugal and Spain looked like the logical, nay, the *prudent* thing to do. After a dozen years in power and countless victories on the battlefield, Napoleon was at the height of his career. Of all his earlier enemies only Great Britain, 'safe behind the shield of her Navy', still held out against him. With the others – Austria, Prussia and Russia – he had reached an understanding. Europe for the moment was at peace. Yet it was a delicate, uncertain peace, one which clearly would not last forever. The Continental powers were only biding their time, waiting for an occasion or a good excuse; and it was plain for all to see that soon France would have to face the coalition on the battlefield again. Napoleon knew he could take them on, any time, any place, in Central and Northern Europe. But there was one weak spot in his defences: the Iberian Peninsula, which offered itself as an ideal beachhead for an English Expeditionary army, right in the back yard of France itself. Consequently Napoleon needed firm friends on his southern frontier. And that was the one thing he did not have.

Portugal, Britain's long time ally and natural trade partner, had been a thorn in the Emperor's side for years. Not only had she steadfastly refused to comply with the Continental System, the Europe-wide embargo on British trade by which Napoleon tried to crush British resistance, but she had also successfully withstood his many attempts at intimidation. The more pressure he brought to bear, the more stubborn Lisbon became; and the way things looked she would soon welcome, if not simply invite, the British landing which would guarantee her independence. Before that happened, Portugal would have to be invaded. And since the Royal Navy ruled the seas, the only way to Portugal was through Spain. Consequently Spain would have to allow the passage of French troops over her territory, in numbers sufficiently great for a rapid conquest.

Fortunately, Spain was an ally of France; and Manuel Godoy, Spain's young, ambitious prime minister, was perfectly willing to allow such a thing. Godoy was an upstart of few scruples, who owed his elevation to high office, at the stunning age of twenty-five, to the filial – and possibly amorous – attentions he had paid to Queen Maria Luisa, and to his gentle, doting manners with the feeble-minded monarch Carlos IV. This somewhat unsavoury *ménage à trois* had, rather naturally, provoked the resentment of the Crown Prince – the future Fernando VII – who despised Godoy with a vengeance and loathed his parents with all the spite of a spurned child. Godoy, however, was unconcerned; for his ambition was not to please princes, but to become one himself. He dreamed of some day winning a kingdom of his own; and since Napoleon was the great King Maker of Europe, there was little Godoy would not do to ingratiate himself with the Emperor.

One would think that a man who gambles for such stakes will stick to the horse on which he has once bet his money. But not so Godoy, who – in the time-honoured fashion of sycophants – thought it safer to play both warring sides at once. To secure his future in every outcome, he had lately made some clumsy diplomatic overtures to England, and to his great misfortune, Napoleon discovered copies of this secret correspondence in Berlin shortly after the battle of Jena in 1806. The reaction was immediate. In one of his typical Italian temper tantrums, the Emperor vowed to sweep the whole degenerate Bourbon brood and their faithless Prime Minister off the European map; and he decided then and there to conquer Spain and plant one of his brothers on its throne, instead of putting his trust in the doubtful fighting qualities and the even more dubious loyalty of Madrid's *ancien régime*. This he set out to do in the summer of 1807; in a manner which would show Godoy that, when it came to ruse and double dealing, Napoleon was no less of a mastermind than he was on the field of battle.

The prelude to the kill was played out in a string of friendly diplomatic gestures, meant to lull Godoy into a sense of false security and minimize the cost of Spanish conquest. Rather than take Spain by assault, it would be far more expedient to secure Godoy's consent for the passage of troops to Portugal. Once inside Spain, these troops could turn on the ally at any desired moment, which would save valuable time. What is more, the Emperor, brilliant as ever, understood that with only a little cunning, he might convince the Spaniards to contribute lavishly towards their own doom.

With these aims in mind, Napoleon concluded the Fontainebleau Treaty with Godoy – a pact which, whatever way one looks at it, is one of the more disreputable agreements in mankind's long history of shady diplomatic deals. In exchange for free passage of some 28,000 French soldiers, ample Spanish military assistance, and a generous contribution from the Spanish treasury to the French war chest, Godoy was promised the southern half of a dismembered Portugal as a kingdom of his own. Napoleon would keep the rest and be rid of a nuisance that had defied him for so long. Thus two countries agreed to carve up a third one among themselves. The prime minister of Spain squandered the resources of his homeland to serve a purely private interest. And the Emperor of the French never for a moment meant to keep his promises, but merely used the pact as bait to wolf down two neighbours in one bite. It is hard to imagine anything more cynical. But then Godoy was never more than an *arriviste*, and Napoleon had long since lost any moral scruples he may once have possessed.

In the autumn of 1807, Napoleon handed command of the operation to his long-time comrade General Andoche Junot. It was perhaps not the happiest choice of commander. Junot, nicknamed 'The Storm' for his daredevil bravery, was a valiant general, but he lacked all subtlety of mind. Yet Napoleon dispatched him with a complicated triple objective. All at once, he was to conquer the recalcitrant Lusitanian kingdom, stave off an English landing, and prepare for the sudden, but preferably blood-less, take-over of Spain. Given these targets, the true challenge facing Junot was not how to conquer Portugal, whose ramshackle army, badly provisioned and worse led, was no match for Europe's most formidable war machine. No, it was how to leave enough French troops behind in Spanish territory for the future *putch* without causing suspicion, and how to take the greatest possible number of Spanish soldiers out of their homeland, to minimize Spanish resistance once the trap was sprung.

The Fontainebleau Treaty went a long way to solve this latter prob-lem. Under its terms, Godoy put three large Spanish armies at Junot's disposition: one of 17,000 men under General Carrafa to be used for the capture of central Portugal; another of some 8,000 under General Solano for the invasion of the Alentejo province in the south; and up north, a force of slightly bigger size led by Francisco Taranco y Llano, the Captain-General of Galicia, which was to occupy Oporto. These troops, almost 35,000 men altogether, would therefore be removed from Spain; and it was merely a matter of pinning them down when the great coup came. As for the other challenge, Junot solved that one with a flair appropriate to his old nickname: by plain bluff and bluntness. From mid-October onward, even before the Fontainebleau Treaty was properly signed, he simply ran his columns into Spain whenever and wherever it pleased him. Then, without giving notice or seeking consent, he moved the army down the road to Portugal and as he marched, planted gar-risons in all the strategic fortresses along the way, ostensibly to secure his communications; in reality to gain control of the defensive infrastructure of the land.

Once the French army was well under way, Napoleon declared war on Portugal, and Junot was given *carte blanche* to unleash his well-planned *Blitzkrieg*. At Valencia de Alcántara he joined his own forces to those of Carrafa, then breached the border on November 17th. One after another the Portuguese frontier towns, Segura, Castelo Branco and Abrantes, were taken, reduced, and sacked. As Junot pushed on unstop-pably towards the capital, burning, killing and plundering as he went, Carrafa and his Spaniards were sent northward, and ordered to occupy the central regions between Coimbra and Tomar. There was nothing the decrepit Portuguese army or its distant British ally could do against the onslaught, except a quick and general *sauve qui peut*. On English advice, the Portuguese fleet set sail for the high seas, where the French could not capture it, while the royal family and some 2,000 courtiers were hurriedly embarked in British battleships and evacuated to Brazil[3]. On the last day of November, Junot occupied Lisbon with 15,000 men, weary not so much from warfare, as from fast marching and looting at every step along the way.

The stage was now set for the parallel invasions of the north and south. On December 1st, the first of Solano's four columns crossed the Portuguese border at Badajoz and occupied Campo Maior. A few days later his remaining forces stormed the frontier town of Elvas and pushed on to Estremoz and Setubal. There was little resistance. By now the Portuguese army had evaporated, and in a textbook operation of mopping up behind a spear point, Solano's troops fanned out into the Alentejo and Portuguese Extremadura, until the whole area south of the Tajo was in Spanish hands.

Meanwhile, up in Galicia, General Taranco received orders to concentrate his army in the town of Tuy, and to begin his occupation of *Entre-Douro-e-Minho*, Portugal's strategic, northernmost province. Taranco's army, which consisted of local, Galician line regiments, crossed the river Miño on December 10th and after a practically unopposed march, occupied Oporto pacifically three days later. It was by far the most civilised of all three Spanish assaults. While Solano's troops had hacked their way into cities and taken fortresses by assault; while Carrafa's soldiers, imitating their French marching-buddies, had committed an endless succession of plunder and atrocities, Taranco's soldiers behaved in an exemplary fashion towards the city and its inhabitants, avoiding all bloodshed and pillage, and observing the strictest discipline.

One reason for such laudable behaviour surely was the close ethnic and linguistic kinship which Taranco's Galicians felt for the equally 'Celtic' Portuguese. But another may have been that they were so few in number

---

3 It is a wry comment on the character of these monarchs that, as the royal carriage rushed towards the harbour through the narrow Lisbon streets, the Queen yelled at the coachman: 'Not so fast! Not so fast! People might think that we are fleeing!'

and could not afford to antagonise the local population. Taranco was extremely short of troops. According to the Fontainebleau Treaty, he had to occupy northern Portugal with 10,000 soldiers and two dozen cannon, but those numbers proved to be too optimistic. Some 6,000 men and twelve pieces were the most which Taranco could assemble. Yet he had to secure all of northern Portugal with these troops, and was even looking at the prospect of having to beat off a British landing. Consequently he solicited reinforcements from Junot as soon as he had reached Oporto, and was sent, in response, some 2,000 men from Carrafa's army, who marched north in mid December under Carrafa's personal command, arriving in the city shortly before Christmas 1807. There both armies were to remain another four immobile months before history caught up with them again.

When it did, the military landscape had changed completely. For in the first months of the new year, it finally began to dawn on the Spanish king and court that the troops which Junot had left behind 'to secure his lines of communications', and those that kept streaming in day after day, were far more numerous than necessary to garrison essential roads or to occupy the Portuguese neighbour. The Fontainebleau Treaty had only allowed the passage of 28,000 men in total; but each of the new French armies that now crossed the Pyrenees counted nearly as many, and they even infiltrated regions which had nothing to do with the route to Portugal: the Levantine coast, the mountains of Aragon, Madrid itself. Soon some 100,000 French troops were camping in Spain, and the conclusion could no longer be overlooked or ignored: the French had not come to cross, they had come to conquer.

Only now Godoy understood how masterly he had been cheated. At a loss what else to do, he advised old King Carlos to flee to Cádiz and from there to South America. The king agreed and hurried preparations were made in the deepest secrecy, because it was plain to see that the Spanish populace would not tolerate such cowardice from the very same dunces who had sold the land to its enemies. They almost got away. But Carlos and Godoy had counted without Fernando, who now saw his chance to get even with his parents and Godoy in one swift stroke. The vengeful crown prince sent his agents into the town and the barracks of Aranjuez, where the court was residing at the time, and raised an impromptu rebellion by revealing the plans for the royal getaway. Furious, the populace stormed the palace. Godoy was discovered as he lay hidden in a roll of matting up in an attic, like some male Cleopatra scorned by his Caesar, and thrown in jail. King Carlos was confined to house arrest. Fernando assumed royal authority, and immediately approached Napoleon to beg the Imperial blessing for his palace coup. This was an even better development than the Emperor had hoped for. Contemptuously, he summoned the whole Bourbon bundle to the Chateau Marrac in Bayonne: King Carlos, his Queen, Godoy and Fernando; and after a farcical semblance of negotiations, forced both father and son to abdicate in favour of his brother Joseph, arrested everybody and packed them off to exile in the heart of France. With only a bit of bullying and a little cheating, the Emperor had filched a throne for his brother and a satellite for France. And it had barely cost him a penny or a soldier.

Or so, at least, he thought.

And he could not have been more mistaken.

As soon as the news of the Bayonne trickery reached Spain, the entire country rebelled. With the exception of a tiny group of die-hard, ultra-Liberal collaborators so very eager to see the benefits of the French Revolution introduced to Spain that they were willing to accept French conquest, the whole nation, left and right, rich and poor, clerics, peasants, burghers and soldiers, rose in indignation against the foreign invader. In the provinces, old enemies and new friends joined hands to form defensive *juntas*, who arrogated government power to themselves to organise and lead the counterattack against the French. Barracked troops spontaneously marched out and either arrested or massacred Junot's left-behind garrisons. All over the land *guerrilla* bands sprang up, led by priests, or prominent tradesmen, or even common bandits, who ambushed French convoys and patrols wherever they were found. On the 2nd of May 1808, the population of Madrid staged a sudden violent revolt, immortalised by Goya in several breathtaking paintings. The French beat back the rebellion with bayonets and sweet promises; but as soon as order was restored they took vengeance by shooting scores of arrested insurgents. It was the most foolish thing they could have done; for this treachery did nothing to intimidate the angry Spaniards; yet it created a saga of martyrdom that would fuel the national crusade for the rest of the war. From here on, the French were not merely the enemy, they were the devil. And it was as devils that the Spaniards would treat them henceforth.

For a considerable while, the Spanish troops in Portugal were kept in the dark as to all these events. Junot, dead set on retaining every last Spanish soldier well within Portugal to soften resistance, kept a tight restriction on letters and messengers. As the tension rose throughout the spring, he even did what he could to separate the Spanish troops from their commanders. Early in the year, General Taranco unexpectedly died of some traumatic, internal disease. In principle, Carrafa, the highest ranking officer, now ought to have taken command in Oporto. But Junot, who did not trust Carrafa, decided otherwise. He bestowed command on Quesnel, the French general who was billeted in Oporto with a small squadron of dragoons, and ordered Carrafa and his troops to return to central Portugal, where he could control them better. Unwilling to take the initiative while the political issue still hung in the balance, Carrafa obeyed. In early April he marched his men south; and Junot immediately divided these forces into tiny units and scattered them over a huge area south of the Tagus, with orders to guard the coast and patrol the left bank of the river. Carrafa found himself without an army and without freedom to move. He was, effectively, a prisoner in Lisbon.

At last, in late May, the news of the Madrid massacres and the spontaneous war which the Spanish populace was now waging on the French, reached Oporto, together with belated, last-minute orders from Godoy to Taranco to return his fourteen battalions to Galicia. Understanding that the French were now officially the enemy, the ranking commanders of the force, the Conde de Maceda and Brigadier Domingo Belestá, acted swiftly. They arrested Quesnel and his staff, and by a surprise raid overwhelmed the eighty French dragoons in their barracks. That done, they made their peace with the Portuguese, handed back authority to an interim council, and on June 10th marched their troops and their prisoners back over the Miño river into Galicia.

When Junot heard of these events he took immediate countermeasures. He ordered all of Carrafa's soldiers to be disarmed, arrested and locked up on the floating pontoon prisons in the Tagus estuary. It was none too soon; for secret directives had also been sent to Carrafa, ordering him to disengage as quickly as he could and return his army to Spain. That movement was now forestalled. Only Solano and his southern division escaped Junot's grip. They made it back to Spain before Junot could stop them, because the main part of the force had been withdrawn to Badajoz and stationed along the border early in March, to cover the abortive flight of King Carlos to Seville.

By the summer of 1808, Junot found himself alone in Portugal, surrounded by enemies everywhere. The Portuguese were in the hills, the Spaniards at his back, and the English on the ocean off the coast. Though long expected, the swiftness of the British arrival may still have surprised Junot, for it was the result of a coincidence. Spain and Portugal had both been quick to solicit assistance from Britain; and as luck would have it, an expeditionary force of some 15,000 men stood ready at Cork under an unknown commander, one Arthur Wellesley, the future Duke of Wellington, to sail for Buenos Aires on a trivial mission. London understood the urgency of the new situation, and what an excellent opportunity it offered to pester Napoleon where it would hurt most. So Wellington's force was quickly rerouted to Portugal, where the troops were disembarked in the first week of August at Mondego Bay, near Figuera da Foz.

Almost as soon as they had landed, Junot – true to his old nickname – stormed their positions with everything he had, so as to hurl them back into the sea. It was far too thoughtless an assault. The unknown Wellington, who had learned his trade fighting the equally impulsive Indian tribes, received the onslaught in perfectly chosen positions near the village of Vimeiro, with a foolproof battle plan worked out to the last detail. Like a *tsunami* that knows not where it's going, Junot's charge floundered on the impregnable defences. And before the day was done, the stormy French general had to withdraw from the battlefield, leaving behind his cannon, thousands of dead, and his aura of invincibility. It was the end of a mad adventure. Junot's position had become untenable. The following day, an armistice was called, and a week later, when the British had landed in force, Junot accepted negotiations. By the Sintra Convention of August 30th 1808, the two sides agreed that the French, in return for surrender, would be honourably repatriated in British warships, with their weapons, their personal possessions and even their accumulated loot – something which caused a colossal scandal when the news reached Britain. Over the next few weeks Junot's men were embarked and shipped out, and by the autumn Portugal was free of Frenchmen.

The first Napoleonic invasion of Portugal had come to an ignoble end.

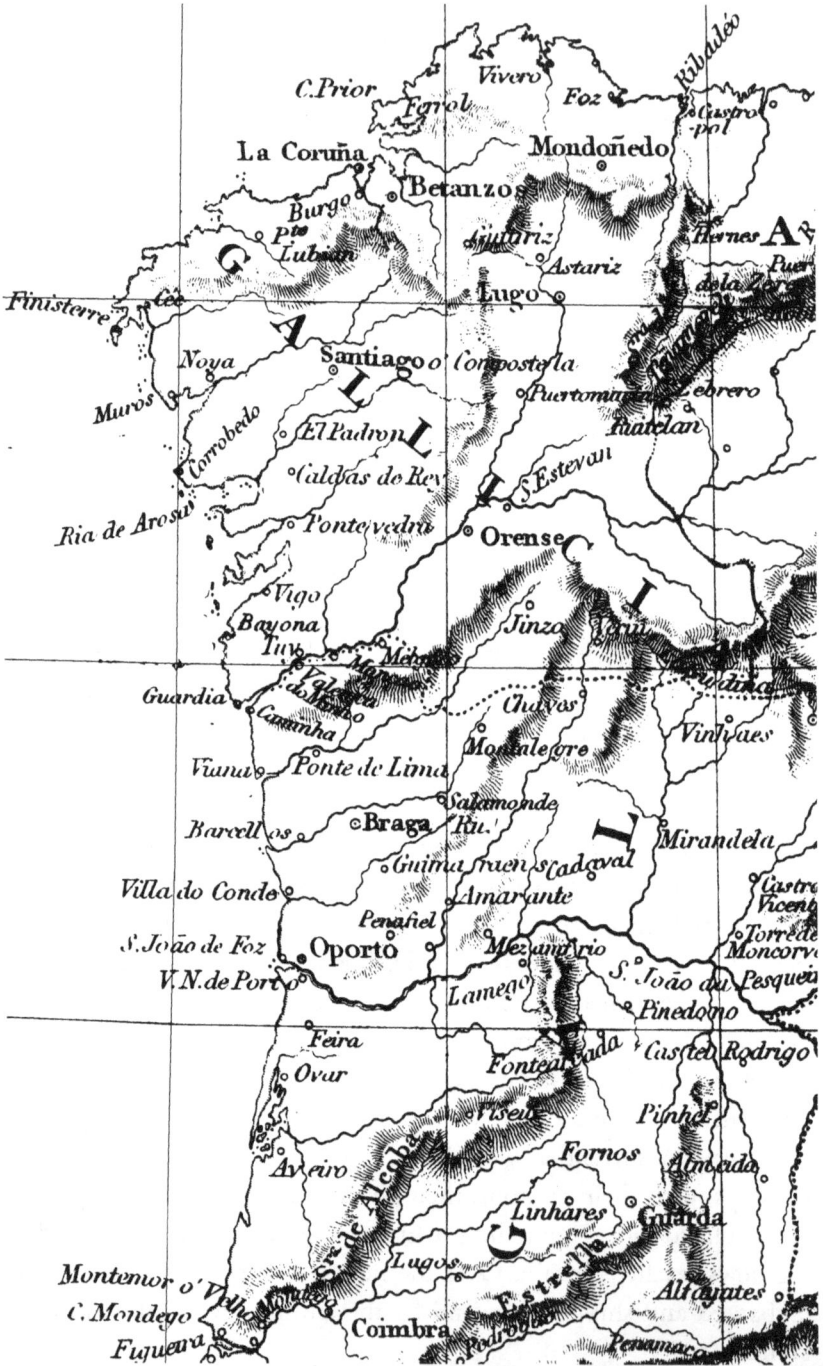

Map 1. **Galicia and Northern Portugal**

6

Lies and Looters

THERE IS nothing we know about the ghastly Peninsular War which speaks against the possibility of a soldier acquiring treasure through theft. On the contrary: such things happened daily and as a matter of course. For this was a time when pillage abounded; when many a fortune was made through torture, blackmail and murder; when each and every man did all he could to exploit the golden opportunities which war invariably offers.

Looting, one of the perennial curses in the history of human conflict, was not merely a cruel fact of life in the early 19th century. It was the fuel of fighting armies and – worse still – a recognized, legitimate instrument of war. The unwritten law which ruled such sanctioned rapine was simple. If, on the arrival of the enemy before the gates, a town chose to resist and was then conquered, it was given over to pillage by the troops. For a set number of days the soldiers were allowed to engage in 'a multitude of favourite sins, beginning with robbery and ending with rape', unpunished, unchecked and unlimited. Neither the persons nor the property of the civilian population enjoyed any protection. The luckiest of them might flee with their shirts on their backs. What happened to the rest needs no elaboration.

To the common soldiers, the prospect of plunder was one of the main enticements to enlist. They rarely got paid in full, never got paid on time, always got paid a trifle. If they were to put their lives on the line, risk death, disease, mutilation and torture, something extra had to be tossed into the bargain over and above their official pittance. That 'something extra' was the chance to enrich themselves beyond all the opportunities of peacetime and civilian life, at the cost of conquered lands. Some officers – mainly the aristocrats and the independently wealthy – thoroughly despised the practice. Others, like Michel Ney, who sometimes tried to stop the worst, were basically indifferent. Others yet again – men like Soult, Junot and many another French general of plebeian extraction – participated to their heart's delight in stripping foreign cities of their accumulated wealth.

The pillage suffered by Spain and Portugal during the Peninsular War was so much the worse because the conflict was fought out by foreign armies on the soil of third nations. Whether it concerned the French conscripts with their revolutionary zeal, or the enlisted dregs of society from which the British armies were composed, nobody harboured any respect for the lives, property or well-being of the native populations. The post-revolutionary French, atheist, iconoclast, and inured to all moral restraint by years of *sans-culotte* excess, felt no qualms at all about robbing the Peninsula's fabulously rich churches, convents and palaces. The British foot soldier, in his turn, never developed the notion that the Peninsula's inhabitants were allies. In his first General Order of the war, issued just before the landing at Mondego Bay, Wellington insisted that 'the troops are to understand that Portugal is a country friendly to His Majesty'. But there is no sign that they ever learned; and against this practice of the ages, even the Duke's famous ingenuity stood helpless. With grinding teeth he had to allow the sack of such cities as Badajoz, Ciudad Rodrigo and San Sebastian, all of which belonged to the allied nation of Spain. And when it came to the frequent *unauthorised* plunder, neither floggings, nor hangings, nor strict control by officers and military police could ever stop the angry young men of the army from raping nuns, digging up corpses in search of jewellery, or roasting people over a slow fire until they revealed the whereabouts of their savings. All such acts of barbarity were perpetrated by the theoretically civilised and 'friendly' British troops. So one may imagine the kind of things done by the hostile and deliberately *uncivilised* French, whipped up to unequalled heights of fury by the constant ambushes, knifings, killings and torture visited upon them by the peasant *guerrilleros*. The horror stories to come out of this lawless mixture, pale the fantasies of Poe, and only equal those of the Marquis de Sade.

With things in such a state, there is nothing improbable in the idea that a foreign soldier fighting in Portugal might have come back to Spain with pillaged treasure the way Benedict Mol described. And yet it could not have happened as George Borrow tells it, because cold, historical fact simply will not fit with that smooth tale. As we have seen, Mol's affirmations were very precise. '*Nearly thirty years ago,*' he told Borrow, '*amongst the sick soldiers who were brought to Madrid, was one of my comrades of the Walloon Guard, who had accompanied the French to Portugal.*' The man was at death's door, but just before expiring, he revealed to the Swiss the precise hiding spot in Santiago where he and two fellow soldiers had buried a treasure looted during that joint invasion. In the spring of 1836, on the banks of a Madrid canal, this may have sounded plausible. But it stops being so when checked against the troop movements described in the previous chapter; since it implies that some time in 1807 or 1808, units of the Walloon Guard, after fighting in Portugal, would have passed through Santiago on their way back into Spain. And such a movement is simply unthinkable.

Some clarification is needed here. It is true that the *Guardia Valona* – crack troops of the Royal Bodyguard who were proud of their unshakeable loyalty to the throne – were often attached to armies in the field as a reliable fighting force, or stationed at essential strategic points away from the palace, the king or the residence. It is even true that a unit of this corps participated in Junot's invasion. But the problem is that they did so at the wrong end of the land. The unit in question – the 3° battalion of Walloon Guards – formed part of Solano's Andalusian division which occupied southern Portugal in early December 1807. History has little to say on how much these men looted. But no matter how much they *stole*, they were not in a position to *bury* their plunder in the appropriate place, for they never went near Compostela in the whole of the war. Once they had occupied their allotted area, they stayed put for almost half a year, until they were quietly withdrawn to Seville in the first week of March 1808, to be incorporated a little later in the regular Andalusian army which went on to battle the French for Madrid.

Admittedly, their presence in Portugal – something of which no stranger to the invasion could well be aware three decades later – does make one wonder where and how Benedict Mol may have been employed during this particular stage of the war. But no measure of speculation about Mol's own adventures can alter the fact that no '*Walloon Guard who had accompanied the French to Portugal*' ever got as far as Compostela. There is, in fact, no sign of them at all. Not even the most detailed histories of the time – which frequently cite names and numbers of the regiments stationed there – ever mention Walloon Guards in Galicia; while, during the crucial period, the whereabouts of most of the Walloon Guard battalions – a mere 4,300 men at best – are known in such places as Barcelona, Aranjuez and Madrid. Consequently the margin to find any of them at the correct time and place for hiding Portuguese loot in Galician churches becomes narrow in the extreme; not to say that it looks like a sheer impossibility.

There is clearly something wrong here, a clumsy mistake, or more likely: a deliberate untruth. And were one only eager to do so, this historical incongruity could easily serve to disqualify the whole of Mol's fabulous tale. Fortunately there is no immediate need to bow to that conclusion, because there are good reasons to think that this particular detail of the Walloon Guard is one of the things which George Borrow added to the narrative when he polished up his book. One can only speculate why he did so or where he found the inspiration; but turn it any way you like: the regiment of the *Reales Guardias Valonas* is really a very strange unit for a Swiss like Benedict Mol to serve in.

Set up sometime in the 1590s, when the Hapsburg monarchs still reigned over the Spanish Netherlands, the regiment was originally conceived as a typical non-native corps which Renaissance princes liked to have at hand as a bodyguard whose loyalty would not falter when their own subjects got restless. Once Spain lost Belgium, the Guard was retained for reasons of prestige, but it soon became so difficult to find enough true 'Walloons' to replenish the ranks, that reforms had to be made. In the mid-18th century, the language of command was changed to Spanish, men of other nationalities were allowed to enrol, and it was decided that one quarter of Belgians was more than enough to justify the time-honoured '*Valona*' label. For a while the Guard therefore functioned as a Foreign Legion *avant la lettre*, a peculiar, mixed, multinational hotchpotch of a force. But the honour to serve the King's own person was not lost on the nationals; willing Belgians became even rarer than before; and by the early years of the 19th century, the Guard had become a fully Spanish regiment. With the exception of an occasional relative of some foreign official looking for status and splendid uniforms, all recruits and officers were native Spaniards. And this was definitely recognized in 1817, when the word 'Walloon' was quietly dropped, and the corps got renamed as 'the 2° regiment of *Guardias de Infanteria*'.

For Mol to belong to such a fully Spanish contingent is extremely strange. If serving in the Royal Bodyguard at all, one would rather expect him in one of its *Swiss* regiments, which the King of Spain employed as well – clearly a far more logical place for a native Swiss to serve. Or one might even go further, and suppose him to be a simple, run-of-the-mill Swiss mercenary, enlisted in a common Spanish line regiment. This in turn would perhaps permit us to stretch the evidence still more, and assume that Mol's looting comrade was no Walloon Guard either, but, just like him, a simple Spanish soldier in some random Spanish outfit, whom we then might try to find. But alas, it is all to no avail. For *where* in the whole of the Junot invasion shall one find *any* Spanish soldier who could both have plundered a treasure in Portugal and buried it on the sly in the city of Saint James?

The first place to go look is, obviously, General Taranco's Oporto army, which came from and returned to Galicia. Since some of its withdrawing units must have stopped over in the Santiago barracks on their way to further battles, this option at first sight looks promising. And yet it is highly unlikely that we would ever find such a looter here, because Taranco's forces did not pillage. In fact, they conquered and occupied Oporto in a manner so exemplary and pacific that they even earned the praise from their Portuguese opponents, a thing nearly unheard of among foes. Accursio das Neves, a contemporary 19th century Portuguese historian, was so struck by the contrast with the behaviour of the barbarian French, that he went out of his way to praise these Galician troops for their great discipline and humane attitudes. And even before the occupation ended, the town council of Oporto directed a most laudatory letter to the Spanish government, in which it poured many florid expressions of gratitude and acclamation onto Taranco and his troops for their 'dexterity and mildness' and the admirable way in which peace and order had been preserved.

Of course, no measure of academic or municipal praise can guarantee that not a single soldier ever stole a single thing of value. Even the friendliest, most well-behaved armies contain rotten apples; and it can never be excluded that somewhere, between the rough lines of the history book, some criminal mind did an unseen criminal thing. Yet this is clearly not the context in which one expects to find a looter of major treasure; and what is more, it is hard to see what might have driven such a man to bury his hoard the way Mol said. As far as we know, Taranco's army consisted entirely of local, Galician troops, who possessed homes, friends and family in their native province. Why would such a soldier, on withdrawal, have buried a treasure in a public place, where it lay unguarded and might accidentally be found? Here in his own land, among his own people, he had many better, safer and more secluded hiding spots: the cellar of his home, the terrace of his vineyard. Or he might simply invest his new fortune in a nice house with a few hundred acres, for his wealth, gained honestly in warfare for the fatherland, was his legitimate possession, not threatened by confiscation on discovery at all.

Consequently, it makes more sense to go look elsewhere for a looting Spaniard; and the only alternative left are those 2,000 men from Juan Carrafa's army who were sent north in the final days of 1807 to reinforce Taranco in Oporto. These men admittedly had done a lot of looting, for they were the same troops who had so enthusiastically pillaged central Portugal in imitation of the French. It is therefore conceivable that a number of successful marauders found themselves, together with their valuable plunder, in Oporto as the new year broke. And yet none of them could have carried such plunder to Santiago; because Junot recalled them to Lisbon in April 1808, and they ended up south of the Tagus before being disarmed and imprisoned in early June. It is unthinkable that one of them could have held on to a veritable hoard through many months of French captivity until Junot's defeat at Vimeiro finally set him free. And even if he did, how, once again, could he ever have come to Santiago?

In short: the Spanish troops who plundered never came near to Compostela; those who were withdrawn to Compostela famously never plundered. Between these two established facts, no room is left to find what we are looking for. Even the least critical, the most *permissive* scenario, which supposes unnoticed looters among Taranco's troops or stragglers from Carrafa's column staying put in Oporto, leaves us with only a tiny handful of men *hypothetically* able both to steal so much and to bury it so far away. And the chance to find one among these very few who possessed something like a kettleful of gold is simply negligible.

This conclusion, however, leaves us with a serious dilemma. Junot's 1807 invasion was the only joint operation of French and Spanish troops in Portugal throughout the whole of the Peninsular War. Therefore it is the only occasion on which any comrade of Mol might conceivably have 'accompanied the French to Portugal'. But if no Spanish soldier, Walloon Guard or otherwise, could very well have carried a heap of stolen booty from Portugal to Compostela, then a rather consistent picture begins to emerge of a theft and concealment which could not very well have taken place in the alleged manner. What is wrong here? Was Mol's tale a total hoax after all? Was it a lie from the first to the last? Well, no, not really; or at least… not *all the way*. But to solve that little riddle, we must first turn to other evidence, and unearth a darker secret still.

7

The French Connection

THERE ARE, in fact, many more things wrong with the treasure hunter's tale than we have seen so far. To begin with 'Benedict Mol' was not the man's real name; or if it was, the facts which he told about his childhood must be false. Some years ago, Sir Angus Fraser, perhaps the most dedicated investigator of George Borrow's works ever, engaged the help of the City Archivist of Lucerne to trace Mol's father, that *'hangman of Lucerne'* whose *'body was seized to pay his debts'* on death. Given the famous Swiss accuracy and the fact that the office of Public Hangman was both hereditary and rare, the search should have been a piece of cake. Yet it was not. The archivist, a Herr Reinhard, studied the files for the last half of the 18th century, the time when Mol's father ought to have plied his trade, and found only three families of hangmen for that period in the area. Their names were Grosholtz, Mengis and Volmar, and in none of these families a son called 'Benedikt' was born between 1760 and 1800.

So where does the name come from? Probably the best guess is that Borrow – who was wont to change personal names in his writings – plucked it from the front page of the *Eco del Comercio*, a radical Madrid daily which broke the news of the Santiago Treasure Hunt in late August 1838. The *Eco* dedicated four substantial articles to the scandal in the course of a week, and, since various bits and pieces contained in those articles also pop up in Borrow's own dramatised version of the event, it is evident that Borrow knew them. In the case of the *Eco's* main report, published in a large front page article on September 1st, the similarities become so striking that it is hard to escape the conclusion that Borrow – who is known to have hoarded his papers obsessively throughout his life – held on to his copy after reading it, took it home with him to England, and kept it at hand while writing 'Mol's' adventures four years later. The *Eco* itself gives no name for the treasure hunter; it simply calls him 'the Swiss'. But on the same page, immediately above the Santiago report, there is a lengthy feature on the deliberations of the Helvetian

Diet, dated 'Lucerne, August 17', which among many other things mentions a prominent delegate from the Tesino canton called *Molo*. Coming
to the spot in his composition where he needed a name and a birthplace
for his treasure hunter, Borrow – who perhaps had never heard the man's
true name and town of origin – may simply have adapted 'Molo' and
adopted Lucerne.

But of course that is only one possible explanation; and there is a
perfectly good alternative. It is no less conceivable that the Swiss himself
invented his pseudonym and false birthplace, and that Borrow merely
copied what he heard. Why would the treasure hunter use a false name?
Well… for the same reason that any man ever does: because he wishes to
conceal an inconvenient identity which he fears may cause him trouble.
The public *persona* of Benedict Mol – a name to which I will stick for
lack of a better alternative – certainly suggests such a thing. What most
catches the eye when one studies his story closely, is how very *good* it all
sounds, how ethically impeccable. It is a tale coated with moral teflon
on every conceivable side. Nothing in the Swiss's background is wrong;
there is nothing that anyone could hold against him. He had arrived in
Spain forty-five years ago, in the 1790s, looking for an honest job. For
decades he was a loyal soldier to the king of Spain, part of the prestigious
Royal Bodyguard. Afterwards he married a respectable Minorcan wife
and raised a pair of upright children. While they grew up, he waited
patiently for a chance to recover a treasure which had been stolen from
foreign owners, by a soldier equally loyal to the Spanish King and since
deceased. It is a veritable marvel. Few greedy men have ever been so
blameless! Neither Spain herself nor any of her subjects had ever been
harmed by this decent, upright fellow!

Tales so good are rarely true; and Mol's is no exception. In the absence
of his real name, most of this unfortunately allows no verification. But
on one vital matter – his veteran status – the documents do occasionally shed some oblique light; and when they do, the discrepancy is
striking. For there are strong indications that Mol never served in the
Spanish army at all, but that he had come to the Peninsula as a hostile
Napoleonic soldier. Neither later historians, nor the press contemporary
with the treasure hunt ever took him to be anything else. One of the
Eco's articles even quotes him as saying that he had spent some time in
Paris in the past – a minor but significant detail which Borrow made

sure to keep out of *The Bible in Spain* – while in 1843, when he staged his second attempt to locate the treasure, the papers stipulated explicitly that the hoard had been buried by French soldiers, that it was sought by an aged Frenchman, and that this person came to Compostela with the local French consul in his wake. Such wide coincidence of opinion does not perhaps prove Mol's identity beyond all doubt; but it does provide good reasons to mistrust his own more rosy affirmations, and explains why we encountered such trouble in finding an adequate *Spanish* looter of the hoard.

If Mol really were a French veteran, there would be nothing uncommon in his continued presence in the country as late as the 1830s. Many Napoleonic veterans – both native Frenchmen or auxiliary troops from occupied countries – stayed behind after Bonaparte was driven out of Spain in 1814. Decades later, we still find scores of them, settled in Spanish cities, married to Spanish women, working in the local sweatshops or running their own thriving businesses. On the whole, such stay-behind French veterans were fairly well accepted by the populace; yet they never became really popular. Napoleon's armies had behaved so barbarously; patriotic feelings had soared so high among Spaniards; chauvinism had been whipped up to such near hysterical levels by priests and propagandists, that to have French roots almost equalled holding a birth certificate from hell. Any man who had a ghost of a chance did well to invent himself an alternative past; and Mol just happened to have that chance. As a native Swiss from a Germanic canton, he could pass for anybody's soldier, because there were Helvetian mercenaries in every army which participated in the Napoleonic Wars. The French certainly had them, but so did Wellington, the Prussians, the Dutch and – as we have seen – the King of Spain.

From here on, one might speculate endlessly. Speculate, for instance, whether Mol himself invented his service in the Walloon Guards after all, to have a nice, politically correct past with which nobody could find fault. Speculate also whether he really stayed behind in Spain after the war, or if even his Minorcan wife and family were only an alibi to cover up a life-long residence in France. The dismal quality of his spoken Spanish, after allegedly spending four decades in the country, certainly suggests as much; and it would explain why it took the man *so very long* to come looking for his hoard. But all of that would only lead us into a jungle of fruitless conjecture based on ever more hypothetical assumptions. And it would distract us from what is truly crucial here, to wit: that if Mol was a French soldier, then naturally his looting comrade must have been one as well.

This, of course, opens sudden and much wider prospects for locating our man. French soldiers looted heavily and everywhere. They fought in Portugal for many years on end and moved from there to Spain and back continually. The chase, therefore, is on again, with the game much thicker on the ground. Yet, as before, we may fairly exclude all of Junot's French troopers from the list of possible looters; for much as these men committed unspeakable pillage, they were all repatriated, with their booty, directly from Portugal to France in British warships, and never came close to Santiago. Only a handful of them ever set foot in Galicia at all: the men aboard a couple of vessels which took refuge from a storm in Vigo harbour; and those eighty French dragoons of General Quesnel, who were arrested in Oporto and marched off to internment in Ferrol in the summer of 1808. All those, however, were prisoners of war of the now hostile Spaniards; and prisoners of war are not, on the whole, allowed to hold on to kettles full of '*gold moidores and diamonds from the Brazils*' during captivity.

Necessarily, we must find such a looting Frenchman elsewhere; and this is none too difficult, for there were two other, consecutive French invasions of Portugal during the remaining years of the Peninsular War: one under Marshal Soult in the Spring of 1809, and a final one in the summer of 1810 led by André Massena. This last one, doomed to founder on Wellington's famous 'Lines of Torres Vedras', does not concern us here. With its 65,000 crack troops under Napoleon's most dashing marshal, the 1810 invasion was by far the most formidable of all three. But by the time Massena moved his mammoth army over the Portuguese border, the whole of Galicia had already been freed from French occupation for more than a year, and lay effectively outside the theatre of war. Consequently none of Massena's soldiers could have reached Santiago, with or without his accumulated loot.

The same, however, does not hold true of the Soult invasion, which was staged out of Santiago, and was to return to Galicia in the course of the war. So it is to this event that we must now turn.

8

Soult in Oporto.

BY THE autumn of 1808 Napoleon was not a happy Emperor. He had planted his brother Joseph on the Spanish throne, and had lent him his best and brightest generals to pacify the country quickly, but the plan had backfired. Each of his commanders made a mess of it. In Madrid, Murat had been surprised by the *Dos de Mayo*, the fierce popular uprising on the 2nd of May. The columns marching south along the Mediterranean coast had failed to push through and had turned around mid-way. Marshal Lannes, sent against Saragossa, encountered such stiff resistance from its civilian population that it took him two months to reduce the un-walled city by siege and bombardment. General Dupont, instead of quickly securing Andalusia, had wasted precious time and effort in pillage, got bogged down by his booty-train, hesitated for weeks, walked into a trap at Bailén, and surrendered his whole division. Last but not least, Junot had lost Portugal by storming at the English like a frenzied bull. By all these setbacks, Madrid was left exposed on three sides and became untenable. In September King Joseph decided to withdraw from the capital and retreat behind the Ebro river, on the doorstep of France itself. Napoleon must have been astonished when he heard the news. What had been meant as just a sideshow was quickly turning into a lethal menace. Complaining that his marshals 'understand nothing of the greater picture of the war' Napoleon decided that he'd have to take command in Spain himself.

This he did, and if any proof of his military genius were still needed, the autumn campaign of 1808 would convince even the greatest sceptic. From the moment Napoleon took control, the situation changed drastically in France's favour. He arrived in Spain in early November. A few days later he broke through the Spanish defences with one big punch, crossed the Ebro, defeated a last Spanish corps at Somosierra on the 30th and marched back into Madrid on December 4th. It had taken him less than a month to wipe out the whole Spanish army, and now it was time to occupy the rest of the land. From Madrid, he dispatched columns in all directions, with minute instructions on what to take and how to take it. Two of his best marshals, Nicolas Jean de Dieu Soult and Michel Ney, were sent north-west, to rout the British Expeditionary Force that was belatedly coming up from Lisbon, take Galicia, and re-occupy Portugal from the north. With two full-strength veteran corps – Soult's 2nd and Ney's 6th – counting some 70,000 men between them, the two famous marshals set out on the chase.

Brought forward at the pace of the ox-cart, the British army – the same one that had beaten Junot out of Portugal – had at this moment only reached Salamanca. Its new commander, Sir John Moore[4], knew he could do nothing with his puny 20,000 men against the overwhelming numerical superiority of the French. He decided on evacuation. The nearest harbour where the fleet might meet the army on short notice was Coruña on the northern coast. So Moore gave warning to the Admiralty and set a hurried course towards Galicia. It turned into the most terrible of retreats. Today, people remember Dunkirk as a by-word for a narrowly escaped military disaster. But until June 1940 they remembered 'Corunna', with similar misgivings[5]. The time was late December; the land one of the most primitive in Spain; the circumstances desperate. With the rapid French army forever on its heels, the British column crawled forward through a hostile, freezing winter landscape that was getting ever more mountainous and inhospitable as it got closer to its goal. From Salamanca to the border of Galicia the going was still easy. But there the road led over the brutal Bierzo mountain range, with its snowed-in, 3,300 feet high Pedrafita pass, a mastodontic barrier which often becomes impassable even in our motorised age. The column stumbled on, with the animal courage of despair, shedding ever more of its baggage and its surplus stocks in an attempt to lighten the march. At Corcul, where a three-arced bridge spanned an abysmal precipice,

---

4 Moore – reputedly the best and most popular general of the day – had assumed command when Wellington was recalled to England to defend himself against political accusations over the excessively favourable terms granted to the French in the Sintra Convention. As we shall see, this was a stroke of luck for Wellington, and a giant misfortune for Moore.

5 A full century later, at the height of WWI, Winston Churchill warned General Monro, who was on his way to organise the evacuation of the Allied forces from Gallipoli, that 'a withdrawel from Gallipoli would be as great a disaster as Corunna'.

Moore's troops even tossed the whole of the war chest – many thousands of pounds in gold *duros* – over the cliff to keep it out of French hands. It helped but little. The roads were mud tracks covered with knee-deep snow. There was no food for man or beast. The temperatures dropped to Siberian lows. The tired soldiers, the exhausted beasts of burden, the luckless camp followers got massacred in droves by the elements. Doctor Adam Neale, an army physician, wrote that:

> Broken waggons and carriages, money-carts, dead animals, and the bodies of human beings, who had perished from the inclemency of the weather during the night, strewed the way for miles. Never had I conceived, much less witnessed, so awful a scene. In one baggage-waggon, which had overturned, an unfortunate soldier's wife, with several children, were frozen to death.(...) Our soldiers lay down and died in the ditches without a struggle. Few women were now to be seen, the greater part had perished.

In early January, after a horrid march lasting weeks, the army finally reached Coruña. Like a godsend, the British ships sailed in in time, but as the boarding started, the French appeared on the horizon, and began a cannonade of the harbour and the transports that were embarking the army. On January 16th Moore engaged the French with a small rearguard near the village of Elviña on the plateau just above the city. The sally gained the necessary time to finish the embarkation, but Moore himself was mortally wounded when a howitzer shell ripped his arm from his shoulder and his belly to shreds. He died a few hours later in a Coruña mansion, and was hurriedly buried on one of the bulwarks near the sea, where his tomb may still be seen. 'Corunna' had cost England its best commander plus 6,000 men and 3,000 horses; not counting the women and children who also perished. Soult and Ney had done their Emperor's bidding well.

Coruña defended itself a few days longer, but had to capitulate on January 19th. Two days before the city fell, on the 17th, Soult sent a vanguard under Franceschi south to occupy Santiago. Franceschi encountered no resistance, but he did find a city in uproar, half-deserted and stripped of its war supplies. Days earlier, as the news of the French advance trickled through, a massive exodus had taken place, partly of the people who had distinguished themselves in the rebellion against *El Rey Intruso*, the Intruder King Joseph Bonaparte, and partly of the rich, the timid, and the religious, who feared French pillage and retaliation. Only a few local *afrancesados*, and a large unruly mob of rabble stayed behind. Together, these had thrown the city into anarchy. Pro-French partisans had ransacked the palace of the archbishop, an active opponent of King Joseph. The bishop's partisans in their turn had nearly lynched people whom they considered traitors. Simultaneously both bands settled a number of personal scores under the convenient pretence of dealing with treachery.

The French wanted a base for operations against Portugal, not some new hotbed of rustic revolution. They made short work of the anarchy. As an example, a firing-squad executed two *saboteurs* on the day Santiago was occupied, and left them lying around in the square for several days until at long last a religious brotherhood got up the courage to seek permission to bury them. All refugees were formally summoned to return, on pain of being considered hostile, and shot on sight. To fill the void of authority, they named friendly officials to positions of power. There was some difficulty in finding candidates, since few men were willing to collaborate; but at long last they hit upon two university professors with the right credentials, convictions and courage: one Manuel Fraguio, who became mayor, and Pedro Bazan y Mendoza, who would act as Director-General of Police. The main buildings of the city were requisitioned: the archbishop's palace as a residence for Soult; the gorgeous *Casa del Dean* for General Marchand; the top stories of the former Inquisition's Palace for Bazan's French police, while its famous dungeons were turned into a magazine for war material and loot. Fonseca College, the monastery of Santo Domingo, and the *Hospitalillo de San Roque* were seized for use as military lazarets. Finally, the French called together all the citizens of note, and forced them to sign an act of allegiance to King Joseph.

Once all this prosaic business was concluded, Soult – who arrived on February 3rd – began to prepare for the invasion of Portugal. If the battle for Spain were to be won, the British had to be denied the beachhead which Junot's fiasco had returned to them. Using Santiago as a springboard, Soult drew together some 40,000 troops and – leaving a garrison of 1,300 men under Marchand in Santiago – moved south by the coastal road in mid-February. Caldas, Pontevedra and Vigo had already been taken early in the month by an advance guard; so without much trouble, the French column reached Tuy, the ancient bishop's see and fortress town poised on the cliffs above the Miño river. Portugal lay on the opposite bank, only a boat ride away. But Soult discovered that Tuy's Portuguese twin, the bastion of Valença, was well-prepared and far too strong to take with the clumsy amphibious techniques at his disposal. It would have to be taken from the land side, from across the river. So he left another garrison at Tuy, together with most of his unwieldy cannon, and went in search of a place to cross.

He first marched west but, arrived at A Guarda on the coast, discovered that the bridge there had been demolished, and that Caminha, on the opposite bank, was well guarded. Turning back again, he marched east along the river bank until he reached the spot where the Miño curves north, and an unencumbered crossing could be made. On the 3rd of March he breached the border by the 'dry route' and took Chaves. The dilapidated Portuguese army put up a brave but futile fight, and once over the border, Soult cut through the defences like a hot knife through butter. First Vila Real fell, then Braga, and by the 28th of March he reached Oporto, the great prize of Northern Portugal.

That a city of such size and importance would not be defended better is a telling sign of Portuguese weakness. Oporto was held by a mere 30,000 armed citizens and disorderly troops, entrenched in hurriedly constructed outworks above the city, and commanded erratically by the local bishop. All semblance of public order was missing. Officers were quarrelling, soldiers were insubordinate, personal and political scores were being settled by a populace that lived in a state of perfect licence. It took little to throw the place into total chaos. At midnight before the French assault, a violent thunderstorm broke over the city, and the besieged, mistaking the claps of thunder, the roaring winds and the flashes of lightning, for the sounds and sights of a French attack, called their fellow citizens to arms by the pealing of the church bells. To the amazement of the slumbering French, they opened a dense and futile fire of cannon and muskets which only wasted ammunition and the opportunity to rest before the battle.

In the morning, when the weather cleared, Soult executed a classic pincer movement on the fortifications of both flanks, followed by a punch in the middle as soon as the Portuguese had stripped their centre of troops to strengthen the wings. The thin defences collapsed like straw and the French streamed in, cutting their way with ease through the barricades erected in the streets. A city-wide panic broke out, and the capricious topography did the rest. Oporto is built on steeply descending slopes that form the gorge of the Douro river at its narrowest point. It is a crammed city, whose structures only find an awkward foothold between rocks and boulders, and whose street plan is a maze of precipitous alleys and stairways that all run down to one jam-packed quay-side at the riverbank. Here lay the one escape route: a single bridge of sloops and planks that connected the north part of the town to the Vila Nova de Gaia suburb on the opposite bank.

Into this lethal funnel streamed the doomed: thousands of fugitives, in hysterical fear of the enemy, the old, the weak, the worn, the attractive young women, the helpless infants... Laden with their most precious belongings, leading little children by the hand and squealing pigs by rope, pushing handcarts and wheelbarrows, they thronged *en masse* towards the river, and scrambled onto the fragile contraption to cross the hundreds of yards of cold and whirling water. Those in front were ruthlessly pressed forward by the weight of those coming behind. The retreating Portuguese soldiers were pushed onto this human mass by the advance of the triumphant French. Soon people were elbowed over the edge of the quays, off the sides of the bridge itself. One impatient Portuguese cavalry squadron simply cut its way through the terrified crowd, callously impervious to the cries of despair or the fate of those they pushed into the river. As soon as French uniforms came into view, the Portuguese artillery, positioned on the heights above Gaia, opened up a roaring cannonade; but since their range was short and they fired indiscriminately into the melange of Frenchmen, Portuguese troops and fleeing civilians, they killed as many compatriots as enemy soldiers, only adding to the general panic. Soon the sheer weight of the throbbing mass tore cables and sank boats. The bridge broke in two and its halves floated off in the current. Those in the middle vanished into the wine-dark stream; those at the ends recoiled in terror. Crossing was now unthinkable, but ever more fugitives poured down the slopes to the wharves, and by sheer weight and pressure tumbled those at the edge towards a certain death in the waters. 'The river was covered with floating corpses,' writes Marbot, and the drowning, grabbing hysterically at passing oars and hulls, capsized the overloaded sloops by which others tried to cross to safety.

Even British historians agree that the French soldiers, stunned by the infernal scene they saw when coming in view of the river, threw down their weapons and began to pull people out of the seething waters. But this unusual attitude of compassion quickly gave way to the normal bestial fury when some companies discovered, in one of the public squares, the bodies of thirty French POWs, who had been horridly tortured the day before, 'their eyes burst asunder, their tongues torn out, and their whole bodies mutilated; while the breath of life still remained,' as one historian put it.

The news of the discovery spread like wildfire among the French soldiers; and from there on, all attempts at control were in vain. 'Exasperated at this horrible sight,' writes Marbot, 'the soldiers thought no more of anything save vengeance, and began to take fearful reprisals.' The welcome pretext of retribution mixed itself liberally with the usual love of loot, and the city was subjected to the most horrendous pillage. 'The streets of Oporto ran blood,' wrote one observer, and between the massacre at the bridge, which drowned 4,000, and the indiscriminate killings during the sacking, some 10,000 citizens of Oporto are thought to have perished.

So far Soult's campaign had all the looks of yet another unstoppable French advance. But it was precisely this rapid progress which now brought about its doom. While Soult was marching through southern Galicia, his troops met ever more resistance from *guerrilla* fighters. Stragglers disappeared without a trace; patrols were ambushed; one ragtag irregular force had even managed to block the French advance over the bridge at Mourentán. Soult, the professional soldier, shook them off like so many flies, but he was in for a surprise. The hit-and-run bands he encountered were not, as everyone supposed, the usual last bursts of sabotage from a beaten enemy, but a growing popular resistance movement of unexpected magnitude and strength. Known as the *Alarmas* – a name which explains itself – the Galician peasantry had risen massively under the leadership of abbots, village priests, local aristocrats and retired army officers. With sickles and pitchforks, with butcher's knives and rusty old hunting rifles, they took to the hills, to cut the throats of the godless foreign invaders. And far from gradually fading away, as Soult expected, they now closed in behind his column like water in the wake of a ship, cutting his communications and his road of retreat, and isolating the French garrisons.

On the 23rd of March a peasant army, over 3,000 strong and led by the formidable Abbot of Couto, suddenly appeared before the walls of Vigo, while two British frigates sailed in to block the harbour. The French garrison was taken completely by surprise and at a loss what to do. With only 1,200 men inside a hostile city, they could not defend themselves against so great a force. Yet both honour and caution forbade capitulation. The besiegers were irregulars, to whom a professional soldier ought not to bow his head. What is more: chances were slight that such furious peasants would recognize the few laws of war which the 19th century allowed, and guarantee French lives. Not until the arrival of Pablo Morillo – a young officer recently dispatched from Seville on an official mission – did the French commander dare to capitulate. Vigo was back in Spanish hands, and the road between Santiago and Portugal definitely cut, on March 28th, ironically one day before Soult crowned his campaign with the conquest of Oporto. To make matters worse, a Portuguese column under Brigadier Silveira retook Chaves at roughly the same time, while yet another force under General Botelho de Sousa bottled up the French garrison in Braga.

These setbacks left Soult triumphant but immobile, locked up in a golden cage. Suddenly there were no more communications with Ney's corps in Galicia, nor with Madrid, nor with the garrisons he had stationed on the road. For more than a month the haughty marshal lived in total darkness. The last Imperial message had reached him two months earlier; the most recent one from Ney was four weeks old. Eager to re-establish contact and recuperate the artillery he had left behind, Soult sent General Huedelet north to Valença and Tuy. Huedelet got through and was even let into Valença by its defeatist Portuguese commander, but he found Tuy besieged by a combination of the *Alarmas* and the Portuguese Legion, and heard for the first time of the fall of Vigo. It was disheartening news, and although the enemy had not made much headway against the 6,000 heavily armed French in Tuy, Huedelet decided to cut his losses. On April 13th, he shipped the entire garrison over to Valença by rowing-boat, after spiking the thirty-six precious cannon, and redeployed in northern Portugal. The movement left Soult even deeper in the mud. He could move neither up nor down. Unknown to him, a worried King Joseph in Madrid had dispatched several columns by a variety of peculiar routes to re-establish contact, but each of them had run into unbreachable forces of Spanish and Portuguese *guerrilleros*, or – of a sudden – into battle-ready units of the British army.

These unexpected redcoats were the first drops of a devastating storm. Back from Britain, Wellington had landed fresh troops in Lisbon on April 22nd, and understanding as no other man the strategic priorities and opportunities of a war, he had moved north as fast as his ox-carts would carry him. On May 12th, 23,000 British soldiers reached the southern bank of the Douro at Oporto. Hearing of their arrival, Soult had the repaired bridge blown up again, and all the river boats withdrawn. But Wellington was a *lucky* general. A patriotic Oporto barber, spotting some forgotten wine-sloops anchored beneath an overhanging cliff, paddled over in a skiff and gave notice. In shiploads of thirty men at a time, the British storm troopers were swiftly carried across and fortified them-selves in the seminary on the opposite bank. It was such a masterstroke that Soult, when studying the English through his looking glass from a distant tower, would not believe they were anything but 'a party of red-coated Swiss who've been down to bathe'. Within hours he knew better. The French sentries at the riverbank were quickly driven off. The assembled barges were abandoned by their guards, the citizens of Oporto manned them and sailed the bulk of the British army over. Soon the whole French army panicked and fled the city in confusion. At four in the afternoon, Wellington had the satisfaction of sitting down to a lavish dinner originally prepared for Nicolas Soult in the Carrancas Palace.

North of the city walls Armageddon was taking shape. The French, so arrogant in triumph, turned into a horde both pitiable and barbaric in defeat. With the British cavalry forever snapping at their heels, a vast, chaotic throng of soldiers, camp-followers, retainers and collabo-rators clambered towards the rugged mountains in the east, the blind leading the blind, the cowardly hurrying on the hopeless. Panic was complete, defence did not exist. Even the elements participated in the rout. Torrential rains turned dirt-tracks into rivers of mud, while hunger and cold reduced the proud French soldiers to beasts.

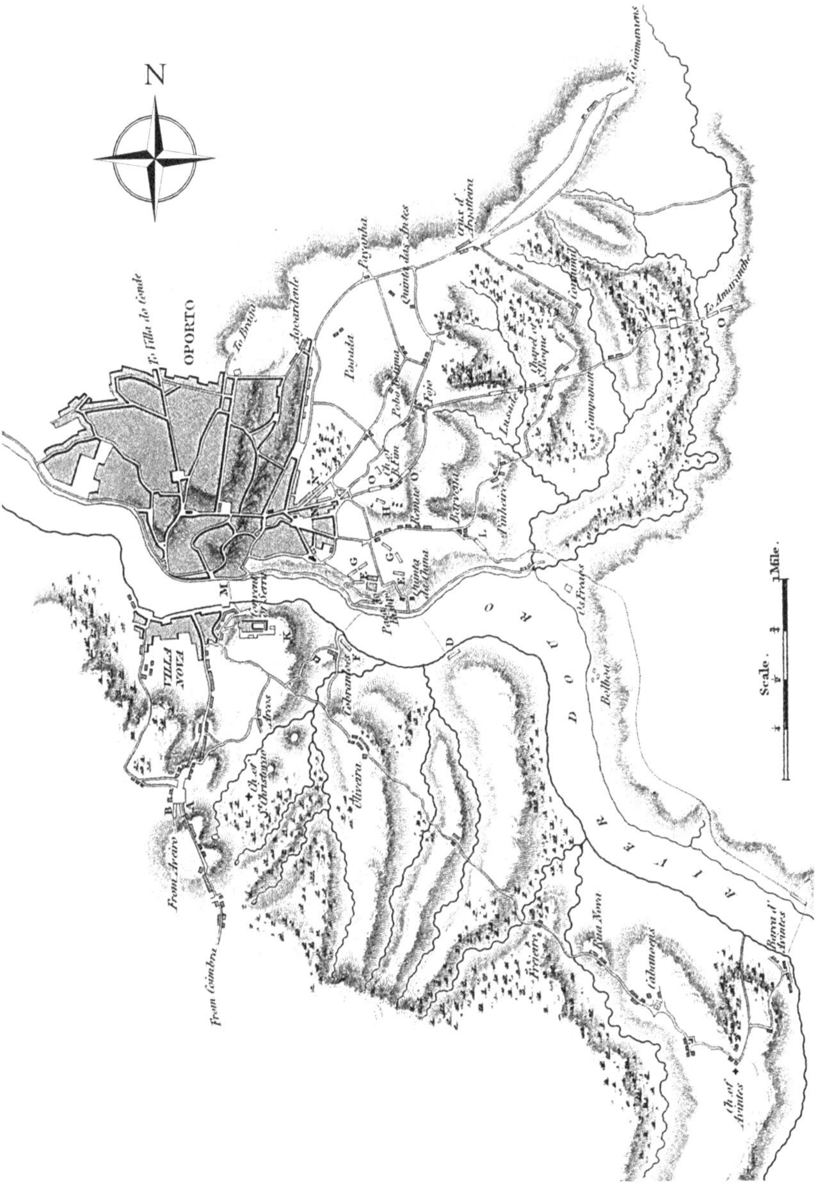

Map 2. **Oporto in 1809**
The position of the bridge of boats is indicated
by the **M** in the centre of the river.

The flight from Oporto was one of the most bloody retreats of the 19th century, 'unequalled in horrors', comparable only to the retreat from Moscow. In British eyes it formed a just revenge for the chase of John Moore's moribund army four months earlier. The beaten French army had to pass through the barely civilised ridges of *Tras-Os-Montes*, today an area of picturesque underdevelopment, then a gloomy highland where people still lived in the Stone Age. Food, wine and fuel were scarce here even in prosperous peacetime. Yet the fleeing French were determined to survive, and did not mind killing half of mankind in order to survive themselves. For five long days they visited such death and devastation on the countryside that it looked as if they wished to end the world then and there. Peasants were hung on roadside trees by scores, for no apparent reason. Arson was a matter of course. 'The route of their column,' says one historian, 'could be traced by the smoke of the villages to which they set fire.' Torture was applied indiscriminately to find out the whereabouts of stores of food and wine, which the French soldiers said they could smell even if hidden below ground.

In furious retaliation, the natives, whose hostile attitudes were inspired as much by primitive bloodlust as by French cruelty, visited agony upon every Frenchman whom they caught. Stragglers were tortured, maimed, emasculated or buried alive. One wounded Frenchman was thrown into a circle of blazing straw, surrounded by an almost ritual circle of peasants armed with pitchforks, who pushed him back into the inferno whenever he crawled out. One French officer was actually *sawn in half...* It was hell on earth, which made the French run so much the faster. 'In vain,' writes Elizabeth Longford, 'Soult's fleeing army, always just ahead, jettisoned more and more of their baggage, cannon, arms and even wounded, whenever their pursuers showed signs of gaining on them. Sodden carcasses of horses and mules and piles of human debris choked the eddies under every rickety bridge.' British soldiers jumped down into this soup of death, to drag up booty from among the bodies... Only by May 18th, Soult crossed back into Galicia at Montalegre, having lost 5,000 soldiers and all of his fifty-eight cannon but one. Even then the barbarous sacking did not stop, churches and villages being pillaged and devastated with abandon. Yet this was no longer a victorious army taking what it liked. It was a beaten horde of 'famished wolves, in almost a state of nature', visiting vengeance on those who had opposed it. In the hands of the harassed, hell soon becomes a purpose in itself.

But it is high time we left behind these tales of bloodshed, and returned to tales of treasure. It will be obvious that, if the Santiago treasure truly came from Portugal and was stolen by a Frenchman, its most likely time and place of origin is Oporto during Soult's occupation. Oporto, grown fat on the export of Douro wines and its trans-Atlantic trade with the Brazils, was a wealthy city, the richest in all Portugal. If gold *moidores* and outsized diamonds were to be found anywhere, this surely was the place. Nor was there a lack of opportunities to steal them, for the sack of the city in the last days of March was a terrible affair, and the French stayed put for six licentious weeks. In such circumstances anything may happen.

Yet there are problems with this scenario; problems no smaller than those we met when it came to the French and Spanish armies of Junot. The main one is that it would have been equally impossible for a soldier of Soult to return to Santiago with his treasure intact. Soult's army was completely cut off from Compostela days *before* his troops sacked Oporto. The swarms of *Alarmas* that surrounded the marshal on his march controlled the whole countryside, and definitely cut the return road to Compostela when they conquered Vigo one day before Oporto fell. Soult's isolation was total; not even a messenger got through. And when the garrison of Tuy decided to evacuate, they found themselves so thoroughly bottled up on the Spanish side that they beat an ignominious retreat south into Portuguese territory. Therefore it is unthinkable that any looting Frenchman could have returned to Compostela with a treasure while the Oporto occupation lasted.

Consequently, such a looter must have marched back with Soult's retreating army after Wellington's dashing strike in May. Yet that retreat was so immensely hurried and horrid that the French, as they were chased through the hellish mountains, discarded whatever they were carrying, including the very weapons they needed to defend themselves. Surely diamonds are a thief's best friend; but in such circumstances, even a treasure becomes a burden, not an asset, and it is hard to imagine a man letting himself be slowed down by such weight while his life hangs in the balance. If he had no time to bury it, he would simply have thrown it away in the anguish of the moment; as was done, for instance, by Hernan Cortés's *conquistadores* – the most gold-obsessed maniacs in history – during their equally desperate run from Mexico in 1520[6].

And then, last but not least, even supposing that our looter did not shed his spoils; even supposing that he did somehow carry this unwieldy hoard – not just a little bag of coins, but a treasure for which Mol's imagination required the muscle power of three men! – all the way into Galicia… then how could it have ended up in Santiago? Soult rallied his forces in Orense on May 19th, and marched on to meet Ney in Lugo the following week, but he and his army never again returned to Compostela. After some fruitless manoeuvring in a half-hearted attempt to recapture southern Galicia, they withdrew to the highlands of Castile, never again to return to the Atlantic seaboard. In short: far too many hurdles of implausibility stand between a looting French trooper from Soult's army and a treasure buried in Santiago; and for all its original appeal, this is, yet again, not how Mol's hoard could have come into being.

---

6 Even during such lethal retreats, soldiers did sometimes hang on doggedly to plunder. Usually they then died. Those of Cortés's men who did not remove the ingots from their boots either drowned in the lake or dropped behind and were slaughtered. The same happened to soldiers of Soult's, on whose corpses, when pulled out of a river by the British, money belts were found. These were, however, the treasures of the dead, and only very few surviving soldiers could have got through with their bloodstained gains intact.

9

The Silver of Saint James

HERE IS however a perfectly fine alternative to all those swaggering soldiers of Soult, Carrafa, Taranco and Junot; one borne out by sources perhaps a wee bit more reliable than *The Bible in Spain*, since they do not reflect the tricky tales of Mol, nor their dramatised reproduction by George Borrow. Called upon to explain the origin of the fabled Santiago treasure in 1844, a local Galician magistrate did not speak of Portuguese '*moidores and diamonds from the Brazils*', but described the hoard as '*a treasure which the French concealed before retreating from this province at the time of the Peninsular War*'. A contemporary Coruña newspaper was even more precise. In an article titled 'The Treasure of Ney', it revealed that this hidden hoard consisted of '*gold and silver church plate*', rumoured to be worth the fabulous sum of sixty million *reales* (some € 125,000,000 today). As we shall see, this Treasure of Ney proved no less elusive than its Portuguese twin, but that matters little for the present argument. The description still reflects the factual beliefs of the public officials who sponsored the treasure hunts – people such as the civil governor, the chief tax inspector, the French consul, and even a Minister of Finance.

If the hoard in question was indeed a Treasure of Ney, it must have been seized in Galicia itself instead of in Portugal, for Marshal Ney never made it over the border at this stage of the war. When Soult marched south in February 1809 for the conquest of Oporto, Ney remained behind to rule Galicia and to guard against a British maritime invasion. With the *Alarmas* all over the countryside and the city folk either uncooperative or plainly hostile, it was a truly thankless task. Yet Ney was not there to make friends; he was there to make a killing. The innovative French method of provisioning which historians commonly label with the famous phrase 'living off the land' did not merely involve robbing the harvest from the fields, the stores from the barns and the roofs and furniture from peasants' huts for fuel. There was absolutely nothing new in that; all armies in all wars did just the same. No, what it meant first and foremost was 'forcible requisitioning amounting to robbery', as Elizabeth Longford put it. While other armies still made do with voluntary loans and war chests carried down from distant capitals, the French demanded monetary contributions and free deliveries of supplies from the local authorities. It was the logical consequence of their modern tactics. If Napoleon's conscript armies were exceptional in anything, it was their extreme marching speed, meant to give them the decisive edge of mobility. While the rest of Europe still marched at a leisurely 70 steps a minute, the French did an astonishing 120! The only possible way to reach such speeds was by freeing themselves as much as possible from cumbersome baggage-trains and the task of maintaining long lines of communication. And if, in the absence of these, they were not to die of hunger and cold, they had to extort whatever the army needed in every place they occupied, unscrupulously confiscating money, food, fuel and clothing, from private citizens, municipal corporations and church treasuries, without an eye to the damage done. '*La guerre*,' wrote Napoleon, '*doit nourrir la guerre*'; even if that meant starving huge chunks of native populations[7].

Compostela got to know the full burden of the method. Barely had Soult marched off, than Ney set briskly about the task. On 13 February 1809 he filed his first claims for monetary contributions, demanding a full two million *reales* from the Santiago township to pay for the occupation and the hospitals for his troops; another four million from its regular and secular clergy; and an additional 'forced loan' of ten million from the Galician Church, which the cathedral's chapter was instructed to allocate and collect, and which had to be handed over in three monthly instalments, the first due on March 10th. Meekly, the town council replied there were no such funds available in the city, while the cathedral chapter in its turn stalled, wrote wriggling letters, and, pleading poverty, filed petitions

---

7 In all fairness it must be pointed out that, much as Napoleon's armies perfected the method, such techniques of stripping town and countryside, and blackmailing local communities into handing over hefty contributions, were already well in place by the mid 18th century. Frederick the Great applied them throughout his remarkable career, while in the French army unchecked marauding 'had an almost institutionalised status, which enabled French soldiers (long before the Revolutionary Wars) to develop a high degree of skill in living off the country,' as the historian Christopher Duffy put it.

to have the sums reduced. The protestations of poverty may have been true, or they may merely have been the obligatory patriotic lies. In any case, the French wouldn't take No for an answer. Ney's representative in Santiago soon turned up his tune, threatening all prominent citizens with imprisonment unless the money was forthcoming, and even hinting subtly at a firing squad. When there still was no satisfactory answer, a handful of notables and cathedral canons was arrested, transported to Coruña, and locked up as hostages in the Castillo de San Anton, a horrid little Alcatraz-style jailhouse on a rock in the harbour. This ugly measure finally stirred the Santiago authorities to action.

In early April, after a long and complicated correspondence, the *Cabildo* of the cathedral informed the French that they had collected what money could be found. The amount fell far short of the sum required, but the canons offered to cover the deficit by handing over the church plate from the cathedral treasury and from various city parishes and convents, with the exception of some pieces necessary for 'the dignity of the mass'. The French were happy to agree. They took the money, then set out to collect the plate. In the afternoon of April 17th, whole cart-loads of silverware and jewellery were hauled out of the religious buildings of Compostela, and handed over to an inspector of the French police, the collaborator José Vivas. Vivas deposited the booty in the cellars of the former Inquisition palace, of old the safest place in Santiago, which the French had turned into their police precinct. It must have been a painful moment for lovers of religious art, for the French made no secret of their intentions. The plate – 14,000 *onzas*, or over 400 kilograms of gold, silver, emeralds and pearls, not counting fifty-seven large brass and silver lamps and other trinkets – was to be 'conveyed in bars to Coruña, where a mint will be set up.' The treasures great and small, many centuries' worth of donations and religious adornment, would be tossed into the melting pot of the modern revolutionary Moloch[8].

---

8 Even so the French were sadly disappointed. Jean-Baptiste Bory, member of Ney's staff and a future botanist of fame, complained sourly about the bad taste and low quality of the booty. Far from being the world-famous treasure of Santiago, he wrote, the supposedly solid statues and candelabras were all merely '*revêtus de lames d'argent beaucoup plus minces que du billon*' ('dressed with silver thinner than sheet metal'); the lamps and church plate were 'of little weight', and St James's massive gold statue with diamond eyes was merely a gilded puppet with fake stones for

As such things go, when the forces of Evil are almost triumphant, the forces of Good appear on the horizon. In this case relief came in the shape of an improvised Spanish army, put hurriedly together from scattered *guerrilla* bands. Having taken Vigo in March and Tuy in mid-April, the ragtag collection of *Alarmas* had been reorganised into a serious corps, some 16,000 strong, called the Division of the Miño. Now, armed by British frigates which had quickly run rifles into Galicia's *rias* and led by officers newly arrived, they came marching north to Santiago. To their luck, Ney himself had left Galicia in the early days of May to conquer neighbouring Asturias with the main part of his army. This left only a garrison of 3,000 troops, with fourteen cannon and 300 horse, to block the Spanish advance at Santiago. The two armies met on May 23rd. After a preliminary skirmish in the early morning some ten miles south of the city, in which the *guerrilleros* of the Abbot of Couto dislodged a French advance guard by a crushing bayonet charge, the Miño Division reached the outskirts of Santiago. Maucune, the acting French commander, had taken one look at Santiago's ramshackle walls, and decided to make a stand outside the city. He ordered his men to dig in on the bulging hill of Santa Susana and on the small plain of the Campo de Estrella a hundred yards south of the city gates. It was a strong, elevated position, which dominated the road by which the Miño Division would have to approach. Some ruinous old walls and ancient oaks trees offered the French soldiers ample cover; while on its extreme south side a high ridge and deep precipice protected them from frontal assault.

In this position, the French might have withstood almost any impromptu attack. But Martin La Carrera, the Spanish commander, had foreseen stiff resistance, and had prepared his forces well. He made sure

---

pupils. From half this wealth, 'of which the Santiago chapter *made a gift* to the army of Marshall Ney' [my italics – PM], 'not even 100,000 *ecus* worth of ingots was obtained.'

Richard Ford, who could be as slanderous a church-basher as Borrow, had a different explanation for the poorness of the catch. According to him it had long ago been embezzled by the canons themselves. 'The chapter thus took in both the intelligent French and the pious pilgrims,' he wrote, 'by converting the solid offerings into dollars *for themselves*, and cheating the vulgar eye with tinsel substitutes.' Avaricious churchmen were no rarity in Renaissance Spain; yet it is far more likely that the Santiago chapter had made good use of the interval between Ney's demands and the April delivery by hiding more valuable pieces in a safe place.

to have all his artillery in excellent shape and brought up before any action was taken. A long cannonade opened the hostilities, in which – as Carrera later wrote proudly – 'our own artillerists were as good as theirs were poor'. For roughly an hour both sides exchanged a fierce fire, while the French unsuccessfully staged several sorties. Then, once the adversary was numbed, Carrera ordered his right wing to envelope the French position, while he himself led a frontal charge. Twice the French withdrew to prepared positions, twice they were dislodged anew. Maucune himself was wounded, and at long last the French line broke. The beaten French soldiers ran for their lives towards the nearest city gate, where some artillery had been stationed to cover a retreat. However, the furious Spaniards quickly overran the battery and pursued their prey right into the city streets, and after a lot of ugly street fighting, they chased them out the other end of the town, and ten miles up the road towards Coruña.

It was a resounding victory, the significance of which was raised to near mystical levels owing to two most welcome coincidences. It was fought on the Campo de Estrella, where legend said the tomb of Saint James had been first discovered in the 9th century. On top of that it took place on the very same date as the famous Battle of Clavijo, a desperate encounter of Christian hosts with the Muslim Moors back in the year 844, where, as the day seemed lost, the Apostle himself had miraculously appeared on a shiny white battle steed, to chop off so many Moorish heads that a glorious victory was won after all. No wonder that today's battle had been barely less miraculous! The French – theologically recognized as the atheist heirs of the infidel Moors – lost all their cannon and some 500 men between casualties and captured, while Spanish losses were so small that their wounded reputedly 'fitted into a single room of the *Hospital Real*'.

Once the town was firmly in their hands, the Spanish made a thorough search for much needed supplies and provisions. They were lucky. The French had blown up two ammunition depots on withdrawal, but two other arsenals were found intact, and so were various magazines containing clothing, some 600 rifles and a number of horses. Most importantly, however, in the dungeons of the Inquisition Palace, the soldiers discovered the French foundry, where forty-one *arrobas* of silver melted into bars lay waiting. Depending on what '*arroba*' the scribes had in mind when noting this down, the hoard may have weighed anywhere between 450 and 600 kilos. In any case, the total considerably exceeded the weight of the church plate officially handed over in April, which shows that Ney's men must have done a good deal of robbing elsewhere as well. And yet, this hoard was still only a part of the all precious metals they had collected, as was to be discovered in the course of the day.

Being a Spanish city, Santiago could not, of course, be given over to pillage, in spite of its resistance. But such patriotic privilege did not extent to the houses of prominent collaborators, all of whom had wisely fled with the retreating French. Their houses were now wrecked and robbed by the soldiers and the loyal inhabitants of the town. In the home of Vivas, the police inspector who had rounded up the church plate, a collection of the original pieces was found. A friend of his wife, a woman only identified by the somewhat disreputable nickname *La Liracha*, was also caught with various trinkets from the original payment. And in a chest in the archive of the town hall, Manuel Fraguio, Civil Governor for the French, had stored away a sum of 8,401 *reales* in money, together with a dozen small, broken chunks of religious silverware tied into a common handkerchief. Naturally these finds represented no more than the crumbs from the French table. Yet they showed what use the French had made of the silver: they had broken up the lot in little bits and pieces, and handed those out to loyal supporters and civil servants, to meet daily expenses.

Carrera was told about all these rediscovered valuables, and he made the best dispositions he could. The bars of silver, whose origins and owners could no longer be traced, he shipped out behind the lines to pay for the costs of the war. What pieces could be identified as belonging to the cathedral were duly returned to its treasury. And loose trinkets such as those from Vivas' cupboards and Fraguio's handkerchief, were deposited with a newly founded Security Council for safekeeping, from where, in later years, they were transferred to the army's paymaster to pay for British weapons. Consequently: anyone who would like to reconstruct the whereabouts of the Santiago church plate, can start to despair right here, with the breaking up and dispersal of the various recuperated hoards, of which no inventories have survived, and whose total volume cannot even be roughly computed.

And this confusion was to grow still worse. On May 22nd, the day before the Battle of Campo de Estrella, Ney returned victoriously to Galicia from the Asturias, where he had occupied Oviedo and Gijón. At

Lugo, he found the beaten Soult waiting for him with the remnants of his routed Oporto army. The news of the Spanish advance onto Santiago reached the two marshals almost before they had shaken hands. They held a strategic conference and decided to make one last attempt to subdue Galicia with the 25,000 troops not needed for garrison duty. Picturing Galicia as a giant disc, Soult would march clockwise inland to the southwest region of the Miño river, while Ney was to go counter-clockwise by Coruña and the coastal route, retake Santiago, and push on to Pontevedra and beyond. At Vigo, the southernmost city of importance, the two armies were to meet.

In the first days of June, Ney's forces approached Santiago. The Spanish commanders understood that they could not hold the unfortified city with their peasant army against a large number of the veteran French soldiers under one of Napoleon's best marshals. Wisely, they decided to evacuate, and dig in at a stronger position further south. On June 2nd they withdrew. Next day, Ney's advance guard marched in. Hurt in their 'invincible' pride, vengeful and furious, the French soldiers behaved barbarously on return. Santiago had shown itself a hostile city, and it was now to pay for the offence. All churches, chapels, convents and monasteries were indiscriminately sacked. At the monastery of Saint Augustine – the only one of which a report has survived – the soldiers accused the monks of having taken pot-shots at them from the windows during their retreat in May – something which is not wholly unthinkable given the patriotic hatred of the times and the robust nature of Galician friars. In retaliation, they mistreated the monks, destroyed the furniture, broke up the altars, the statues, the glass windows and everything else sufficiently fragile, burned the library, robbed the remaining jewellery from chapels and treasuries, and even stripped the gold leaf off the woodwork of the altarpiece. It seems similar scenes took place at the other great temples and monastic institutions. What little church plate the French had allowed to remain in the churches for the saying of mass – and such pieces which the clerics had managed to hide! – were now taken by brute force and indiscriminately carried off.

Then, on June 6th, Ney marched his men southwards. The Miño Division was waiting for him at the bridge of Sampayo, a strategic crossing over the firth between Vigo and Pontevedra. With foresight, the Spanish commander, Don Pablo Morillo, had fortified the spot weeks in advance, and the *Alarmas* were perfectly dug in, with breastworks on the riverbanks and even gunboats on the river. Ney, however, had no choice but charge. If he ever wanted to join up with Soult and keep hold of Galicia for France, he had to break through at this point. On the morning of the 8th, he ordered a kamikaze style assault. Time after time the French columns charged over the bridge. Just as often they were thrown back before they could reach the opposite bank. The position proved simply impregnable and at the end of the day the French had to give up. Reputedly for the first time in his career, 'Brave Ney', Napoleon's most celebrated marshal, had lost a battle. And to add insult to injury: he had been beaten by a bunch of peasants of whom almost a third went unarmed. Wellington had indeed shown great foresight when after the conquest of Oporto, he declined to pursue the French into Galicia with the remark that he would leave Marshal Ney 'to the war of the peasantry, which has been so successful.'

The battle of Sampayo bridge was the straw that broke the camel's back. On June 11th Ney returned to Santiago disheartened and began to prepare for a definite evacuation. Soult – who had managed to do little more than march fruitlessly to and fro between the Miño and the border at Sanabria – agreed. He wrote a bitter and frustrated letter to King Joseph, explaining his retreat with the observation that 'this province is in continuous fermentation. The soldiers are either doomed to perish from pure want or from assault by the peasants, who, through a system of incessant pestering and the evasion of all open battle, would succeed in wiping out even the strongest army; and unless that army be constantly replenished anew with fresh men, [these peasants] would manage to destroy it without any combat.' The 'Spanish Ulcer' was playing up; and it finally began to dawn on the overconfident French marshals that one may perhaps battle a country, but never beat a nation. With less than 20,000 men left to them out of the splendid 70,000 with which they had marched in, the two marshals abandoned Galicia in the final week of June, burning and sacking as they went, and being ambushed in return by the *Alarmas*. On July 1st not one French soldier remained in the province.

The further adventures of Santiago's church plate remain to be told, but only a muddled story can be made of it. We do not know how much of their booty the soldiers who pillaged the churches and convents in the first days of June ceded to the army paymaster, and what they kept for themselves. It seems that part of it was salvaged from Ney's baggage train after Sampayo bridge; but other than that all trace is lost of these valuables. Nor has it ever become clear how much, or little, it may have amounted to. As for the church plate which had not been shipped out by the Spanish in May and had not been looted by the soldiers, the French tried to recuperate it. On June 7th, Pedro Bazan, the collaborating Chief of the Police, demanded that these remnants be handed back again, together with all the trophies of the Battle of Campo de Estrella which Carrera had piously deposited in the cathedral as offering to the Apostle during a great Thanksgiving mass. What there was – or perhaps better: what the *Cabildo* was unable to conceal – was duly handed over. It wasn't much, only some caliches, statues and small trinkets. These were collected once again at Bazan's police station in the Inquisition Palace. Then, at the ultimate moment, on June 16th, four days before final evacuation, Bazan ordered the accumulated church plate, new and old, to be sent to Marchand's offices. There is no evidence that it was ever moved there, but neither is there any proof to the contrary. We simply lose sight of the hoard in these final chaotic days of occupation.

The small rearguard garrison that remained in Santiago to the last, marched out – with Bazan in their midst – on the 20th of June, never to return again. It was a petty, feeble force that had to pass through hostile country, infested with vengeful *Alarmas* who would gladly come in for a final kill. Speed was vital if they wished to survive. Therefore they had to march light and there could be no question of loading up with booty. So what did they do with their accumulated loot? It is said, by the reliable Santiago historian Lopez Ferreiro, that once again they left much of their plunder behind with loyal supporters, but how much of it and where is not explained. Some choice pieces pop up unexpectedly in later months: an inscribed silver tray from the convent of San Payo, returned by the cathedral on the abbess's request in August; a monstrance restored to the church of San Francisco in October, and so on. A few miserable pieces were put back in the misnamed 'treasury' of the cathedral itself and could be seen there, decades later, in a gloomy room behind the altar. All those, however, are but drops in an ocean of vanished plate, and can never account for the towering pile of silver and jewellery whose fate remains unknown. The truth is that nobody has an inkling as to the final account of the valuables looted, lost, destroyed and returned. How much was ever really robbed in Galicia during the six months of French occupation, how much was recuperated, and how much of those rescued goods were turned over to the Spanish army, or stolen again by the French, or appropriated by individual soldiers and collaborators, will remain, forever, a mystery.

Reading all this, one gradually begins to see how a belief in a Treasure of Ney could have emerged in later years. In this self-propelling tangle of requisitions, confiscations, the breaking up and scattering of hoards, the undocumented additions and the spontaneous grants to the national war chest, all track is lost of the whereabouts of Santiago's church plate. And where such obscurity reigns, where even one single piece of the pie seems to be missing, there will always be some chatterbox who suggests that a major part of the fortune was in reality buried on the sly, on a mountainside, in the dark... It only has to happen once, and a vigorous legend, a true Hydra of Hidden Hoards, is born. And it is after monsters of this breed that huntsmen like Mol come chasing.

10

Red Herring, Rara Avis

T HE TALE which Benedict Mol dished up to George Borrow – and most likely to everyone else willing to listen – was a sophisticated cover story, carefully adapted to the prejudices of his audience and his own deep need for secrecy. Neatly plotted and seamlessly assembled, it possessed all the strength and cohesion of cyclopean masonry. And now, at last, with the historical context sketched in minute detail, we may weigh its truth, discover its defects, and see how it came into being.

If we take Mol at his word, the Santiago treasure was stolen in Portugal, by a Walloon Guard and two fellow soldiers, who participated in a joint invasion of the Lusitanian kingdom by the French and Spanish armies, and later buried their hoard *'in a certain church at Compostela'*. Our other historical source, the *Eco del Comercio*, seems to bear out this scenario. In the summer of 1838, at the actual time of the treasure hunt, the newspaper twice told its readers that – according to the Swiss – *'there lay buried in the city of Santiago, ever since 1809, a great treasure consisting of Portuguese gold'*. With such close agreement between two different sources, the time and the place of provenance would seem to be indisputable, even if we allow for the assumption that Borrow himself took some of his cues from the *Eco*.

But the previous pages have shown that it is nearly impossible to reconcile this scenario with the facts of recorded history. No Walloon Guard could have reached Santiago, with or without any valuable plunder. Only the tiniest handful of Spanish soldiers ever had the opportunity both to steal so much and then bury it in the right place. And not even a *French* soldier belonging to the armies of Junot or Soult could, in any plausible way, have made it back from Portugal to Compostela with such fabulous loot in his knapsack. The conclusion is therefore warranted that Mol's hoard had not been carried off from Portugal at all, but that it consisted of the church plate which Ney had confiscated from the Galician churches and convents in the spring of 1809.

Mol surely was aware of this; but to admit so would be folly. Had he told the truth, people would at once have recognized him for what he was: a castaway French veteran, party to pillage and murder, who was trying to benefit from sacrilegious church theft on Spanish soil. The disclosure would not only have stigmatised him dreadfully in the eyes of Spanish patriots; but the revelation of the hoard's true provenance would also have triggered instant claims to its return from its rightful owner: the formidable, all-powerful Church of Santiago. Consequently, Mol needed to conceal these facts as best he could. He had to draw a fat red herring over the trail, to make his audience believe that no national had been harmed, that he himself had nothing to do with the theft, and that no legitimate owner needed to be traced.

And so he did. Making the best possible use of historical obscurity, he created for himself a new, immaculate *persona* as a loyal Spanish veteran and an upright Catholic, whose only association with the loathsome act of looting was one of vague *camaraderie* with wayward characters. And he recast that magnificent heap of Spanish church plate as a treasure looted abroad, from nameless owners, in exonerating circumstances of war, by thieves who were conveniently dead and buried. Only in this manner could the hoard pass for the rightful property of the honest fellow who raised it from the bowels of the earth. And only in this way would there be no dreaded claims from abbots and archbishops.

But even though his cover story was bogus, Mol's faith in his treasure was not. His later behaviour shows every sign that he truly believed it existed. In his quest to obtain it, he took far greater risks than your average impostor would be willing to run. He sold himself to the powerful government of a nation, who would not lightly forgive a swindle. He went digging for his treasure in plain daylight, with an outsized audience in tow, nearly got lynched, was thrown in jail and 'disappeared'. Then, five years later, he returned and sold himself to that selfsame government again! No true fraudster will ever be so brainless. A true fraudster pockets whatever petty cash is offered first time around, then vanishes over the horizon as soon as the ground becomes too hot under his feet. Benedict Mol did no such thing. He hung on doggedly till the very end and paid the price for his persistence. That leaves only the conclusion that he truly supposed his treasure might be found.

Why he felt so confident is anyone's guess. He cannot have buried the hoard himself – otherwise it is impossible to explain why he had such trouble to locate it later on. He obviously only possessed some vague and inexact indications as to its hiding place, second-hand hearsay, which may have come from a rumour that made the rounds in his regiment while stationed in Spain, or, indeed, from a comrade who pretended to have seen the hoard buried with his own eyes.

This possibility steers matters back to the identity of his 'looting comrade'. Obviously, we shall never know who this murky fellow was. The information which the Swiss provides on him is far too vague and fragmented; his story resembles that of too many soldiers in too many similar situations throughout the Peninsular War. Find him? One might as well go look for a straw in a haystack! But perhaps the man's name, his regiment, his origins and his tiresome marches up and down the goat-paths of Iberia matter nothing. For turn it anyway you wish: this part of Mol's tale is really bursting at the seams from phoney stuffing. The eagerness of this looter to disclose the whereabouts of his hard-earned hoard is just as unnatural, if not more so, as Mol's own 'remarkable willingness' to tell every detail of his story to George Borrow. People do not work that way. If they themselves cannot enjoy the fruits of their one lucky break in life, they usually prefer to carry such secrets with them to the grave; rather than reveal them, to no particular advantage, to casual 'comrades'.

So we may well wonder if Mol, the little swindler, was not himself a little swindled. The story really smacks too much of a moribund man, lying sick in some beastly hospital – be it in Spain in the 1810s, or in France decades later – where food and medical care are scarce and dear, and who tries to lure a gullible old acquaintance into lending the help he needs to survive. Instead of deathbed generosity, then, the tale of treasure may simply have been last-minute bait, thrown out in despair to a credulous simpleton, in search of mercenary charity. If that is the case, then the whole tale of treasure is a hoax, and no hidden hoard ever existed.

But *is* that the case? *Was* it a hoax? Or is there a ghost of a chance that the treasure really existed? Usually, the answer to that question must be a most resounding *No*. Both common sense and a hundred known fiascos suggest that all such 'military' hoards like the Treasure of Ney are sheer nonsense. Countless fables of the kind have risen to fame throughout history. Every major war gave birth to a number, and people have gone looking for buried military bullion in every conceivable country and time. But whether one speaks of the Hoard of the Persians, the Tomb of

Alaric, the Confederate Gold or the countless Nazi war chests sunk into inky Alpine lakes, not one such treasure has ever come to light. Nor has anyone ever been able to prove that one was truly entrusted to the earth at the end of any war.

And yet, bizarre as it may sound: the Santiago treasure may be the one exception to the rule, the *rara avis* among the shabby lot. There are many things wrong with that tale of Mol: his name, his life story, his allegiance during the Peninsular War and perhaps even the bare existence of that looter friend of his. But just possibly his claim that there was a treasure hidden in Santiago was not so terribly far-fetched; for the circumstances under which Ney's church plate disappeared are essentially different from those of all other fabled 'military' hoards. It was not hidden, like the Confederate gold reserves or the Nazi ingots, by a defeated army in the chaotic last days of a lost war, but only at the time of a temporary setback. The Peninsular War was still young in June 1809, and far from lost. The notion that Napoleon's invincible armies would in the long run be beaten by a motley bunch of stone age peasants armed with pitchforks and led by priests, was totally absurd. Therefore a return to Santiago when French fortunes had improved, must have seemed quite conceivable to Marchand and his staff. Under such circumstances, to bury a heap of confiscated church plate, which you cannot take along but are loath to leave to your enemy, makes perfect sense. And the fact that we do not know what happened to the recollected remnants of the church plate at the time of the final French withdrawal, speaks in favour of such an almost 'inconceivable' possibility.

However that may be, the fact remains that earnest, well-informed government officials lent Mol a willing ear, and considered his tale of treasure sufficiently plausible to sponsor his cause. How that perplexing business came about, we may now find out and see.

1: **Portrait of George Borrow**
Painted by Henry Wyndham Phillips in 1843

2: Manuel Godoy

3: Andoche Junot

4: Nicolas Soult

5: Michel Ney

6: Sir John Moore

7: **Memorial plaque to Moore** commemorating the Coruña mansion where John Moore died on January 16th, 1809. The actual house was demolished years ago and replaced by a bank.

8: **The tomb of Sir John Moore on the Coruña bulwarks**

9: (left) Location of the bridge of boats over the Douro at Oporto
10: (right) The *Altar to the Martyrs of 1809*, on the northern quay
where the bridge was moored, showing French soldiers
massacring citizens, the throng of refugees crowding the broken
bridge, and God the Father beholding the scene in awe.

11: The hotel built on the site of the Santiago Inquisition Palace
(Plaza Galicia). The famous cellars now house a café.

12: **Santiago de Compostela seen from the Santa Susana mountain**

13: **Borrow's Oviedo** *posada*
in the former palace of the Marques de Santa Cruz, where
Mol supposedly visited him in late September 1837

14: **The Alameda of Santiago**
where Borrow supposedly met Mol in August 1837

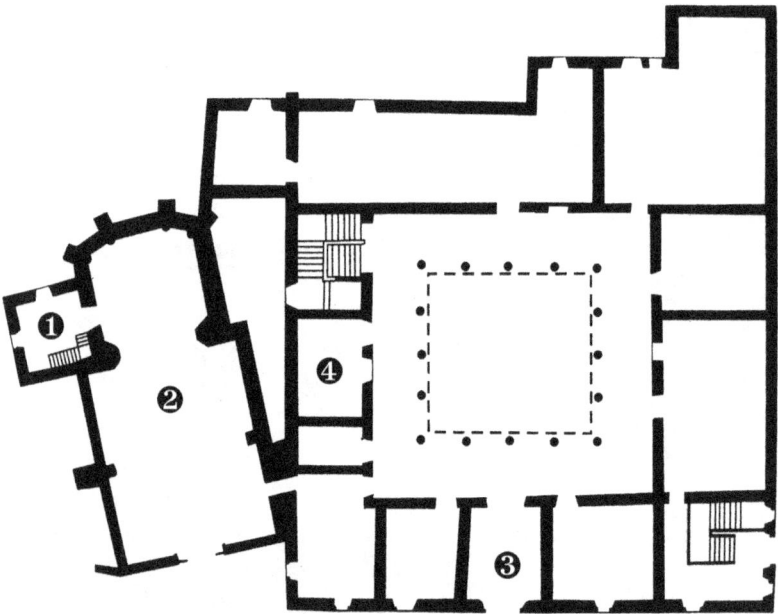

15: **Ground plan of the San Roque complex**
❶ Sacristy   ❷ Chapel   ❸ Hospital entrance
❹ Position of today's bathrooms (it is, however, uncertain
if the 1838 latrines were in this same spot)

16: The San Roque chapel from the north

17: The statue of San Roque carried in procession on August 16th

18: The statue of San Roque above the chapel door

19: The statues of Cosme and Damian above the entrance to the *Hospitalillo*

20: The *Hospitalillo de San Roque* from the south

21: The patio of the *Hospitalillo de San Roque*

22: 'Dig Here!' Benedict Mol showing where his treasure lies buried
From *The Recreation*, 4th series, Edinburgh: John Menzies; London:
Robert Tyas, 1844. Note the 'Horrid Haxweib' right behind Mol
and the greedy canon on the left. (Courtesy of Dr. Ann Ridler)

23: The inside of a Spanish prison from '*Maria Espanhola ou A Victima de um Frade*' by Wenceslau Ayguals de Izco, Lisbon 1849

24: *Eco del Comercio* nᵒ 1,584 of 1st September 1838, with the report of the treasure hunt at the bottom.

25: Baldomero Espartero

26: Jeronimo Valdés

27: The church of San Martiño of Laraño

28: The chapel of Santa Susana at Santiago

29: **Alejandro Mon**

III

The Search

11

Narrative Fraud

FOURTEEN CHAPTERS after introducing Benedict Mol, roughly a quarter of his book later, Borrow returned to the theme of the Treasure Hunter of Saint James. In chapter 27 of *The Bible in Spain* he describes how he and the Swiss met by coincidence in Santiago de Compostela. Then he thickens the plot in a most ingenious manner by describing the discovery, no, not of the treasure itself, but of the spot where it must lie buried. With its sprinkling of magic, its meeting with Carlist bandits and its violent, greedy, quite ungodly canon of the cathedral, the episode is one of the most entertaining in *The Bible in Spain*. Yet it is also the most treacherous, because the whole thing is a hoax. It never took place. It never was. While the other 'Benedict Mol' episodes in Borrow's book have all the look of being – if not factual reports – at least a fair reflection of something which truly happened, the events in this part sprang only from George Borrow's imagination.

The introduction of an entirely fictional segment in an otherwise reliable narrative is a curiosity which begs explanation. As we saw before: Borrow rarely did such things. He sometimes tampered a bit with the truth, he embellished a little and improved his stories where the need arose; but he usually stopped short of pure invention. Why then do so in the case of Benedict Mol? The answer lies in the complicated genesis of *The Bible in Spain*. When first written, Borrow's travelogue was nothing more than a serial compilation of the letters he had written to friends and employers during his Spanish years. These letters were far more than dry reports talking missionary shop. They were long florid discourses on the land, its people, their customs and beliefs, the political and martial trouble of the decade, and the traveller's many adventures. The letters were, in fact, so very complete and exciting, that in most cases all he needed to do to create a chapter was to cut away the address and the signature. The first draft of the book was effectively produced this way, more by scissors than by pen. But no matter how admirably the letters were done, taken together they were only a collection of loose, haphazard anecdotes dealing mostly with the delights and worries of the day, and vaguely held together by the ups and downs of the author's missionary efforts. When in late 1841 he submitted this first draft for publication, his publisher, the great John Murray, found the book a little short and lacking in cohesion. So he suggested that the unity be improved and some extra flesh be put onto the skeleton of the correspondence by adding fresh material and more *Leitmotiv* to bind it all together.

Borrow cheerfully obliged. In the course of 1842, he thoroughly reworked the book, adding no fewer than 389 new manuscript pages to the original 770, and introducing a host of new characters, events and anecdotes. Mol's adventures belong entirely to this 'second stratum' of the book: the parts and layers added during the rewrite, and placed at regular intervals to lend the narrative more consistency. Most of that material is authentic, either quarried from Borrow's own memory or copied from the press reports. But coming to the point of his Santiago visit, he added an episode which Should Have Been But Never Was. The treasure hunter seen at his preposterous labours in the very city where the gold lies buried! The gold-digger helped along by the author, who all the while exhorts the man to return to his senses! How could any wannabe author say No to such a thing? How could he refuse a golden opportunity to improve his book, to please his readers and – in passing – to enhance his own importance?

Two large portions of *The Bible in Spain* were conceived this way: one which is set in Santiago, another in Oviedo. That it is all make-believe and fraud can be shown beyond all reasonable doubt. But that does not make these episodes completely worthless, for Borrow was still more inclined to rehash pieces of reality than to fabricate them; so that we find here, embedded in a heap of fiction, some stirring echoes of the true events. It is only a matter of sorting them out.

12

The City of Santiago

BORROW LEFT Madrid in the spring of 1837 for a long, Bible-peddling journey through northern Spain which took him in some six months to Salamanca, Valladolid, Coruña, Santiago, Oviedo, and Santander. More than a *Tour d'Espagne*, it was a *tour de force*, one which no ordinary missionary would ever have undertaken. Spain was dangerous ground to travel at the time. Although the true civil war, that war of battlefields and cities under siege, raged only in the Basque lands and Navarra, the remainder of the Peninsula got its share of bloodshed as well. Apart from the common bandits and the gangs of Carlist partisans who infested every hill and highway, incursions by columns of Carlist soldiers were frequent in the north; riots and town uprisings broke out without warning; taverns and inns were few, flea-ridden and miserably run. Especially in the wilder, more marginal areas which Borrow insisted on visiting, living conditions were so utterly primitive that even the moneyed foreigner found neither beds for the men, nor fodder for the beasts. Borrow was undoubtedly a dedicated servant of his God and Faith, and a well-paid one for that. But he would never have embarked on such an expedition had he not been a consummate, obsessive traveller, whose courage could feed on curiosity alone. Even a concise inventory tells it all: during this single journey, he was held up by armed robbers on one occasion, was twice arrested as a spy and once nearly shot by firing-squad, got lost in the wilderness at least three times, found himself in two towns on the brink of revolt, was hunted down by a Carlist band alerted to his presence by informers, nearly tumbled down the slippery precipice of a mountain pass, and caught fever, dysentery and an awful eye disease on the way. Few booksellers ever go to such tremendous lengths to peddle their wares to a lukewarm public.

In early August, after three months on the road, he reached Santiago de Compostela. Predictably, a visit to this old Catholic pilgrimage town, once the third holiest shrine of Christianity after Jerusalem and Rome, triggered mixed feelings in a Protestant as thoroughly allergic

Map 3. **Santiago in the 1830s**
(after Madoz, 1848)
❶ Santa Isabel Barracks   ❷ Road to Coruña   ❸ San Roque
❹ Cathedral   ❺ Cárcel   ❻ Santa Susana   ❼ Alameda
❽ Inquisition Palace   ❾ Road to Padron and Pontevedra
❿ Cruz de Gallo crossroads

to Papism as he. Although he felt a certain awe for Santiago's age-old spiritual magnitude, both the letter which he wrote home from here and the chapter he dedicated to it in his book abound with scorn for the empty – if gilded – shell of religion. The splendour, the jewellery, the magnificent ritual of the masses, so Borrow reckoned, served only to camouflage a lifestyle of generalised vice. Here, in a city nominally dedicated to Christian virtues, he noted filth, simonism, prostitutes and venereal disease, theft and cruelty on an unparalleled scale, debauchery and superstitions abandoned and forgotten elsewhere.

The cathedral, where the relics of Saint James have lain buried ever since their discovery in the 9th century, he thought 'a majestic, venerable pile, in every respect calculated to excite awe and admiration', and he adds that 'it is almost impossible to walk its long dusky aisles and hear the solemn music and the noble chanting and inhale the incense of the mighty censers, which are at times swung so high by machinery that they smite the vaulted roof, (…) and entertain a doubt that we are treading the floor of a house where God delighteth to dwell.' And yet, he hurries to add, 'the Lord is distant from that house. He heareth not, He seeth not: or, if He hear and see, it is with anger.' It was all idolatry and the travesty of true faith to the Anglican; and he even goes so far as to suggest, with brazen exaggeration, that 'God and His will are less known and respected [here] than at Pekin or amid the wildernesses where graze the coursers of the Mongol and the Mandchou.'

Beside such inflated indignation, the feeling which most dominated the ten days of Borrow's stay was simple boredom. Perhaps it surprised him. Like most travellers then and now, the massive, romantic repute of Compostela had misled him to expect an Urban Giant, a City of God, able to offer significant answers to those yearning for spiritual guidance. What he found instead was a small, anaemic little town, provincial to its core, a backwater whose fame far outstripped its size and purpose. Borrow describes a city where everything is slowly falling into ruin, where every institution is faltering for lack of funds or *raison d'être*, where the splendid chapels, churches and charities of yesteryear have lost their majesty and pomp, and everything is caked with mud, disease and rubble.

This decline was largely the price which greatness ultimately pays for age. On a local scale, Santiago was still a city of importance. With its 18,000 inhabitants it was in fact the biggest urban centre in Galicia.

But the waning of the Middle Ages, the erosion caused by science and Enlightenment, and the last four years of vicious civil war had exacted a heavy toll. Compostela was no longer the bustling medieval metropolis which yearly welcomed a million pilgrims, people who came, on their knees, from places as far away as Scotland, Hungary, and Lithuania, to pray at the tomb of the Apostle and gain remission for their sins. In Borrow's days, barely a pilgrim arrived here. The famous *Camino de Santiago*, the walking route which devout travellers had to follow from the Pyrenees to the Atlantic Ocean, ran right through the worst war zone of Navarra and the Basque lands. No foreign pilgrim could possibly pass through there, and even if they did, they found no shelter and no food, because the recent disentailment had wiped out the Church's road-side inns. We learn from the books of the Great Hospital of Santiago, which lodged those fallen sick, that the handful of the devout who still visited the city in these years, were mostly *Gallegos* from the immediate neighbourhood, with an occasional family from the adjacent province of Asturias thrown in. Santiago, by this year 1837, was reduced to a shadow of its former self and had practically dwindled to the equivalent of a petty local shrine, a wallflower place of worship, clad in magnificent buildings, venerable rites, and glorious traditions, all of them too big now for its shrunken size. 'The carcass remains,' wrote Richard Ford, who visited the city some years earlier, 'but the spirit is fled'.

That deadly judgement needs some qualification. Ford, the sarcastic aesthete, certainly had a point where the volume and *grandeur* of the pilgrimage was concerned. But he was quite mistaken when it came to the ancient Spirit of Crusade which was equally at home here. *That* spirit had never died or vanished. It still reigned supreme, unbroken, and vital; as battle-ready now as it had ever been in the days of the *Reconquista*, of the subjugation of the Americas and during the Counter-reformation. Perhaps few pilgrims came here now, but that was really immaterial; for Santiago had always been far more than a mere service station for pious pedestrians. In a unique symbolic way, it loomed large in the Spanish conscience as the emblem of resistance to the forces of heresy and hea-thendom. It embodied the immoveable rock of apostolic truth in a sea of apostasy and paganism. The Lord's disciple who rested here was the incarnation of Spanish Christianity itself. He was credited with having personally converted the country shortly before being martyred. And once buried on these distant shores, he had patronised, in his guise of Santiago *Matamoros* – Saint James the Moor-Slayer – the century-long combat to break the rule of the infidel Muslim over the Peninsula.

In the eyes of the Santiago clergy, that fight had never ended, nor would it ever until the Day of Judgement; for this was the eternal, on-going struggle of the Faith against the Forces of Evil, whatever shape or appearance those forces might assume. The Muslims, the Jews, the Lutherans or the French philosophers, the satanic conspiracies of Freemasonry or the atheist hordes of Revolutionary France… All these were merely variations of the same undying evil. Today, in the heart of the fatherland, there was Liberalism, which wanted to close the great monastic institutions and strip away their mammoth landholdings; and the Church regarded this movement as only one more fresh disguise of the Dark One. Consequently, there could be no question about where that Church stood in the present conflict between the partisans of Don Carlos and those of the child-queen Isabel. From the first to the last, from the highest member of the hierarchy to the humblest village priest, that Church was Carlist.

The Liberal authorities had done everything in their power to reduce this outspoken bulwark of the rebellion. Its archbishop, the venerable Fray Rafael de Velez, had been exiled to the Balearic Islands in April 1835, together with his closest collaborators and many of the cathedral canons. Hard-pressed and harassed, other members of the hierarchy had chosen voluntary exile. They fled to Portugal, or went to France, or joined Don Carlos's rambling court in Navarra to participate actively in the struggle. In one case a great dignitary of the cathedral even took up arms himself. He was the formidable canon-cardinal Francisco de Gorostidi, a Basque by birth and a former partisan leader in the Peninsular War, to whom the switch from vestments to armour and back again came as easily as breathing. A known reactionary, Gorostidi escaped from the choir when some bailiffs came to fetch him for interrogation, took to the hills, and started a *guerrilla* band with plans to storm and occupy Compostela for The Cause. In May 1835, just as he was about to descend upon the city, he and his party were surprised by a passing patrol on a nearby mountain. A short skirmish followed; the band dispersed; but Gorostidi was dis-covered hiding in a maize field, taken to the city, furtively interrogated and shot that very same evening for high treason. His death was a major loss for the local Carlist cause; but it was worsened by the capture, in his luggage, of a suitcase full of compromising letters written by fellow conspirers in Santiago. This priceless discovery enabled the authorities to make a clean sweep of the city's hidden Carlists, many of whom were deported or locked up, and – since there were many friars and clerics involved – it gave the Liberals a fine excuse for the premature closing of all the convents and monasteries in town.

A year later, in July 1836, a Carlist expeditionary force led by General Miguel Gomez y Damas occupied the city for a brief spell. As if on some bellicose pilgrimage, the column had come marching all the way from the Basque countries with the object of inciting war in other provinces. It was received with cheers and jubilation – some of the inhabitants are said to have kissed the feet of the lancers as they rode into town – and for one fleeting moment it looked as if Compostela might become the nucleus of yet another Carlist combat zone. But Gomez could not hold what he had captured. He had arrived with ten regiments of veteran Liberal soldiers on his heels, led by the greatest and most ruthless of Liberal generals, Baldomero Espartero, and after a mere forty hours of occupation, Gomez was obliged to sneak off in the dead of night and find safer base elsewhere. The open demonstrations of joy at the Carlists' arrival, and the involvement of many of the inhabitants in pro-rebel activities during the day and a half of the occupation, were sure to bring repercussions. Consequently no fewer than 400 Carlist sympathisers – over 2 % of the population! – left the town in the tail of Gomez's column, escaping the wrath of the Liberal troops. Many of those who stayed behind, either because they were too old to march or because they thought themselves safe, were later prosecuted, exiled or imprisoned.

By August 1837, when Borrow arrived, the backbone of local Carlism had been broken, and Santiago had been reduced to a bucolic little town, living at uneasy peace under martial law. It was a sleepy place. Nothing much happened here, for everything that *could* conceivably happen carried grave political danger. What is more: the inner city, a tangle of small streets and dark alleys, cramped within the limits of ancient walls and alleviated only by an occasional *plaza*, was half depopulated. Gone were the friars, the students, the pilgrims and the civil servants. Pigs ran freely in the streets. The sick of the surrounding countryside huddled in the gutters, hoping to find charity. Beggars crowded the porches of the churches. Starving lepers trespassed into the town. Whatever was vital was missing; whatever was present was poor.

Borrow was blind to economy, and one can read between the lines of his carping descriptions that he blamed Santiago's decay on her spiritual backwardness and the lack of uplifting – read: *Protestant* – devotion. Yet the reasons for Santiago's decline were of a simpler, material kind. The city had been so utterly dependent on medieval-style income and expenditure, especially on the ecclesiastical tithes, tenths, rents and donations, that a few years of civil war, combined with some ruthless anti-clerical reforms, had sufficed to bleed the life out of the system. Hundreds of craftsmen and suppliers had been put out of business when in 1835 the wealthy monastic institutions were closed and abolished. The great reforming overhaul of the same year, known as the *Desamortización* – which in simple terms comes down to the wholesale confiscation of Church lands by the state – had stripped the ecclesiastical institutions and their charities of their rents. Much as the Liberals had solemnly pledged to replace the lost income from endowments with regular salaries, the costly war effort, the rot of corruption and the Liberals' hostile attitudes towards the Church, ensured that no such funds ever arrived. For similar reasons, the large royal subsidy to the Church of Saint James, known as the yearly *Voto de Santiago*, had been abolished early on, because – as Pablo Morillo, the Captain-General of the day, aptly put it – it was madness for the Crown to donate money to an institution which would immediately pass it on to the Crown's own mortal enemies.

Such deliberate measures aside, the local *guerrilla* war that raged all around the city had exacted a heavy toll. In the surrounding countryside, the Carlist bands – largely financed and supplied by the Church – were roaming freely. Their frequent assaults on merchants, stagecoaches and fairs brought commerce practically to a halt. Their raids and robberies often impeded the harvests from being gathered in, or from being transported to the town. And their presence on the roads choked off even the feeble trickle of pilgrims who still dared to set out on the *Camino*. Cold, mercantile statistics bear witness to the erosion of municipal wealth. During the seven lean years of the Carlist War the number of silversmiths – a prominent trade in a town keen for religious souvenirs – plummeted from nineteen to only four; the taverns which used to lodge pilgrims, merchants and students halved in number from 235 to 120; the bookshops of this grand university city were reduced to two, both owned by one family; the textile and leather workshops worked half time, if at all.

In short, there was little left to see, and less still to do in Compostela for a travelling Victorian. Obviously bored, Borrow had to make the most of it. He struck up a friendship with the bookseller, Francisco Rey Romero, 'a venerable man of seventy, very wealthy and respected' who desperately tried to survive the economic slump. Rey Romero was a man of some Liberal sympathies, but – having already run into trouble with the ecclesiastical authorities during the reign of Fernando – he had learned the value of extreme political caution. He agreed to sell Borrow's vernacular Testaments, but he did so on the sly, without publicity, and perhaps more from an astute business sense than from any divinely inspired idealism, as Borrow would have it. The two men spent much time together. They made long walks through the scenic old town and its pleasant, wooded neighbourhood. They visited the sights to see – mostly such remaining charity institutions as the Great Hospital, which Borrow found dirty and overcrowded, and the leper house of Santa Marta on the Padrón road, which he viewed with outright horror – and spent many afternoons in animated conversation in Borrow's *posada*, speaking a little on politics and a lot on religion.

It was, no doubt, an agreeable ten day stopover in an otherwise agitated journey. But this bucolic calm also carried disadvantages. Santiago failed to supply the future author with the remarkable characters, the weird meetings and the juicy anecdotes with which to fill the pages of his book and the lacunae in this chapter. So something more was needed. And since it was desperately needed, it was conveniently found, in the shape of a passing Swiss pilgrim...

13

The Pauper from the Machine

BORROW EMBARKED upon his little narrative fraud one pleasant moonlit evening among a grove of oak and chestnut trees on the southern outskirts of Santiago; the same spot, incidentally, where thirty years before the great Battle of the *Campo de Estrella* had been fought. 'I was walking late one night alone in the Alameda of Saint James,' he wrote years later, 'considering in what direction I should next bend my course.'

> The moon was shining gloriously, and illumined every object around to a considerable distance. The Alameda was quite deserted; everybody, with the exception of myself, having for some time retired. I sat down on a bench and continued my reflections, which were suddenly interrupted by a heavy stumping sound. Turning my eyes in the direction from which it proceeded, I perceived what at first appeared a shapeless bulk slowly advancing: nearer and nearer it drew, and I could now distinguish the outline of a man dressed in coarse brown garments, a kind of Andalusian hat, and using as a staff the long peeled branch of a tree. He had now arrived opposite the bench where I was seated, when, stopping, he took off his hat and demanded charity in uncouth tones and in a strange jargon, which had some resemblance to the Catalan. The moon shone on grey locks and on a ruddy weather-beaten countenance which I at once recognized: 'Benedict Mol,' said I, 'is it possible that I see you at Compostella?'
>
> 'Och, mein Gott, es ist der Herr!' replied Benedict. 'Och, what good fortune, that the Herr is the first person I meet at Compostella.'
>
> MYSELF. – I can scarcely believe my eyes. Do you mean to say that you have just arrived at this place?

BENEDICT – Ow yes, I am this moment arrived. I have walked all the long way from Madrid.

MYSELF – What motive could possibly bring you such a distance?

BENEDICT – Ow, I am come for the schatz – the treasure. I told you at Madrid that I was coming; and now I have met you here, I have no doubt that I shall find it.

MYSELF – In what manner did you support yourself by the way?

BENEDICT – Ow, I begged, I bettled, and so contrived to pick up some cuartos; and when I reached Toro, I worked at my trade of soap-making for a time, till the people said I knew nothing about it, and drove me out of the town. So I went on and begged and bettled till I arrived at Orense, which is in this country of Galicia. Ow, I do not like this country of Galicia at all.

MYSELF – Why not?

BENEDICT – Why! because here they all beg and bettle, and have scarce anything for themselves, much less for me whom they know to be a foreign man. O the misery of Galicia. When I arrive at night at one of their pigsties, which they call posadas, and ask for bread to eat in the name of God, and straw to lie down in, they curse me, and say there is neither bread nor straw in Galicia; and sure enough, since I have been here I have seen neither. (...)

MYSELF – And yet you have come to this country, which you call so miserable, in search of treasure?

BENEDICT – Ow yaw, but the schatz is buried; it is not above ground; there is no money above ground in Galicia. I must dig it up; and when I have dug it up I will purchase a coach with six mules, and ride out of Galicia to Lucerne (...)

MYSELF – I am afraid that you have come on a desperate errand. What do you propose to do? Have you any money?

BENEDICT – Not a cuart; but I do not care now I have arrived at Saint James. The schatz is nigh; and I have, moreover, seen you, which is a good sign; it tells me that the schatz is still here. I shall go to the best posada in the place, and live like a duke till I have an opportunity of digging up the schatz, when I will pay all scores.

'Do nothing of the kind,' I replied; 'find out some place in which to sleep, and endeavour to seek some employment. In the mean time, here is a trifle with which to support yourself; but as for the treasure which you have come to seek, I believe it only exists in your own imagination.' I gave him a dollar and departed.

It is, of course, as difficult to prove somebody's absence as it is to prove a negative. One only stands a chance if the person in question is famous, and his presence at that precise moment can be shown elsewhere. But that is not the case with Benedict Mol. Tramps leave few traces. Once the wind fills in their footsteps with the dust of the road, nothing remains to prove their whereabouts, or even their bare existence. Borrow probably counted on that when he invented this miraculous nocturnal meeting with Mol. But let us be frank here: the coincidence is really too good to be true. Precisely during the ten short days which the Bible salesman spent in Santiago, his old gold-digging Madrid acquaintance just happens to turn up there to come looking for his *Schatz*! What greater boon could Fate bestow on an ambitious author with budding plans for a book of travel and adventure? This is no longer a 'meaningful coincidence' – it is Destiny brazenly ghost-writing a best seller!

Needless to say, like any master fabricator, Borrow took good care to keep Lie and Truth in perfect harmony. Not one iota of the above scene is out of place. All its details are correct: the description of Santiago's Alameda; the location of its benches near the spot where the road to Padrón meets the southern city limits; Mol's itinerary from Madrid; and yes, even that glorious full moon shining up above! For there was indeed a full moon in the sky on the night when this encounter supposedly took place, the 16th or the 17th of August 1837. One cannot help but picture Borrow, sitting on an Alameda bench, taking in the pleasant evening air and – turning his eyes towards the sky – dreaming up the arrival of a friend…

The stage was now set for a glimpse at the treasure hunter at his ludicrous labours. So a few prosaic pages later, Borrow summoned the

Swiss for yet another sham encounter, this time in the company of the bookseller Rey Romero.

Two or three days after this, as we were seated in my apartment in the posada, engaged in conversation, the door was opened by Antonio, who, with a smile on his countenance, said that there was a foreign *gentleman* below, who desired to speak with me. 'Show him up,' I replied; whereupon almost instantly appeared Benedict Mol.

'This is a most extraordinary person,' said I to the bookseller. 'You Galicians, in general, leave your country in quest of money; he, on the contrary, is come hither to find some.'

REY ROMERO – And he is right. Galicia is by nature the richest province in Spain, but the inhabitants are very stupid, and know not how to turn the blessings which surround them to any account (...) There are riches all around us, upon the earth and in the earth.

BENEDICT – Ow yaw, in the earth, that is what I say. There is much more treasure below the earth than above it.

MYSELF – Since I last saw you, have you discovered the place in which you say the treasure is deposited?

BENEDICT – O yes, I know all about it now. It is buried 'neath the sacristy in the church of San Roque.

MYSELF – How have you been able to make that discovery?

BENEDICT – I will tell you: the day after my arrival I walked about all the city in quest of the church, but could find none which at all answered to the signs which my comrade who died in the hospital gave me. I entered several, and looked about, but all in vain; I could not find the place which I had in my mind's eye. At last the people with whom I lodge, and to whom I told my business, advised me to send for a meiga.

MYSELF – A meiga! What is that?

BENEDICT – Ow! a haxweib, a witch; the Gallegos call them so in their jargon (...) So I consented, and they sent

for the meiga. Och! what a weib is that meiga! I never saw
such a woman; she is as large as myself, and has a face
as round and red as the sun. She asked me a great many
questions in her Gallegan, and when I had told her all she
wanted to know, she pulled out a pack of cards and laid
them on the table in a particular manner, and then she
said that the treasure was in the church of San Roque;
and sure enough, when I went to that church, it answered
in every respect to the signs of my comrade who died in the
hospital. O she is a powerful hax, that meiga; she is well
known in the neighbourhood, and has done much harm
to the cattle. I gave her half the dollar I had from you for
her trouble.

MYSELF – Then you acted like a simpleton; she has
grossly deceived you. But even suppose that the treasure
is really deposited in the church you mention, it is not
probable that you will be permitted to remove the floor of
the sacristy to search for it.

BENEDICT – Ow, the matter is already well advanced.
Yesterday I went to one of the canons to confess myself and
to receive absolution and benediction; not that I regard
these things much, but I thought this would be the best
means of broaching the matter, so I confessed myself, and
then I spoke of my travels to the canon, and at last I told
him of the treasure, and proposed that if he assisted me we
should share it between us. Ow, I wish you had seen him;
he entered at once into the affair, and said that it might
turn out a very profitable speculation: and he shook me by
the hand, and said that I was an honest Swiss and a good
Catholic. And I then proposed that he should take me into
his house and keep me there till we had an opportunity of
digging up the treasure together. This he refused to do.

REY ROMERO – Of that I have no doubt: trust one of
our canons for not committing himself so far until he sees
very good reason. These tales of treasure are at present
rather too stale: we have heard of them ever since the time
of the Moors.

BENEDICT – He advised me to go to the Captain General and obtain permission to make excavations, in which case he promised to assist me to the utmost of his power.

Thereupon the Swiss departed, and I neither saw nor heard anything farther of him during the time that I continued at Saint James.

For all its charm and appeal, none of this dialogue needs to be taken too seriously. A three-way conversation such as Borrow here describes, between himself, the bookseller and the treasure hunter simply never took place. We know so because some two years later, Rey Romero, in response to a query, broached the subject of the treasure hunter in a business letter; and there he treats the Swiss as a total stranger, one on whom he had never laid eyes, let alone spent a goodly hour talking to the man. At some point, probably much later than the summer of 1837, Borrow obviously mentioned Mol to Rey Romero, seeing that the same letter speaks of a 'recommendation'; and the two friends may very well have tackled the subject of hidden hoards and the madness of gold fever. But if they did, it must have been in the absence of the Swiss.

We see Borrow at his best and at his worst in this last scene. He was being perfectly plausible, and one might even say convincing. And yet he was lying through his teeth with nearly every word he wrote. A master of fabrication if he had to be, he pulled in every useful bit which he could pillage from his sources, then recycled the lot to compose Mol's spectacular monologue. That witch, for instance, Mol's horrid *Haxweib* with her deck of Tarot cards, was taken straight from one of the minor articles which the *Eco del Comercio* dedicated to the Santiago treasure hunt in 1838. There, she figures in a trivial supporting role to Mol's self-defence, as 'the woman who laid the cards for him in Paris', and who had fooled him to believe that his gold really could be found. We never learn anything else about her, and she did not matter to the tale. But Borrow's keen eye perceived a welcome opportunity to introduce some thrilling Galician magic into his book. And so he lifted her from his prime material, swept her, as if by broomstick, from Paris to Santiago, and put her to much better use in the Apostle's City than she ever could have served him in the City of Lights.

Perhaps the identification of the treasure's burial spot as 'beneath the sacristy in the church of San Roque' came about in a similar way. That element also figured initially in the *Eco* articles; and it is not unthinkable that this is where Borrow took it from. Yet one needs to be a cautious here, for the better question is how that phrase – which is a patent untruth – found its way into the *Eco* in the first place. As we shall see, the real treasure hunt did not take place in the *chapel* of San Roque, but in the adjacent *hospital*. Nobody, however, knew this was the true objective of the search until the day the Swiss actually set out to dig. So possibly this was another standard feature of Mol's cover story, that clever little tale full of false clues which he told people when – by way of bait – he had to reveal some appetising titbits about his hoard. If meant to throw other prospectors off the track, it was truly well-chosen; for who in these tense religious times would dare to go dig in a functioning chapel and commit a screaming sacrilege?

Borrow, incidentally, never corrected the fact. Throughout his book, he maintained that the chapel was the object of the treasure hunter's search, and in a later chapter he even describes Mol digging there, in flagrant disregard of the truth. His motives are not hard to guess: once more he meant to vilify the Church of Rome, and sticking firmly to the chapel as the burial spot enabled him to do just that. Throughout the tale of Mol, Borrow never misses a chance to hint at dark, illicit Church involvement in the scandal, as if some secret cabal of black-clad prelates was really pulling the strings on which the treasure hunter dangled. That Santiago Canon, greedy, violent, and scheming, the perfect opposite of a Christian shepherd, comes from the same unsavoury stock. Admittedly, there was a cathedral canon responsible for the administration of San Roque. His name was Don Ramón Boán, and he held the office from the early 1830s to his death in 1857. If Mol wanted to prospect anywhere in the complex, this was indeed the man to see. But there are no reasons to believe that Don Ramón, or any other ecclesiastic, was ever involved in the scandal. No other source beside George Borrow says so; and for all we can tell, the treasure hunt was exclusively a government affair. Yet for Borrow that was not good enough. He always had to gratify his obsessive urge to calumniate the Church; which is why he added such little slanders and innuendos, of which there were more, and worse, to follow.

14

Canon and Blunderbuss

AFTER TEN days in Santiago Borrow decided to move on. In late August 1837, he packed his bags and travelled south, to Vigo and Pontevedra, where he tried to peddle his Spanish New Testaments without much success. On the way back, he took his large detour to the *Costa da Morte* – the 'Coast of Death', so named for the innumerable ships which foundered on its treacherous, rock-infested shores – to see Cape Finisterre. It was a rough journey. Despite the services of a guide, he got lost in the wilderness of the western hills, spent a miserable night in a flea-ridden turf hut among half naked peasants, and once in Finisterre nearly got shot for being a Carlist spy. After all this he had had his fill of Galicia. He returned to Coruña, and from there set out by the coast to Oviedo in the Asturias. There – just in time to provide yet another lively chapter – Benedict Mol put in one more miraculous appearance. One rainy morning, Borrow writes, he was seated in the large room of his gloomy, gothic Oviedo inn,

> when the door was flung open and in bounded Antonio.
>
> 'Mon maitre,' said he, quite breathless, 'who do you think has arrived?'
>
> 'The pretender, I suppose,' said I, in some trepidation; 'if so, we are prisoners.'
>
> 'Bah, bah!' said Antonio, 'it is not the pretender, but one worth twenty of him; it is the Swiss of Saint James.'
>
> 'Benedict Mol, the Swiss!' said I, 'What! has he found the treasure? But how did he come? How is he dressed?'
>
> 'Mon maitre,' said Antonio, 'he came on foot if we may judge by his shoes, through which his toes are sticking; and as for his dress, he is in most villainous apparel.' (...)
>
> In a few minutes Benedict Mol found his way upstairs; he was, as Antonio had remarked, in most villainous

apparel, and nearly barefooted; his old Andalusian hat was dripping with rain.

'Och, lieber herr,' said Benedict, 'how rejoiced I am to see you again. Oh, the sight of your countenance almost repays me for all the miseries I have undergone since I parted with you at Saint James.'

MYSELF – I can scarcely believe that I really see you here at Oviedo. What motive can have induced you to come to such an out-of-the-way place from such an immense distance?

BENEDICT – Lieber herr, I will sit down and tell you all that has befallen me. Some few days after I saw you last, the canonigo persuaded me to go to the captain-general to apply for permission to disinter the schatz, and also to crave assistance. So I saw the captain-general, who at first received me very kindly, asked me several questions, and told me to come again. So I continued visiting him till he would see me no longer, and do what I might I could not obtain a glance of him. The canon now became impatient, more especially as he had given me a few pesetas out of the charities of the church. He frequently called me a bribon and impostor. At last, one morning I went to him, and said that I had proposed to return to Madrid, in order to lay the matter before the government, and requested that he would give me a certificate to the effect that I had performed a pilgrimage to Saint James, which I imagined would be of assistance to me upon the way, as it would enable me to beg with some colour of authority. He no sooner heard this request, than, without saying a word or allowing me a moment to put myself on my defence, he sprang upon me like a tiger, grasping my throat so hard that I thought he would have strangled me. I am a Swiss, however, and a man of Lucerne, and when I had recovered myself a little, I had no difficulty in flinging him off; I then threatened him with my staff and went away. He followed me to the gate with the most horrid curses, saying that if I presumed to return again, he would have me thrown at

once into prison as a thief and a heretic. So I went in quest
of yourself, lieber herr, but they told me that you were
departed for Coruna; I then set out for Coruna after you.

MYSELF – And what befell you on the road?

BENEDICT – I will tell you: about half-way between
Saint James and Coruna, as I was walking along, thinking
of the schatz, I heard a loud galloping, and looking around
me I saw two men on horseback coming across the field
with the swiftness of the wind, and making directly for
me. Lieber Gott, said I, these are thieves, these are fac-
tious; and so they were. They came up to me in a moment
and bade me stand, so I flung down my staff, took off my
hat and saluted them. "Good day, caballeros," said I to
them. "Good day, countryman," said they to me, and then
we stood staring at each other for more than a minute (...),
till at last one asked me who I was, whence I came, and
where I was going. "Gentlemen," said I, "I am a Swiss, I
have been to Saint James to perform a religious vow, and
am now returning to my own country." I said not a word
about the treasure, for I was afraid that they would have
shot me at once, conceiving that I carried part of it about
me. "Have you any money?" they demanded. "Gentlemen,"
I replied, "you see how I travel on foot, with my shoes torn
to pieces; I should not do so if I had money. I will not
deceive you, however, I have a peseta and a few cuartos,"
and thereupon I took out what I had and offered it to them.
"Fellow," said they, "we are caballeros of Galicia, and do
not take pesetas, much less cuartos. Of what opinion are
you? Are you for the queen?" "No, gentlemen," said I, "I
am not for the queen, but, at the same time, allow me to
tell you that I am not for the king either; I know nothing
about the matter; I am a Swiss, and fight neither for nor
against anybody unless I am paid." This made them laugh,
and then they questioned me about Saint James, and the
troops there, and the captain-general; and not to disoblige
them, I told them all I knew and much more. Then one of
them, who looked the fiercest and most determined, took

his trombone in his hand, and pointing it at me, said, "Had you been a Spaniard, we would have blown your head to shivers, for we should have thought you a spy, but we see you are a foreigner, and believe what you have said; take, therefore, this peseta and go your way, but beware that you tell nobody any thing about us, for if you do, carracho!" He then discharged his trombone just over my head, so that for a moment I thought myself shot, and then with an awful shout, they both galloped away, their horses leaping over the barrancos, as if possessed with many devils.

MYSELF – And what happened to you on your arrival at Coruna?

BENEDICT – When I arrived at Coruna, I inquired after yourself, lieber herr, and they informed me that, only the day before my arrival, you had departed for Oviedo: and when I heard that, my heart died within me, for I was now at the far end of Galicia, without a friend to help me. For a day or two I knew not what to do; at last I determined to make for the frontier of France, passing through Oviedo in the way, where I hoped to see you and ask counsel of you. So I begged and bettled among the Germans of Coruna. I, however, got very little from them, only a few cuarts, less than the thieves had given me on the road from Saint James, and with these I departed for the Asturias by the way of Mondonedo. Och, what a town is that, full of canons, priests, and pfaffen, all of them more Carlist than Carlos himself.

One day I went to the bishop's palace and spoke to him, telling him I was a pilgrim from Saint James, and requesting assistance. He told me, however, that he could not relieve me, and as for my being a pilgrim from Saint James, he was glad of it, and hoped that it would be of service to my soul. So I left Mondonedo, and got amongst the wild mountains, begging and betting at the door of every choza that I passed, telling all I saw that I was a pilgrim from Saint James, and showing my passport in proof that I had been there. Lieber herr, no person gave me a cuart, nor even a piece of broa, and both Gallegans and Asturians laughed at Saint James, and told me that his name was no longer a passport in Spain. I should have starved if I had not sometimes plucked an ear or two out of the maize fields; I likewise gathered grapes from the parras and berries from the brambles, and in this manner I subsisted till I arrived at the bellotas, where I slaughtered a stray kid which I met, and devoured part of the flesh raw, so great was my hunger. It made me, however, very ill, and for two days I lay in a barranco half dead and unable to help myself; it was a mercy that I was not devoured by the wolves. I then struck across the country for Oviedo: how I reached it I do not know; I was like one walking in a dream. Last night I slept in an empty hogsty about two leagues from here, and ere I left it, I fell down on my knees and prayed to God that I might find you, lieber herr, for you were my last hope.

MYSELF – And what do you propose to do at present?

BENEDICT – What can I say, lieber herr? I know not what to do. I will be guided in everything by your counsel.

MYSELF – I shall remain at Oviedo a few days longer, during which time you can lodge at this posada, and endeavour to recover from the fatigue of your disastrous journeys; perhaps before I depart, we may hit on some plan to extricate you from your present difficulties.

One need not look too closely to find the flaws in this here piece. The fact that all of Mol's travelling adventures are practically a carbon copy of Borrow's own, is almost enough to give the game away. Those Carlists *guerrilleros* who almost shoot the Swiss, dove-tail perfectly with a pair of bandits who tried to rob the Bible salesman at the Castellana bridge, near the town of Lugo. The troublesome journey through the Asturian mountain range called 'the Seven Bellotas', Borrow himself had just negotiated and had described at length in the preceding pages. But how fantastic all this is, shows clearest in the grotesque sequence of religious hypocrisy which pervades the entire episode. One might still overlook the oddity that Benedict Mol, former member of the Papal Guard and scion of a good Catholic Swiss canton, somehow shares George Borrow's ultra-Anglican prejudices against the Church of Rome. But what to think of canons of the Santiago cathedral who rob their own charities and dabble in Greek-Roman wrestling? How can it be that Gallegos and Asturians, who, led by their priests, gallantly battled Napoleon's armies under the war cry '¡Santiago y a Ellos!' would openly laugh at the Apostle Saint James? And how does one explain a Bishop of Mondoñedo who talks in so laconic a way about some of the most sacred tenets of his own apostolic faith?

Let us not linger on the fact that this is most uncharacteristic of Galician bishops of all times. Let us also ignore the fact that even Spanish bishops must have had better things to do than to receive foreign vagrants in private audience. Let us merely point out that this entire meeting is totally impossible, since this Bishop of Mondoñedo, a staunch and well-known Carlist called Don Francisco López Borricón, was nowhere near Mondoñedo in September 1837. Hassled and molested for his reactionary opinions, Don Francisco had fled from his See to the Basque countries in October 1836, a year before Mol supposedly met him. But Borrow had not been to Mondoñedo, so he was unaware of the bishop's absence. And in his eagerness to ladle yet one more infamy upon the Papist Church, he walked straight into a trap of his own making.

It was, by now, enough. Having made good use of Mol in Oviedo, and looking at a score of pages in which to describe his own return to Madrid – pages in which he had no need for the Swiss at all – Borrow then had to lose his man again. He did so smoothly, by bringing in the pretext of fatigue.

> A day or two after this I said to Mol, 'tomorrow I start from hence for Santander. It is therefore high time that you decide upon some course, whether to return to Madrid or to make the best of your way to France, and from thence proceed to your own country.'
>
> 'Lieber herr,' said Benedict, 'I will follow you to Santander by short journeys, for I am unable to make long ones amongst these hills; and when I am there, peradventure I may find some means of passing into France. (...) I will quit Spain as soon as possible, and betake me to Lucerne,

though it is a hard thing to leave the schatz behind me in the land of the Gallegans.'

Thereupon I presented him with a few dollars.

'A strange man is this Benedict,' said Antonio to me next morning as we sallied forth from Oviedo .'A strange life has he led, and a strange death he will die – it is written on his countenance. That he will leave Spain I do not believe, (...) for he is bewitched about this treasure. Last night he sent for a sorcière, whom he consulted in my presence; and she told him that he was doomed to possess it, but that first of all he must cross water. She cautioned him likewise against an enemy, which he supposes must be the canon of Saint James. I have often heard people speak of the avidity of the Swiss for money, and here is a proof of it. I would not undergo what Benedict has suffered in these last journeys of his, to possess all the treasures in Spain.'

15

A Zahori *in the* Cárcel de Corte

THE OLDEST Spanish word for 'treasure hunter', the one most widely used in the days of Mol, is *Zahori*. It is an Arab word, which reached Spain in the linguistic saddlebags of the invading Berber Muslims. Used for a thousand years or more, it has gone through many shifts of meaning. Originally, in North-Africa, it only meant a common divine or geomancer, who owed his occult powers to being born under a particular constellation of the planet Venus (*az-zahura* in Arabic) and was therefore called a 'Venusian' or *Zuhari*. In this same sense of 'sorcerer' or 'witch', the word is sometimes found in old Andalusian texts written during the Muslim rule or shortly after. Later, it seems to have turned into the name for a certain class of faith healers. And later still it came to mean *rhabdomancer*, a village medium who, with a dowsing rod, searches a peasant's fields for subterranean sheets of water. This meaning it still retains today in Spanish and Valencian.

It was, however, in the late 17th century that the word acquired its most extravagant meaning of all. In that wildly superstitious age, the Spanish *Zahori* became a genuine clairvoyant, an optical wonder-worker, who was credited with the faculty of seeing deep into the earth. His eyesight was so good, so sharp, so very intense, that it penetrated through rock and soil as if they were made of glass; and this enabled him to locate valuable hoards of precious metals and buried treasures up to a depth of some 100 feet. According to beliefs still current in the 1830s, *Zahoris* acquired this remarkable talent by being born, not under the aegis of some pagan planet, but during the most portentous moment of the Christian year. 'It is a widespread popular tradition,' wrote Modesto Lafuente, Spain's 19th century Voltaire, 'that those born on Good Friday during the celebration of matins possess this most enviable ability.' That is to say: they saw the light at the time of the *Tenebrae* mass, when all the candles in church are extinguished, and the world awaits, in eerie darkness, the Saviour's gruesome death.

It will not surprise that the *Zahoris*, who came into the world at so gloomy a time, turned out to be people of a profound melancholic disposition. They were forever haunted by spectres, and lived sombre and unhappy lives. Yet the curse also carried some rewards. People who could spot a hidden hoard in the twinkle of an eye, were naturally quite popular in a country where 'ever since the time of the Moors' each village, town and hamlet possessed its tale of buried gold. And so, for centuries on end, countless *Zahoris* made splendid money by swindling poor peasants and simple-minded town folk out of their petty savings, in exchange for a beckoning illusion and some dramatic hocus-pocus.

In his weekly *Fray Gerundio*, Modesto Lafuente himself dedicated a lengthy series of articles to the adventures of such con men, who for a handful of small change located the buried treasures in the vicinity of poor villages and vanished from the neighbourhood just before the peasants understood they had been had. A compulsive merrymaker and the most gifted political satirist of his day, Lafuente did so with a calculated purpose. He liked to draw close parallels between village *Zahoris* looking for imaginary gold and the successive Ministers of Finance looking for phantom revenue. But when he told these stories, in the early months of 1838, even he could not foresee how soon such a real-life combination of a Chancellor and a *Zahori* would come true in Santiago.

Mol, of course, never pretended to see through solid rock and earth. But that mattered little when it came to poking fun at the *Powers That Be*. The man was looking for buried treasure; the word implied all those who swindled dupes with the help of make-believe. So he more than deserved his sobriquet; and when in the following summer the Santiago scandal broke, Lafuente – his tongue in a cheek it rarely left – felt no scruples in baptising Mol *El Suizo Zahori*: 'the Swiss Zahori'. As slurs go, it was not the worst one ever to be bestowed on the man from Lucerne.

Unlike Modesto Lafuente, George Borrow never called his treasure-hunting friend a *Zahori*. Yet it is not unthinkable he was hinting at the very thing when during their next encounter, he presented the Swiss dressed up in a carnival costume. That meeting, in May 1838, took place in a prison cell. But other than one might expect, the man locked up in jail was not Benedict Mol, the mercenary vagrant, but George Borrow, the respectable English Bible salesman. It was he who got imprisoned for his religious activities; while Mol, the petty swindler, was received in the offices of power.

The events and causes which led to Borrow's bout in jail are many and complex, and it would take too long to spell them all out. Suffice it to say it was the inevitable outcome of his labours in a land like Spain. Borrow had moved here to peddle vernacular Scripture; and there was nothing which the Spanish Church feared and hated more fiercely than this. Such translations, which laymen might read and *misinterpret*, and which could easily lead them to heresy and critical views of the priesthood, were in fact qualified – rather astonishingly – as '*books and pamphlets against religion and Christian morals*'. For centuries the Inquisition had done what it could to suppress such works, to intercept them and destroy them. Now, on the brink of modern times, the churchmen were fighting a rearguard action, which turned particularly bitter because they knew they were losing. Four years earlier, when the Liberals had come to power, they had taken immediate steps to strip the Church of its book-burning privileges. The Inquisition was abolished; a free press promulgated; censorship reduced to a minimum. The bishops retained some minor rights to approve or forbid religious works, but this privilege was largely a dead letter, whose enforcement usually depended on the personal goodwill of individual magistrates.

But political constellations change, especially in the context of a civil war and an endless string of popular rebellions. After two or three radical left-wing governments, Queen Regent Maria Cristina began to tire of ministers who kept chopping away at her prerogatives. To stem the tide, she appointed a government of so-called *Moderados* – 'Moderate Liberals' – a term sufficiently elastic to allow the party to be led by a man like Count Ofalia, formerly a faithful servant of Fernando VII, and one who might just as easily have found his niche among the Carlists. Ofalia and his five fellow ministers had excellent, if discreet, relations in ecclesiastical circles. So when they took office in December 1837, the Church leaders saw their chance to regain the momentum in their fight against heresy. They swung into action, applied some pressure, and convinced Spain's new rulers to curb the introduction of dangerous foreign books and propaganda into the kingdom.

George Borrow was an obvious target. He was headstrong, uncompromising and happy to defy the Church every step of the way. He published Bibles and New Testaments in Spanish, Gospels of Luke in both Caló and Basque. He hung out with thieves, with vagabonds, with smugglers, and harlots. He opened shops to sell his Lutheran literature, and went on long tours through the provinces to spread his venomous books all over the land! Worst of all, however: he never really gave offence. In all his private battles with the Church, he took care never to insult, never to break laws openly, never to do anything which might be turned into a reason for a crack-down. This most irritating habit made him nearly untouchable; but fortunately, in April 1838, another Bible-selling agent, one Lieutenant Graydon, caused a major riot in Malaga by spreading tracts which insulted the Virgin Mary and the Catholic hierarchy as a whole. The scandal gave the government its pretext for intervention; and when Borrow, provoked by a plain-clothes policemen he found rummaging through his papers, threw the man out of his quarters by force, the authorities had their excuse to lock him up in the *Cárcel de Corte* – the huge, fortress-style jailhouse in the centre of Madrid.

Borrow did not mind at all. On the contrary: he enjoyed it, he loved it, he cherished his arrest as a personal triumph! It enabled him to cast himself as the innocent yet fearless victim of Papist bigotry, a Christian Soldier Marching Onward in defence of the Gospel of the Lord. It was to make his name and reputation. It was to bring him national fame back home. How delighted he was with the martyr's bonnet gleams through the subscript which he added to the title of his book: '*The Bible in Spain* or *The journeys, adventures, and imprisonments of an Englishman in an attempt to circulate the Scriptures in the Peninsula*'. Surely the public would appreciate his upright British probity. Surely they would admire a man who once dared to tell Ofalia to his face, that 'it is a pleasant thing to be persecuted for the Gospel's sake'. For good measure, Borrow suppressed all mention of Graydon in the book, arrogating all the laurels of religious persecution to himself, and 'extended' the length of his imprisonment from the nine days that it actually lasted to an heroic 'three weeks'. Of course it wasn't all a joyride. The Madrid prison was a filthy and dangerous place, and one of his servants caught the jail fever there and shortly after died a horrible death. But Borrow's confinement was nowhere as dramatic as he pretended. He had money, in a jail where famously 'the situation of every prisoner depends not at all on his crimes, but on his purse.' What is more: both he and his jailers were well aware of the diplomatic protection which the British Ambassador granted him. And further in the background still loomed the British government, without whose help even the *Moderados* could not run their civil war. So Borrow was treated well, kept in a luxurious jail cell of his own, where his servants could come and go as they pleased, where he had all the food, furniture and clean linen he desired, and where he was allowed to receive any visitors who came to see him.

One of those visitors was Benedict Mol. Supposedly by pure coincidence he ran into Borrow's manservant in a nearby street. Hearing that Borrow was in jail, the Swiss decided to pay his respects, and to acquaint his English friend with the windfall which had lately come his way. His luck had changed; his ship had sailed in; and this showed, first and foremost in his extravagant, nearly brand-new costume. His clothes, Borrow wrote,

> were of a much more respectable appearance than any which he had sported on former occasions. His coat and pantaloons, which were of light green, were nearly new. On his head he still wore an Andalusian hat, but the present one was neither old nor shabby, but fresh and glossy, and of immense altitude of cone: whilst in his hand, instead of the ragged staff which I had observed at Saint James, he now carried a huge bamboo rattan, surmounted by the grim head of either a bear or lion, curiously cut out of pewter.

Some dress indeed! An outfit worthy of an Oriental *Zahori*! It would seem that someone somewhere had done his occult homework, and had brought Mol's looks into line with *Zahori* dress-code. Green is the colour of the supernatural in the Middle East, the hue of the sacred, of the mystic and of the magical in all its manifestations. Ancient *grimoires* of astrological magic mention it expressly as the colour of the planet Venus, from which the *Zahoris* took their name and powers. It is anybody's guess where that high coned hat came from; perhaps it was only a stage prop, meant to lend the man the appearance of a soothsayer. But that 'magic rattan' – as Borrow repeatedly calls it – belongs plainly to the *Zahori* tradition. Such a thing gets mentioned, for instance, by the 17th century explorer Lucas in his travelogue *Voyage en Egypte*, where he describes how, as he passed through the Nile valley, he was rumoured by the *fellaheen* to be a western wizard who, *'due to his baton'*, possessed the gift of seeing into the most obscure places, even through rocks and solid walls, 'and that I had thus discovered all the treasures which lay below the mountains by which we passed'.

> 'You have all the appearance of a treasure seeker returned from a successful expedition,' I exclaimed.
> 'Or rather,' interrupted Antonio, 'of one who has ceased to trade on his own bottom, and now goes seeking treasures at the cost and expense of others.'

Neither for the first time nor the last, Borrow's savvy Greek manservant hit the mark. Mol indeed had found himself a sponsor – and not just anybody, but one of the most prominent men in the land. As Borrow explains it: after their separation in Oviedo, the Swiss had wandered through the wilderness, vaguely in the direction of the border, with the aim of returning home to Lucerne. Hunger, cold and rain made his progress miserable. His pockets were empty, but the locals were so poor themselves that it was impossible to survive on alms. Then, one night, almost at the end of his forces, weak from hunger and privation, brought near collapse somewhere in the middle of the Aragon mountains by 'the horror of wandering about the savage hills and wide plains of Spain, without money and without hope', he had a mystical experience. Having appealed for help to higher powers in the depth of a dark abyss, he heard a voice. A voice 'from the hollow of a rock, clear and strong, and it cried: *Der schatz, der schatz, it is not yet dug up; to Madrid, to Madrid. The way to the schatz is through Madrid.*' This was all it took to convince him. 'I brandished my staff,' he told Borrow in the jail cell, 'and my body and my limbs became full of new and surprising strength, and I strode forward, and was not long before I reached the high road; and then I begged and bettled as I best could, until I reached Madrid.'

All this is probably little more than Borrow's ingenious way to patch up the holes left by Mol's intrusive fantasy-trip up north, and to write his treasure hunter back to Madrid after having callously abandoned him in Oviedo. Yet the appearance of the Swiss in the jail cell, and the remaining adventures which he tells from there on, probably do contain a core of truth. For we know from Rey Romero's letter that Mol was able, some three months later, to inform him of Borrow's imprisonment, and that

Borrow in his turn recommended the Swiss to the old bookseller by letter. So the conclusion is warranted that the Bible salesman and the treasure hunter were both in Madrid in the spring of 1838 and maintained some sort of contact; and this puts the rest of the episode in quite another, more veracious, light.

'And what has befallen you since you reached Madrid?' I inquired. 'Did you find the treasure in the streets?'

On a sudden Bennet became reserved and taciturn, which the more surprised me, as, up to the present moment, he had at all times been remarkably communicative with respect to his affairs and prospects. From what I could learn from his broken hints and innuendoes, it appeared that, since his arrival at Madrid, he had fallen into the hands of certain people who had treated him with kindness, and provided him with both money and clothes; not from disinterested motives, however, but having an eye to the treasure. (...)

Who his new friends were, he either knew not or would not tell me, save that they were people in power. He said something about Queen Christina and an oath which he had taken in the presence of a bishop on the crucifix and 'the four Evangiles.' I thought that his head was turned, and forbore questioning. Just before taking his departure, he observed 'Lieber herr, pardon me for not being quite frank towards you, to whom I owe so much, but I dare not; I am not now my own man. It is, moreover, an evil thing at all times to say a word about treasure before you have secured it. There was once a man in my own country, who dug deep into the earth until he arrived at a copper vessel which contained a schatz. Seizing it by the handle, he merely exclaimed in his transport, 'I have it'; that was enough, however: down sank the kettle, though the handle remained in his grasp. That was all he ever got for his trouble and digging. Farewell, lieber herr, I shall speedily be sent back to Saint James to dig up the schatz; but I will visit you ere I go.'

16

His Excellency Alejandro Mon

BY 1842, when writing *The Bible in Spain*, Borrow knew perfectly well whom Mol had had in mind when he mentioned the '*people in power*' who '*treated him with kindness*'. The Swiss was speaking of the Minister of Finance of the Ofalia government, Don Alejandro Mon, who had become the sponsor of the Santiago treasure hunt.

Mon is a strange and aloof figure in contemporary Spanish politics. On the one hand, set among the true and bogus heroes of this agitated age, he dwarfs to insignificance due to his bland bookkeeper's nature and his total lack of glamour. On the other, he looms as large as Goliath in the fiscal and monetary history of his country. So large indeed he looms, that one admiring author from his native Asturias once ventured the daring statement that 19th century Spain was saved 'by the sabre of Narvaez and the brains of Mon'. Whether one should really qualify General Narvaez's role in Spanish history as an act of national salvation may well be questioned. Spain's first true thorough-bred *caudillo* was a most cynical autocrat who ruled the land for decades through intrigue, *coup d'état* and firing-squad. In his first year of power alone, he executed more men than Fernando VII had done in all his reign; and on his deathbed, when invited by his confessor to forgive his enemies, he is said to have replied: 'Enemies? I have no enemies! I killed them all...' Strange words are these in the mouth of a saviour...

When it comes to Mon, however, the judgment makes more sense. There can be little doubt that, in the long run, the Asturian Chancellor had a most salutary effect on Spanish finances. In fact, what economic recovery the land enjoyed after 1850, is very much due to his single-handed, sensible reforms. But that was really only 'in the long run', in the latter half of the century. Mon's influence was not so benign in the 1830s, when he set out on his political career; and still less in 1838, when his Treasury Department was a circus.

Admittedly this was not all his fault. Mon had the misfortune of making his debut in public service during a period of chaos which would have defied the combined abilities of Einstein, Necker and Napoleon. He was a financial wizard in a monetary wasteland; a highly competent man in an utterly impossible age. We cannot really blame him for his failure to mend the irreparable. And yet, his role was not limited to simple impotence in the face of *force majeur*. He also added his own grain of sand to the towering heap of madness. He was a young man when the treasure hunt took place, only thirty-seven, and, although a financial prodigy, he possessed a pronounced irrational streak. Such men often run amok until the wisdom of middle age starts pulling in the reins.

Mon's young years show this erratic trait of his clearest. Born into a prominent Oviedo family in 1801, the future Chancellor first set out to study for the priesthood. He stuck to it for a considerable while; but then, all of a sudden, decided to leave the seminary and switch to the faculty of law. Of course, such abrupt swings of fancy are nothing uncommon in the young; but in Mon's case the change was ambivalent and half-hearted. He might have left theology behind, but clerical lore had lost none of its attraction; and when he took his degree, he graduated both in Civil and in Canonical law. Then, having come this far, he once again swung away brusquely from his former course and joined the ranks of the Church's most irreconcilable enemies. At the time of the ultra-Liberal Riego rebellion of 1820, he – the former seminarist, the doctor in Church Law – participated in the Oviedo riots and enlisted in the local 'Literary Battalion', a student militia formed to defend the new anti-clerical Constitution. Three years went by, the Liberal regime crumbled, Fernando was restored by French bayonets, and like so many other participants, Mon was condemned to death, in absentia, by the king's harsh tribunals of 'purification'. Consequently young Alejandro fled Oviedo and stayed in hiding for the next ten years. Only after Fernando's death was he able to re-emerge under the terms of the political amnesty granted by the new regime.

Perhaps this decade of enforced idleness had not yet sobered him up completely; but it had at least cured his extremism. Never again would Mon support a radical cause. Instead of joining the new revolution, he now attached himself to conventional, modest, mainstream Liberalism. With the help of two influential family-members – his ultra-Catholic cousin Pedro Pidal and the conservative heavyweight Toreno – he embarked upon a political career in Madrid. Somewhere along the way, he had picked up enough financial acumen to be worthy of a post in public finance. The patronage of Toreno – who became Prime Minister in 1835 – did the rest. In quick succession, Mon was appointed secretary to the Treasury, Superintendent in Granada, and Superintendent in Coruña. In each of these positions he impressed the *Moderado* leadership with his expertise and wooden loyalty. In reward he was allowed to stand for Parliament in the 1836 elections, and entered the *Cortes*. Soon, he was chosen as one of its speakers; and in December 1837, when Count Ofalia formed his cabinet, he was invited to join as Minister of Finance.

What he encountered on arrival at the Treasury was chaos and empty coffers. It is not easy for us moderns, used as we are to a large measure of solvency in public affairs, to grasp the kind of tangle which existed at the time. Five years of civil war and political upheaval, of disturbed trade and rampant corruption, combined with a total overhaul of the economic, social and fiscal structure of the land, had wrecked an economy which had not been working particularly well to begin with.

The root of the trouble was that Spain's economy was still languishing largely in the Middle Ages when Fernando died. Taxation was primitive: a haphazard bundle of tolls on the highways, custom duties in the ports, and sales taxes on such everyday things as wine, soap, and salt. Tax collecting itself was done by the wasteful and offensive system of tax farming, which granted individual investors the right to collect state dues in exchange for a lump sum, with the understanding they could pocket any surplus which they managed to extract from the taxpayers. Trade was curbed by monopolies, protective legislation and crumbling roads. Land was held, 80 % or more, by great landowners and mammoth monasteries, who could not or would not sell their holdings, but rented them out to dirt farmers under fixed, oppressive, long-term contracts, so that agricultural production was automatically reduced to the subsistence minimum of the stone age.

All this the Liberals set out to reform as soon as they gained power in 1833. It was perhaps a necessary thing to lead Spain into the modern age, but its timing was madness, for the overhaul was undertaken under the worst conceivable circumstances: during a disruptive civil war and a global economic slump that was certain to defeat any attempt at industrialisation by backward nations. Whatever was done backfired dreadfully. The Liberals freed trade; exports of grain to richer markets instantly caused famines. They tried to rationalise taxation; state income dwindled to a trickle. To solve the dilemma of landownership – and, in passing, to curb the power of the Church – all Church lands were confiscated at the stroke of a pen in 1835, and sold off to private citizens. This might have been a useful measure, had it only been done honestly and well. As it was, it got badly bungled. The land did not pass into the hands of the farmers who worked it, but was scooped up by bourgeois investors, often political cronies, who continued the same decrepit system of leasing, only in a harsher manner still. These investors first acquired their new property at rock bottom prices, and were then allowed to pay for their purchase with government bonds at their nominal value, *even though these bonds had dropped to 18 % of that nominal value* because the operation started when Spain was already defaulting on its debts. Thus the larcenous government was itself robbed of its windfall, as those who claimed to be its most loyal supporters converted their worthless state paper into solid real estate.

The consequences quickly made themselves felt. A bankrupt state was facing ever more obligations, and defaulted on every single one of them, except the kickbacks to political friends. Initially, the proceeds of the land sales had been earmarked to pay stipends to the clergy and the charitable institutions, to compensate for the loss of landed income. Of course, nothing came of that. The cost of the gargantuan war gobbled up the small profits that were made. That same war filled the hospitals with wounded, the roads with refugees, and the cities with widows, orphans, invalids and retired officers. All of these were by law entitled to a pension, and never saw a cent. There are stories – which may be true in substance – that village priests died of starvation after eating *grass* for weeks. It is certain that inmates of hospitals had to resort to begging for their sustenance. And the measure of ministerial despair shows itself most blatantly in the decision of mid 1838 to distribute small rations of military bread to all those widows, orphans and invalids whom the war had cast upon the barren shores of state charity, in place of their pensions. And this at the very time when many of the army's fighting regiments went starving on the fields of battle…

So if we ask why in the world a man as astute in financial matters as Alejandro Mon would listen to the preposterous tales of a small-time Swiss swindler, the answer is simple: for money, or rather: for the lack of it. Mon suffered from a colossal lack of revenue. He needed funds, *any funds*, no matter where they came from! Every cent counted for a Chancellor who in five long months could not fork out more than 275,000 *reales* (barely € 500,000) to the Ministry of State to pay for the entire diplomatic and consular corps, a swollen civil service and bureaucracy, and many other things, such as ransoms for hostages held by the Carlists. Every trickle of revenue was welcome to a Chancellor who had to look on passively as the medical department of the Spanish army *could not pick up its mail* because it lacked the money to pay for the postage; whose best ideas for state obligations and rational taxation foundered on the simple principle that new bonds are unsellable as long as old ones pay no dividends; that nobody will lend money to an insolvent state; and that even tax collectors expect to be paid for their taxing.

On arrival, Mon tried to secure a new state loan of 500 million *reales* which he deemed necessary to lead the Treasury out of its first, worst predicament. Parliament, where the *Progresista* opposition was strong and friends were few, gleefully voted it down; as it was to vote down every future project which threatened to improve the Nation's finances: the bad ones for reasons of probity, the good ones – behold Man at his most fickle! – because they might benefit the government. Since there was no way to cut expenditure (it had already been expertly cut by defaulting!) Mon desperately tried to secure foreign loans. But the international banking community had long since lost confidence in Spain and its ability to drag itself, Münchausen style, out of the mire. All Mon got for his trouble was a tidal wave of fresh new bills, because the mediators of these unforthcoming loans – wonder doctors who did not know the meaning of 'no cure no pay' – demanded and received astronomical stipends for their fruitless labours in Paris, London and Berlin.

In walks this Swiss and tells of a treasure, up for grabs, in distant Compostela. Mon gave him the benefit of the doubt, and it is impossible to blame him. It was admittedly ridiculous to hope for treasure, as the historian Javier de Burgos wrote. But what had Mon to lose? The cost of the trip and the fees for his *Zahori*? Only a fool would begrudge him that. Four of those honest 'mediators' just mentioned had pocketed 100,000 *reales* each to bring in *zilch*! The Swiss can barely have cost more than fifteen *reales* a day, plus a one-way ticket to Santiago and a promise of a nice reward if treasure were indeed secured. In a context sufficiently extreme, even tales of hidden treasure become perfectly reasonable proposals.

But was that all? Was there really nothing else to the decision but despair at state bankruptcy, and a last bout of Mon's juvenile follies? Or did he know something which we today ignore? We will never know. Mon wrote no memoirs, he ordered his papers burned after his death, and he never explained his actions during this episode. Therefore we will never learn what really moved him to undertake such a bizarre adventure. But it should not be forgotten that Mon knew Galicia extremely well. Just before his promotion to Chancellor, he had served as tax inspector in Coruña; over the years he packed the treasury departments there with family-members and loyal dependants; and his local contacts were so good that in later decades he was to use the province as his principal electoral power base. It is not at all unthinkable that during his stay in Galicia, or from one of his many protégés, he picked up some vaguely re-liable hearsay concerning that Treasure of Ney, which the beaten marshal, or his deputy Marchand, was said to have buried in 1809. If that were the case, it would turn mindless ministerial folly into perfectly sensible policy; or at least into something worthwhile trying.

But perhaps it is too much to ask for logic. The spring of 1838 was not Mon's finest hour anyway, either as a minister or as a man. While he was grappling with the finances of his country, while he was scraping together nickels to pay for the war, while he faced popular rebellion, inter-party strife and a host of political scandals, Mon also found himself obliged to travel secretly to Paris with his paramour, the recent widow of a close collaborator, so that she might give birth, without causing the young Catholic minister too much scandal, to their illegitimate son. Under such circumstances, one may forgive a man a minor folly.

17

A Farewell in Madrid

O NE CAN only guess why Borrow never mentioned Alejandro Mon by name. Even half a decade after the events, he observed a most curious silence on the true identity of Mol's patron. Some trivial reasons spring to mind. He may have chosen to remain so hazy because his publisher disapproved of political libel. Or perhaps he preferred to indulge in his customary Church-bashing and male chauvinism, shifting the burden of blame onto Queen Mother Maria Cristina and that nameless bishop who took Mol's oath on *'the Evangiles'*. Or just possibly he no longer cared. With a complex personality like George Borrow's, one can never really tell what lies behind peculiar behaviour…

But whatever the reason may have been, it certainly was not ignorance. The *Eco del Comercio* – of which he made such elaborate use – singled Mon out, specifically and with vitriolic glee, as the sole silly sponsor of the whole affair. And we hear undeniable echoes of that involvement, when he writes in a later chapter: *'it appeared the government had listened to [Mol's] tale, and had been so struck with Bennet's exaggerated description of the buried treasure, that they imagined that, by a little trouble and outlay, gold and diamonds might be dug up at Saint James sufficient to enrich themselves and to pay off the national debt of Spain'.*

This evident awareness makes Borrow's silence even more remarkable, since he had an axe of his own to grind with Mon. The Ofalia government – of which Don Alejandro was perhaps the most auspicious member – had been the definite Nemesis of his gospel-selling mission. They had locked him up, confiscated his stocks, closed his bookshop, and generally made his life miserable. After the British Ambassador applied a copious dose of diplomatic pressure, Borrow was released from jail and offered formal apologies. But it was only a Pyrrhic victory, because the diplomatic tangle gave the cabinet a perfect excuse for a crackdown, and before the month was out a Royal Decree forbade all printing, promotion and sale of vernacular Scripture. Consequently there was little love lost between the Bible salesman and the *Moderado* Chancellor who, with his ecclesiastical leanings and his snug little ties to the Catholic Church, doubtless played a prominent part in the sabotage of Borrow's mission.

The definite prohibition left Borrow with nothing to do, except reading the newspapers and roaming the streets. It was none to his liking. He was restless by nature, and soon his 'spirit chafed under this spell of enforced idleness'. Therefore, in July 1838, when the worst legal battles had been fought and the diplomatic dust had settled, he decided to defy the Law of Man in favour of the Greater Glory of the Lord. He loaded yet another mule with Spanish gospels and rode forth into the countryside, to peddle them – illegally – to the peasants of the Sagra, a wretched and isolated district east of Toledo. Benedict Mol, on the verge of being sent to Santiago, paid him a final visit just before he left. It was to be their last encounter.

'I am come to bid you farewell, lieber herr; I return to Compostella.'

'On what errand?'

'To dig up the schatz, lieber herr. For what else should I go? For what have I lived until now, but that I may dig up the schatz?'

'You might have lived for something better,' I exclaimed. 'I wish you success, however. But on what grounds do you hope? Have you obtained permission to dig? Surely you remember your former trials in Galicia?'

'I have not forgotten them, lieber herr (…). But I must accomplish my destiny. I go now to Galicia, as is becoming a Swiss, at the expense of the government, with coach and mule, I mean in the galera. I am to have all the help I require, so that I can dig down to the earth's centre if I think fit. I – but I must not tell your worship, for I am sworn on "the four Evangiles" not to tell.'

'Well, Benedict, I have nothing to say, save that I hope you will succeed in your digging.'

'Thank you, lieber herr, thank you; and now farewell. Succeed! I shall succeed!' Here he stopped short, started, and looking upon me with an expression of countenance almost wild, he exclaimed: 'Heiliger Gott! I forgot one thing. Suppose I should not find the treasure after all.'

'Very rationally said; pity, though, that you did not think of that contingency till now. I tell you, my friend, that you have engaged in a most desperate undertaking. It is true that you may find a treasure. The chances are, however, a hundred to one that you do not, and in that event, what will be your situation? You will be looked upon as an impostor, and the consequences may be horrible to you. Remember where you are, and amongst whom you are. The Spaniards are a credulous people, but let them once suspect that they have been imposed upon, and above all laughed at, and their thirst for vengeance knows no limit. Think not that your innocence will avail you. That you are no impostor I feel convinced; but they would never believe it. It is not too late. Return your fine clothes and magic rattan to those from whom you had them. Put on your old garments, grasp your ragged staff, and come with me to the Sagra, to assist in circulating the illustrious Gospel amongst the rustics on the Tagus' bank.'

Benedict mused for a moment, then shaking his head, he cried, 'No, no, I must accomplish my destiny. The schatz is not yet dug up. So said the voice in the barranco. Tomorrow to Compostella. I shall find it – the schatz – it is still there – it MUST be there.' He went, and I never saw him more.

Borrow's paternal warnings and his prophecy worthy of Cassandra were, of course, a product of pure hindsight. But if any conversation like this took place during their last meeting, he may well have voiced similar worries. Anyone with a grain of common sense can see that adventures of this kind rarely come to a happy end. A wise man will warn against them; a good man will try to persuade his friend to desist. But all such admonitions are in vain. A treasure hunter like Mol, whether he be a true swindler or only a self-deluded dupe, will never be restrained by bad forebodings. Gold fever has munched away his aptitude for common sense. He has no brain lobes left with which to practice logical anticipation. He is, in short, a sluggish zombie, who gets swept along by his evil fortune, which he then – ironically – calls his own Free Will.

18

The Chapel of San Roque

THE PRECINCT of San Roque in Santiago is a small, unobtrusive cluster of buildings on the northern edge of the old city. Constructed over a major period of time, it shows all the signs of having been designed by too many builders working with no plan at all. If a simile were wanted, the image which springs most readily to mind is that of a big male walrus dozing on a beach. The tiny, unremarkable chapel of pock-marked granite would then be the clumsy head, while the bulky body of the Hospital, whitewashed and adorned with the few frills of austere Spanish baroque, towers behind it like a disproportional mount of flesh. A small vestry on the chapel's north-side unsuccessfully tries to compensate for the lack of structural balance. The image of the Saint, dressed in the garb of a 16th century pilgrim and hidden in a dark niche above the church door, is no match for the two massive statues of Cosme and Damian, patron saints of surgeons, which flank the central entrance. It is, in short, one of those wallflower monuments of a less attractive age, the kind at which the passing tourist may take a furtive glance from force of habit, only to come away with lukewarm architectonical bliss, before he hurries on to more promising sights.

San Roque owes its existence to the Plague. Early in the 16th century a devastating epidemic of the Black Death broke out in Compostela, probably carried there by pious but unwashed pilgrims[9]. At a loss what

---

9 San Roque (Saint Roch in English) was a suitable protector for Santiago. He had begun to manifest his sainthood during a pilgrimage to Rome, when he cured the plague in many Italian cities simply by making the sign of the cross over the stricken. He was therefore usually depicted in pilgrim's dress, which by addition of the felt hat, the sea-shell and the staff with pumpkin gourd, could easily be converted into the traditional appearance of the pilgrims who for centuries had come walking to the shrine of Saint James. Roque is usually shown lifting the hem of his garb to show a festering wound on his leg (he caught the plague himself and was cured of it), with at his side the little dog that licked the wound back to health and brought him bread during his convalescence. As a charming detail, it may be mentioned that a narrow side-street across the road from the chapel used to be called after this little 'dog of San Roque'.

else to do against such things in this age of medical ignorance, the town council sought a solution in penitence and piety. In early March of 1517, they staged a solemn nocturnal procession, which marched several times around the city walls in silence, while candles were lit on the battlements above. When this remedy failed, the council met with the cathedral chapter, and together they vowed to build a chapel to San Roque, the 14th century patron saint of those afflicted with the Plague, in return for intercession.

The plague abated; the city owed the saint his chapel. The foundations were laid in 1517, but as such things often go with promises made in distress, the urgency to fulfil the vow faded as fast as the plight which had inspired it. In 1522 the master builder died and shortly afterwards work was altogether abandoned. The Saint was patient; but this was not the deal as he had understood it. Fifty years later, in 1570, the Plague returned; and only then the city elders remembered their solemn promise and hurried to breathe new life into the project. The chapel was finished in 1576 and a year later the foundations were laid for a hospital next door. When this was completed six years later, it was opened not merely to those afflicted with the Plague, but to all those suffering from 'boils and other contagious ailments', and 'to cure secret afflictions', two discreet euphemisms which the documents and guide books use to camouflage a clinic for syphilitics.

As saintly career-moves go, its timing and direction could not have been improved upon; for as the Plague became rare, syphilis conquered the world. Only recently imported from across the ocean in the ships of Columbus, it quickly wreaked havoc on the crowded old continent with its miserable standards of hygiene and its equally dismal moral habits. Santiago de Compostela did not escape the curse. For all its sanctity and its deeply religious traditions, the Apostle's city was not a well-behaved town. Crime was rampant, violence frequent, carnal vice was everywhere. During the first fifty years of the 19th century, roughly one out of every eight children in the city was born to single unwed mothers, while some 250 newborn babies were abandoned to an almost certain death in the foundling ward of the Great Hospital, a staggering number in a town which only registered some 800 births a year. Right in view of the cathedral, in the extramural area of the *Cruz de Gallo* crossroads and the *Calle de Pombal*, stood a block of brothels which had been in business at least since the middle ages. Market stalls, supposed ateliers of seamstresses, and roadside taverns were well-known cover-ups for simple whore-houses. And even the *romerias*, or procession-style pilgrimages to local shrines, were notorious occasions for licence and prostitution, because the pilgrims often spent the night on the floor of the distant chapel before returning home.

Under pressure from the Church, the city authorities did what they could to curtail such licence. Already in the 16th century the town hall passed its first fruitless measures, threatening gentlemen with fines, floggings and the confiscation of their side-arms, if they dared to go strolling along the *Rio del Sapo* to look at, and approach, the washerwomen who plied a double trade on the riverbank. At other times woman were forbidden to live alone; forbidden to go on *romerias*; forbidden to join the troops of migrant workers to Castille unless chaperoned by a father or a brother; forbidden to own shops, market stalls, taverns... All to no avail of course. One cannot legislate against human nature, nor prohibit what is most natural. By the year 1600, San Roque, run by the Order of San Lazarus, already counted thirty-one beds for men and thirty-nine for women and each next century saw that number doubled. But even such dedicated activity did nothing to erase the disease. When George Borrow visited the town in 1837, he wrote home (in a paragraph which he prudently excised from *The Bible in Spain*) that 'prostitution is carried on to an enormous extent, and loathsome concustant [sic] diseases stare the stranger in the face in the street, in the market-place, in the church, and at the fountain'.

The Hospital of San Roque not only cured these diseases; but, in an ironic twist, also promoted them. In the early 1830s, professional prostitutes from out of town flocked to Santiago under the pretence of seeking treatment in San Roque; and while they waited for admittance, they cheerfully plied their trade and 'led honest citizens into temptation'. To stifle this public health hazard, the bizarre and puritanical Captain-General Nazario Eguia passed measures forbidding country women to come to town for treatment unless recommended by their village priest. At the same time he prescribed that patients spent no more time in the city than between admittance and release. Perhaps it helped some. But then the Carlist Civil War broke out, and all attempts at containment became futile.

Syphilis never thrives better than in wartime, when troop movements plough large numbers of horny young men through urban wastelands where unmarried women and professional prostitutes offer their assets in a context of weak social control. So it happened during the Peninsular War, when the Brotherhood of San Roque, which had taken charge of the buildings and the celebrations of the saint, showed a remarkable increase in membership. And it was no different during the civil war of the 1830s.

In the days of Mol and Borrow, San Roque was working overtime. Perhaps to cut the cost of heating, it only functioned in the summer months, between April and October. But during that period it ran like a veritable mill of venereal disease. Every six weeks, a new group of patients was admitted to receive the notorious mercury treatment which was medicine's only answer to syphilis until Fleming discovered penicillin. These were huge groups, often as large as 200 people, and always a most varied bunch. Predictably, there were soldiers, fifteen to twenty in every batch, men officially sent over by the barracks' doctor. Then there were large numbers of lone women who were most probably whores; a great many married couples, who took their children along to live with them in the wards for the duration of the cure, both spouses receiving treatment. There was the occasional pilgrim who had caught something on the road, and sometimes a prisoner, sent over from the jail as a precaution. In one notorious case, an infected inmate from Betanzos prison, the Carlist bandit Tomas Vazques, needed to be transported in a litter the full fifty miles to Santiago because the swollen glands in his groin stopped him from walking. And in another, particularly sad instance, there was a sixteen year old girl, infected by the husband she had married only recently. Some weeks before their wedding, the husband, José Rey, had been laid up in bed with sores of such magnitude that he could not put his legs together. The sores, however, had disappeared, and so he had happily married his young bride. Since he now felt perfectly fine, he categorically refused treatment. It took a petition from the girl to the town hall, a forced examination by the city doctors, and an official court order to get young José to check in for a cure. With attitudes and ignorance like that, one is not surprised that San Roque was doing excellent business...

It was in this building, then, that the Swiss believed his treasure to lie buried. It may seem that he chose the most unlikely place for such a thing, but actually it is not; least of all if what he came to look for was indeed a hoard hidden by French soldiers. As we saw above: when the troops of Ney and Soult took Santiago in January 1809, they immediately requisitioned numerous buildings to serve as military hospitals. San Roque was one of those. The municipal archive of Compostela holds a note, dated February 4th, in which General Marchand informs the city magistrates that his troops have taken possession of the building, after which he demands that it be provided with firewood and other effects needed to set up a functioning sickbay. Frenchmen, sick Frenchmen, were billeted here for the length of the occupation. Among them may well have been a man who looted treasure, and did not know where to put it when told to march away…

Or that, at least, is what Benedict Mol believed.

Perhaps he ought to have been warned by the fact that Cosme and Damian, its patron saints, used to be nicknamed *The Silverless* because they never took payment for the cures they effected…

19

The Opulent Cesspool

EACH YEAR, on August 16th, the chapel of San Roque becomes for one fleeting moment the buzzing centre of Santiago. August 16th is the feast-day of the saint, a day celebrated with great pomp and ostentation. In the morning, a solemn mass is said for the cathedral chapter, whose high dignitaries come walking in procession wearing their most sumptuous dress. A short while later, another mass is celebrated for the municipal council, during which the original vows of the city elders (recorded on a parchment stored in a drawer of the alter) are solemnly renewed. Then, in the afternoon, the San Roque Fraternity carries the saint's statue in procession through the town, below the pealing of the bell in the belfry, the sounds of a bagpipe band, and the ear-shattering explosions of fireworks overhead. It is, in short, a typical Galician feast, one whose traditions have been maintained, almost uninterrupted, for nearly 400 years.

Almost uninterrupted. Not *wholly* so. For even as harmless a celebration as San Roque's feast-day has occasionally fallen victim to the interminable tug of war between Spain's radical left-wingers and its ultra-conservative Church. The 1830s, the decade of the Carlist War, the period of struggle between extreme religiousness and extreme secularisation, was one of these times. Barely had the Liberals seized power, than the bickering over the celebration began; and the conflict reached its pinnacle of zeal and childishness in 1837, a year before Mol's arrival. As always, money made the most convenient bone of contention. The new Liberal Constitution, adopted only a few months earlier, imposed a rigorous separation of Church and State. To the Liberal town council of Compostela this implied that not a farthing of public money should be spent on ecclesiastical affairs. Perhaps this made good modern statecraft, but it clashed with the town hall's traditional obligations towards San Roque's feast-day. Because both the city council and the Church had stood at the cradle of San Roque chapel, the two bodies had always divided the workload between them. The chapter of the cathedral ran the hospital and patronised the chapel, but the municipal corporation had always shouldered the costs of the yearly celebration, such as the handful of *maravedís* for the candles burned, the costs for various decorations, and the gratuities for the organist and the *gaiteros*, the bagpipe players. In 1837, the council refused to do so.

A long and acid correspondence ensued between town hall, *Cabildo* and Fraternity about the funding of the celebration. The aldermen maintained that they had no objection to attending the festivities, but that the new rules allowed no disbursements from the municipal budget. The Chapter and Fraternity insisted that the town had made a solemn, binding pledge – and they threatened a religious strike in protest, i.e. they hinted at not holding the festivities next year unless the town hall came around. Much as the Santiago aldermen, proud in their new constitutional powers, were planning to stand firm, the provincial authorities took a different view. They understood the consequences of such municipal obstinacy. The populace, deprived of its traditional joys and diversions, would surely blame the new Liberal regime. The Church – and the Carlists – could only gain prestige from this. Therefore, when a new clash threatened in August 1838, the provincial authorities in Coruña intervened with a last minute compromise: a few days before the 16th, they pledged themselves to shoulder the costs – some 500 *reales* – so that the festivities could go ahead as planned, while both warring sides could claim victory.

Benedict Mol arrived in Santiago, dressed in his *Zahori* attire, a short while before San Roque's feast-day. The precise date is a matter of conjecture. If he really set out from Madrid on the same day that Borrow started for the Sagra, he must have climbed into his stagecoach on July 10th or 11th, and would have arrived in Coruña, after the long and arduous journey over the dry Castilian plains and the steep Galician mountains, some two weeks later, approximately on July 25th. There are, however, some reasons to think – reasons too long and dreary to repeat here – that Borrow applied some of his customary creative chronology when he described their last farewell; and that Mol only left Madrid a fortnight later, about July 28th, when Borrow himself set out on yet another trip. In that case Mol would have reached Coruña by the 8th of August, and Santiago by the 10th, pretty much at the time when the tension between town hall and Chapter was reaching its zenith.

Naturally Mol was in a hurry to start digging, but with a war on, martial law in force and civil strife reigning all around, he could barely march into San Roque with a pickaxe and start hauling up the pavement. He needed help and a formal permission. To that effect he probably first sought contact with the local officials of the Treasury, Mon's men in Compostela, and put his case to them. One would just love to see the credentials which he showed them: his travelling passport, his recommendation from the Minister, the petitions he may have filed and the answers he received. Unfortunately all of those seem to have been lost or tucked away in files so secret that they never again re-emerged. The Treasury officials were obedient men, exemplary civil servants, so we may trust that they promised the Swiss all the help he might need. But, being cautious as well, they will have warned him that there was only one man from whom both manpower and permission could be obtained: Jerónimo Valdés, the Captain-General of Galicia, the highest civil, military and legal authority of the province, and consequently the only officeholder competent to take charge of such a delicate affair. As luck would have it, this all-important person, who usually resided in Coruña, was in Santiago at this time.

Valdés, an efficient administrator and fine general who had started his career as a *guerrilla* leader during the Peninsular War, was new to the job. He had only taken charge of Galicia in the first week of July, but he had done so with incomparable energy and initiative. The situation clearly demanded it. His predecessor, General José Manso – whose last name, ironically, means 'tame' – had left a mess behind. Too passive a personality for an emergency of the present order, Manso had been unable to face up to growing Carlist audacity while the army's allocations grew thinner. The consequences were visible everywhere: Carlist *guerrilleros* were infesting nearly every corner of the countryside. Merchants and travellers were robbed, garrisons ambushed, towns assaulted, officials murdered in their very own homes at night. To restore confidence, Valdés needed a quick, resounding military success, and so, immediately upon assumption of office, he undertook a thorough reorganisation of the war effort and set out on major-scale military operations against his two worst enemies: one particularly unpleasant young brigand called Mateo Guillade, who ran his *guerrilla* band in the southern mountains; the other Ramón Ramos, the notorious head of the Carlist movement in Galicia, who operated east of Santiago, around Arzua.

Both of these dangers were much better dealt with from central Compostela than from Coruña on the distant coast. What is more, Valdés, who saw his troops starve and go unshod because Alejandro Mon had no money left to spend on provincial armies, had hit upon a plan to raise additional funds from the wealthy Santiago merchants. To be successful, to collect more than a few apologetic pennies, such a plea would have to be made in person. So somewhere in late July or early August, the Captain-General moved his headquarters, his bureaucracy and half his army to the city of Saint James, and began his arduous meetings and military preparations. And here, in the middle of all this momentous, pressing, time-consuming business, he was one day confronted by a delegation from the Treasury Department, with in their midst Don Benedicto Mol, official government *Zahori*, who explained the purpose of his visit as a search for a French treasure, buried thirty years ago by the troops of Ney, somewhere in the San Roque complex…

One can only guess what the Captain-General may have thought of this Swiss nutcase, dumped on him by the very same Minister of Finance who could spare no money to run the starving army… If he had any sense of humour left, Valdés may have smiled wryly. But it is just as likely he cursed the incompetent ministerial accountant under his breath and wished him to places better left unmentioned. Valdés was not a man to lose precious time over other people's antics. His first impulse must have been to dismiss the lot and forbid all disturbances of the peace. But when push came to shove even the Captain-General was only an appointed official, who owed his job to the government of the day, and there must have been some heavy pressure from Madrid. So Valdés had to give in. He read the recommendation and studied the paperwork. He sounded out the local authorities and perhaps even sent someone to check out San Roque for himself. Then at last he cut the Gordian knot. The treasure hunt could go ahead, but it had to wait until after San Roque's feast-day. Someone must have told Valdés of the running dispute between town council and cathedral; and given these tensions, it made sense to restrain the treasure hunter from entering San Roque until all that tricky business had blown over. Especially since Mol, for understandable reasons of secrecy, kept hinting, as he had always done, that he planned to dig in San Roque's sacristy, or even in the chapel itself, and concealed the fact that his true object was the Hospital.

Consequently the search was postponed until after the celebrations. But not a single day longer! As such things go when people are let confidentially into secrets, the sensational news of buried treasure had immediately leaked out. There was no telling what might happen if some wild character got it into his head to go looking for the gold on his own account. A single man might start a riot; a riot would have to be suppressed; the violence might easily trigger an all-out rebellion in as Carlist a city as Saint James. The big day was therefore set at Friday the 17th of August – the day immediately following on the festivities – and preparations were made to ensure that everything would take place in an orderly fashion. A selection of prominent citizens was summoned to attend the search as official witnesses. A number of scribes – most probably Mon's men from the *Hacienda Publica* – were directed to stand by, to count, register and seal the gold and silver which would be dug up. A large team of masons and porters were engaged to perform the necessary labour, and soldiers were allotted to guarantee peace and order during the work and the subsequent transport.

Lodged in luxury, fed like a prince, Mol waited for his dubious Finest Hour to arrive. He was now being kept at the cost of the taxpayer and no longer needed to sleep in cheap pigsties or eat grub from course clay bowls. Even so he must have been anxious for Friday morning to arrive. He had waited such a long time – nearly thirty years – and now, this close to his goal, the remaining week must have felt like a century. There were the persistant uncertainties, the gnawing fears… What if the Captain-General unexpectedly changed his mind? What if some unscrupulous rascal stole into San Roque on the sly? What if…. Oh, a hundred apprehensions must have tormented the poor fellow day and night. If he slept more than an hour all through that endless week it deserves to be called a miracle. He may even have lost some pounds from pure wrecked nerves, in spite of the rich, abundant fare which he now ate.

And then, at last, the great day dawned…

Early in the morning, the large group of official participants gathered at a central spot in town, most probably in the building of the local Treasury Department. If so, there was some irony in the fact; for Santiago's *Administracion de Rentas del Estado* was housed in the former Inquisition Palace, that very same building where back in the days of the Peninsular War the French had stored and melted down their ill-gotten gains of confiscated church plate, part of which supposedly got buried as the Treasure of Ney. It was a large group from the start, but as it left the building, and moved towards San Roque, it was to grow larger still. By now – either through rumour, or through unwise publicity – word had spread like wildfire all through the town that this marvellous, fairy-tale event was to take place this Friday morning. Mankind's undying fascination for hidden treasure did the rest. A large crowd of citizens flocked together, and followed in the wake of this, the most absurd parade ever to be staged on government orders. With the Swiss at their head, the witnesses, scribes, masons and town-folk passed through the city, in the direction of the north gate. As they moved through the narrow streets and over the modest *plazas*, passers-by stopped in their tracks, shopkeepers stepped from behind their counters, housewives leaned out of their windows. At the Campo de Pan the long queue of maidservants waiting in line to fill their buckets at Cervantes's fountain, turned around to stare. People asked what the fuss was all about. In a handful of words, they were told the story of the hoard, the object of the search; and they joined in, swelling the ever-growing throng.

Shortly before 10 a.m. they arrived before the gates of San Roque. Here the first surprise was sprung on the audience. Contrary to what he had always said, the Swiss did not go into the chapel, but opened the heavy oak wood gates of the hospital instead. Followed by his companions and the crowd of onlookers, he entered the patio. There he stopped and took a careful look around. Perhaps he needed to refresh his memory as to what his dying comrade in Madrid had said, those thirty years ago. Perhaps also, the description of the building which his moribund friend had given him did not compare too well with the layout of the *Hospitalillo de San Roque*. He stood still and stared for a considerable while. Then, all of a sudden, he took off, with the workmen and the witnesses in tow. He crossed the patio and entered – of all places – the lavatories. There he stopped, and told the masons to get to work. He told them to dig out the cesspool. The order must have astonished them.

We do not know what the toilets of San Roque hospital looked like at this time. But if they were anything like those built in such public places as the municipal jail a short while later, the reader may imagine a large, flat slab of coarse granite with two or three round holes in it, and a deep, murky cavity beneath. That was all; the primitive contraption where thousands of syphilitic patients had relieved themselves for many generations. And it was the foulest of places. Hygiene had never been a Spanish strong point; Galician hygiene was still worse. Even before the masons set to work, the place must have smelled like a slaughterhouse. The *Eco del Comercio*, which reported the affair in stunning detail, tells how the Swiss had armed himself against this very contingency with a napkin-sized handkerchief and a giant bottle of *Eau de Cologne*. He was the only one halfway protected, for nobody else had been told of the true hiding place of the hoard, and, to their cost, they came unprepared. When the masons dug the stone away, when the workmen began to haul up the buckets of goo that had accumulated in the cesspool underneath, the many years worth of excrement, matured with time, rose to the surface and... No, it is impossible to describe how such a thing must have smelled! Words, sweet words, those clean little sound-bites braided from thought, can never capture sensory perceptions of such magnitude! The reader shall have to imagine the scene for himself...

It took six long hours. Six hours of digging down, hauling up, carrying out and dumping – yes, where exactly? There is little choice. Either out in the public street in front of the gate, or at the back, in the hospital's gardens. In both cases, the grade of the hill running down behind the building, ensured that the debris got well spread. It floated down through the gutters in a gooey mass. Its *essential oils* were picked up by the wind. Slowly but surely, the noxious fumes, carried on the crest of the breeze, trickled into the nearby town, drifted over the rooftops and through the narrow alleys, entered open windows and settled in every nook and corner of the densely built city. The stink brought out more onlookers still, people alerted by their nostrils to some catastrophe taking place.

After some hours the hole was as large as thirty feet. It is difficult to picture how the workmen must have looked by then, stained by their effort, by sweat and by faeces. It is difficult to imagine what they may have said, and how they may have cursed. The Swiss, says the *Eco*, 'dabbed one hankie after another with *Eau de Cologne* and pressed it to his nostrils continually, until his snout swelled up like a balloon; the onlookers, pinching their noses, tried to avoid breathing the fumes even stronger than those which Don Quijote smelled when Sancho *disgraced* himself while listening to the music of the watermills; the other poor fellows, those summoned to bear witness to it all, already had their noses bigger and redder than beetroots; but even so everybody from the first to the last kept his eyes wide open, holding out until the Golden Brick be born.'

And it never was.

Nothing but human manure came up. By four in the afternoon, writes the *Eco*, 'the hole had grown so deep that it touched the roof of hell itself; hell, which surely had swallowed up the treasure'. The men were getting tired. The work was going slower. There were murmurs, murmurs that said it was all a fraud, a bad joke, an insult. How did Mol feel? We may easily imagine. Driven by despair, he must have urged the workmen to continue. He had no choice. He truly believed that his treasure was buried here, here in this pestilent spot, this nightmare gateway from Dante, Swedenborg and Saint John's Apocalypse. Had he been a deliberate swindler, a calculating fraud, would he ever have chosen a spot such as this, sure to inflame the passions of the men put under his charge, for the dirtiness of the work, and the horrid health-risk to which he exposed them? Any other place would have been a better bet for a swindler. No other place would have caused such fury in his victims. So he insisted that they continue, in his illiterate, stammering Spanish, hoping for a miracle, hoping for a Deus ex Machina, hoping for anything except his present plight. But after six hours the workmen had had enough. Who can blame them? They threw down their tools, they left the lavatories, they went to wash at the fountain of the *Placeta de San Roque*, surely scaring, with their looks and smell, the poor stagecoach horses tied up there; and every human being who beheld them. The polite citizens and the scribes followed them out, disheartened and disgusted. Nobody wanted anything more to do with the business.

Mol stayed behind, not knowing whether to follow, whether to hide, whether to try and find some secret passage through which he might escape. But to escape he stood no chance. There were too many people gathered behind him, in the courtyard, below the vaulted arcades around the patio, perhaps in the street in front of the gates: citizens who had come along for the marvellous show six hours earlier, syphilitic patients from the hospital, former whores who lived in the workhouse for *arrepentidas* that occupied a few rooms of the complex, neighbours brought out by the infernal stink that invaded their homes. They were hostile. Some had had their day spoiled by the fumes; some hated foreigners who got chances denied to themselves; the inmates of San Roque had lost their bathrooms and fresh air. And all had seen their highest hopes shattered because of this babbling Swiss swindler in a clown's costume. And perhaps that was the worst of all. People will tolerate a lot, but not the wanton destruction of their dreams. When he did emerge from the lavatories, they crowded around him. He was pushed. He was screamed at. Someone demanded to know what the hell he thought he'd been doing? Another asked him where's your goddamn treasure now?

Desperate, stammering, in bits and pieces, he tried to offer explanations – naive explanations, anything halfway reasonable that he hoped would exonerate him in the eyes of reasonable men, as Germans will do in like situations. But there were no reasonable men here. There were only furious Gallegos, a breed of men able to scare Attila's Huns off their horses. He exclaimed that 'it was all the fault of the woman who laid the cards for him in Paris'. She had told him what to look for, told him where to look, told him – one imagines – to dig in muck. Hoping to reinvent himself as a victim, hoping they would believe him and show mercy, he cried out that she had cheated him, that it was all her fault!

The first punch took him by surprise. He will have protested, will have puffed out an indignant German "*Hooooh!!*" The second blow he tried to stave off. He was a Swiss and a man from Lucerne, a veteran of many wars, burly and big. But no man can successfully battle a crowd. Not even a Swiss; not even a man from Lucerne. They fell on him from all sides simultaneously. He was given a thorough thrashing by the good people of Santiago. Punches, kicks and spittle. And we can only hope that the soldiers sent in to break up the riot did not take too long to arrive. And that they did not wait too calmly on the edge of the crowd, before they pushed their way through with the butts of their rifles, picked him up from the cobblestone floor, and dragged him off to a jail cell.

IV

The Aftermath

20

The Fall of Mon

Spain was lucky that Alejandro Mon was a *francophile*, and no great fan of German drama. Had it been otherwise, our gullible Chancellor might well have read the second part of Goethe's *Faust*, not ten years old in 1838; and there he would have stumbled upon a most baneful scheme to turn Mol's tales of hidden hoards into plenty of good, hard cash. In the first Act of Goethe's sequel, Doctor Faust and Mephistopheles play *voodoo* bankers to the German Emperor, whom they provide with unlimited funds by issuing billions worth of promissory notes backed, not by gold reserves or revenue, but 'by the unfailing guarantee of the countless buried treasures in the earth'; promissory notes which shall be redeemed as soon as those treasures have been dug up! The scheme works splendidly for a mighty long time. After all: *everybody knows* that the earth is full of hidden treasures, and that those treasures belong to the Emperor by the ancient *Bergrecht*. Therefore everybody willingly accepts these notes as payment, or as security for loans, as salary or imbursement… The court spends lavishly on soldiers, luxuries and pensions… In response, the whole populace catches the liberal mood, confident that there will never be an end to this ever increasing wealth… The whole land prospers… *Everybody* grows rich…

A bubble is of course a bubble, and sooner or later it must burst. But that we do not really get to see in *Faust*. So given Mon's despair, his screaming lack of funds, and his great financial acumen, there is a fair chance he might have given Goethe's scheme a cautious try. And Spain, poor, miserable, much-bled Spain, would then have had to foot yet one more costly bill.

As it was, things were bad enough…

Treasure hunts are a tricky business. Like any high stakes gamble, like an *all-or-nothing* bet, a treasure hunt promises the greatest bliss to the lucky man, the deepest despondency to one who fails. Succeed and you will be a god. Fail and you will be an ass. It makes no difference if you're a poor sod digging for nuggets in the mud, an industrial prospector of unlimited means, an ageing Swiss vagrant who believes his own fables or the very government of a nation. The rule is universal and applies to all. If the truth be told, there is no fairer Lady Justice than Dame Fortune. For she is sightless from birth, and needs no blindfold to be impartial.

The news of Mol's treasure hunt hit Madrid on August 29th, more than ten days after it had taken place. Communications were slow in those unmechanised times, when news could not spread faster than at the speed of a running horse. Consequently, what reached the capital was not the outcome of the Santiago dig, but its *announcement*. This was contained in a letter from the correspondent of the *Eco del Comercio* in the small town of Betanzos, just below Coruña, which gave notice of the coming excavation in the church. This Betanzos correspondent, who unfortunately remains nameless, had heard from well-placed Santiago friends about the arrival of the Swiss in Compostela and the authorities' decision to make a formal investigation of San Roque on the 17th. Smelling mighty scandal, the journalistic sleuth immediately notified his newspaper in the following way:

> It seems that a while ago, a Swiss presented himself to the gentlemen of the government, and informed them that in the church of San Roque in Santiago lay buried, ever since 1809, a great treasure of Portuguese gold. The government sent this Swiss to Santiago, and on presenting himself there he solemnly repeated the same declaration. As a result, it was decided to undertake the excavations which the Swiss intends to make; yesterday being the day designated for the job. We shall see what comes out. (...) If nothing is found, the Swiss will surely say that he did see the treasure buried but that somebody must have removed it later on. Behold a way of making a living in the world! For now I prefer to make no further comments, just in case the Swiss does find what he is looking for, and that I myself become the object of ridicule.

The *Eco* – an opposition paper if ever there was one – felt overjoyed to receive notice of such a fine governmental *picardia*. Like any Spanish daily of the period, it was far less interested in providing information than in bending public opinion to its will, if need be by murky hints, falsehood, mockery and lies. Its shameless goal was to erode the *Moderado* government, so any scandal was welcome, the more absurd the better. And yet, political slander is a delicate thing, which must be administered with care. It makes for sensational fireworks, but may just as easily explode in your face as in the sky. The editors understood that this bizarre affair might still turn into a stunning triumph for Ofalia and his team. If gold were really found, the cabinet's standing would instantly be restored in the eyes of the public, forever fascinated by the Dream of Hidden Treasure. So pending the outcome, the *Eco* took no chances. It published the letter in its entirety, but did so on the back page of the issue, in the middle of a host of other items of mediocre weight.

Three days later, however, all *Progresista* prayers were answered. The same correspondent produced a full-length report of the stinking dig in the Hospital, together with positive identification of Alejandro Mon as its sponsor, and a long, indignant, patriotic harangue about the Honour of Spain, perfidious foreigners, and foolish *Moderado* ministers who listened to preposterous tales. 'Praise indeed,' wrote the Betanzon Voltaire at the end of his narrative, with the sweet agreeability of the poisonous snake,

> Praise indeed to his Lordship the minister for listening to the Swiss and for investigating if such a treasure did exist. But was it really necessary to give so much publicity to a disclosure which showed every sign of being a swindle? Would it not have been more prudent to commission a small number of discreet and trustworthy men to attend the excavations, thus avoiding the risk that, in case of this outcome, the public of Santiago would grumble, as they *do* now grumble, against those who have been made the laughing stock of some unknown individual who, to make his mockery even more appetising, ordered the excavation of a pestilent spot, and who in order to avoid his just punishment only needs to say that he did see the treasure buried, but that someone must have dug it up since then (...)?

Here I rest my pen. I am no partisan of the present ministers, because I think they are leading the fatherland to ruin. But I am a Spaniard, and I only wish that the leaders of my country would know how to keep up the prestige and dignity necessary to carry out their heavy responsibility. The Treasure of the Swiss most certainly does not contribute to that end. You gentlemen [of the editorial staff] are free to add what commentaries you see fit; but I for my part deplore this bizarre adventure which harms us more than appears at first sight.

The *Eco* just loved it, and on September 1st published this *Mother of all Scandals* prominently, on the front page of its Saturday issue. The treasure hunt had turned out for the political best! That is to say: it had failed, failed dismally, and revealed the Minister of Finance, one of the up and coming men of the *Moderado* party, as a credulous fool. In *Progresista* eyes the outcome could not have been better. Nor could its timing be improved; for Ofalia's government was like a fruit rotting on the bough and very much ready to drop.

Only nine months in office at the time, Ofalia's team had been in trouble from the first. It had been put in by Queen Mother Maria Cristina as a right-wing compensation for her loss of prerogatives under the new, rigid Constitution of 1837. It was backed by the military power of General Narvaez, the autocrat whose Liberalism was only a rung on the ladder of his own boundless ambitions. But this was all the support it ever had. Ofalia's government had been imposed upon a nation which did not want it. Every radical in the land despised it thoroughly; the people mocked it; and even most prominent fellow *Moderados*, many of whom had coveted the post of Prime Minister for themselves, liked it not. Seeing its weakness and its inability to cope with the war and the financial crisis, the country at large never bothered to give it a moment's trust. With a million enemies and practically no friends, it was open to attack from all sides at all times. In Chinese astrology, its zodiac sign would surely have been the Sitting Duck.

As long as the *Cortes* was in session, the *Progresista* opposition limited itself to taking parliamentary potshots at the regime, chipping away at its prestige and making sure it never stood a chance of finding its balance.

Then, when parliament closed in June, they took their opposition to the streets. Over the summer the concerted action of press, popular riot and institutional paralysis undermined the ramshackle position of the cabinet step by step. Municipal and provincial authorities throughout the land involved themselves in national politics, refused obedience, sabotaged policy. Mon's inability to secure loans, pass taxes or cut costs doomed the cabinet to bankruptcy. This in turn forced the minister to suspend all payments and pensions. Unpaid, unfed, unhoused, yes, even *unshod*, the army was reduced to virtual inaction. General Espartero, the all-important commander-in-chief of the northern armies and himself a die-hard *Progresista*, insisted on Mon's dismissal. Starving soldiers staged mutinies. The notorious left-wing town of Cádiz rebelled, announcing the perennial doomsday scenario of military insurgence. In Seville, the 2,000 working women of the cigar factory – a state monopoly of immense size and crucial importance for revenue – went on strike when they had not been paid for a full three months. And finally there was a succession of petty political scandals over the spring and summer, not surprisingly promoted and kept in the focus of the public eye by *Progresista* MPs and the press at their bidding. There was the case of a *louche* Catalan businessman called Safont, who offered to supply the army for prices that would make usury look like charity. He was almost hired, and only sent packing at the last moment. Another Catalan, who had somehow landed a seat in the French parliament, offered to mediate a French loan in exchange for a 25 % commission *on the principal* and the monopoly on all the mines in Spain. The offer was almost accepted.

Then, out of the *Progresista* blue, came the affair of the 'widows of Comares', a scandal which has all the semblance of another Diamond Necklace, yet stuns the modern reader by its mind-boggling triviality. The wives of two peasants who had died of typhus in Malaga jail when locked up by General Palarea, the town's military governor, were dragged to Madrid to claim compensation from the state. The *Eco del Comercio* itself opened up a subscription for their sustenance. Funds flowed in; the rural widows were fêted with quantities of food, wine and luxury they had never known in their lives. Then the inevitable 'protectors' made their appearance: a clique of Madrid-based Italians, former consuls, tenors of the opera, journalists and divas, who not only altruistically volun-teered to look after the widows' new patrimony, but even presented the two poor things at the palace to Queen Mother Maria Cristina, whose Neapolitan origins granted access. The ministers, shocked at this royal collaboration with an Opposition scheme, presented their resignation; Maria Cristina quickly backed down; the Italians were exiled; Palarea, without ever having performed a single military action, was decorated with the highest military medal; the poor old widows of Comares were summoned to appear before a judge…

In short: the summer of 1838 was a time thoroughly addicted to scandal, and the treasure hunt of Santiago was merely one sordid little *affaire* among many. Perhaps it wasn't the most important of the lot, but it was the last one; the final, if not the biggest, blast of the firework show. The radical press threw itself upon the material with the appetite of starving hyenas. The kill was near; it made them all the more ferocious. During the first days of September, the *Eco* carried a fresh new article on the Santiago infamy in nearly every issue, keeping the bombshell snugly warm. In his turn, Modesto Lafuente, whose *Fray Gerundio* was the most popular weekly of the time, gladly press-ganged the ludicrous story for yet another sarcastic attack on the government. The scandal of this 'Swiss *zahori* who on mister Mon's orders went to dig up a treasure in the lavatories of San Roque hospital' perfectly illustrated, he said, *la miseria de los gobernantes*, the 'depravity of our rulers'. 'The devil take me' he wrote, 'if that *zahori* is not the spitting image of our ministers of finance', who are always on the look-out for new taxes to impose and new wealth to confiscate with which to finance their tottering war. 'They see treasures where there are none, pretend to dig resources from the earth itself, continue to receive their daily bread from the towns and the villages, and forever make us scratch around in the dirt, in the hope of discovering the kettle of our happiness.' And the only result, so Lafuente concluded, is 'that they keep us perfectly hoodwinked.'

The most embarrassing use of the affair, however, was made by the daily *Nosotros*, a paper whose extremism paled even the radical stand of the *Eco*. In a piece so scabrous that it almost makes the historian blush to reproduce it, its issue of September 1st printed a fake letter from the Swiss to Alejandro Mon, written in a Hispano-German Newspeak with a spoonful of crippled Italian thrown in. No translation can do it justice, but the gist may be seen from the following feeble shadow on the back wall of the cave:

Mister Mon searching resources in the Y[10]

The mistake of a mailman has brought into our possession a peculiar document which we shall reproduce for the reader's amusement. Lately the ministers made such a fuss with their remark that we oppose them only because we want to become ministers ourselves (may God bless them in proportion to their truthfulness!) that a mailman, finding an envelope addressed: "Phur ze minnistroh mohst new of ze minnistrows", and thinking that the new minister, once the present crisis had been solved, would be among our number, delivered the letter here[11]. We opened it without more ado and found the following message:

Sant Djames ze 18 Augusto

Meister ministroh,

I just come finding these thing for who you excellentia send mi, to whit these treasure who talked mi to you exselentia of. Ze road through who I has came is damm bad, that ze big donqui on top of who I come not could put foot down. These donqui walk one league for zree hours, and by for leagues tired so, that he have beak as you exsellentia haved yours when I account mi know ein treasure in Chalisia, santo Roco tjapel, in ze sity of santo Djames. At fine I am arrive in these devilled chalician land, and I am said that I has come of meister ministroh Mon, the mohst newest of ministrohs of kingess Cristina. Ies my duty tell you what when geheard you name Mon in theirs ears, these challegos put big laughs on mouths of them,

---

10 An obscure phrase. Perhaps this 'Y' was meant to resemble a dowsing rod; or it may be a euphemism for *bathrooms* which today's dictionaries fail to explain.

11 In Spanish 'among our number' reads '*entre Nosotros*', i.e. the newspaper's title. The mailman gets confused because the letter is addressed to 'el ministro mas nuevo', an ugly little phrase which may mean the 'latest' or 'newest' minister, but also – in Gallego – 'the youngest minister' in the cabinet, i.e. 37-year old Alejandro Mon.

one look at ozer, and more laugh, then say they that the Mon have bean Coruña taks inspektor, and were damm inspektor who not know to inspekt.

I pay them no care, aber say I has came for find treasure for mi ministroh and they go with mi in santo Roco tjurtjs. There, there have a door, and in behind of these door is a sit, and on top these sit is a round whole for to put ze hams when out ze belly come these thing. Come with mi much chalician man and they hold noses with hands of them because there smells much bad, and put laugh in their mouth and sayed: "these ministroh Mon surge ze gold and find ze shit". Mi I put ze silence in my mouth and kommand to dig, dig, dig; and digging with spate mis mans take out lot earth and lot escrement. Mi not know what thing eat ze challegos for to smell so bad ze escrements. And digging make a whole so big for to be in it you escelensia and all ze more ministrows Kolleges of you, I think so true. And because I has see whole so big and nozing find and all laugh much over mi, I tell no more dig.

These letter I writ, meister ministroh, to know like on mi swiss word you can beleeve, none thing of these treasure is there but it is escremento. And I you send a bit escrement with muleteer for to see to be true these thing what I say.

Mi walk to ze Sweiss soon; because no good wine in these land; these wine is bad as ze ministrows, and ze ministrows are like ze treasures.

Am yours, meister ministroh,

Frederic Switzemerd.

This then is the letter, of which, to speak the truth, we would not have understood one iota, had we not known that recently a Swiss presented himself to mister Mon, saying that he knew of a treasure in Santiago de Compostela. It seems that mister Mon, credulous as every ignoramus is, swallowed the bait and authorized the Swiss to go to Santiago and excavate. It is said that the Swiss chose the very dirtiest place of the church of San Roque and that the

filthy operation took place the 17th last. The letter tells the
rest, and it shows how low mister Mon is willing to stoop,
and how truly admirable are the talents of a minister who
in the absence of loans and taxes goes searching for resources in a cesspool.

When educated men speak in such terms of the highest dignitaries of
the land, there is little hope left for a government, no matter what its
political colour. At roughly the same time as these newspaper articles
appeared, nightly mobs had been going around Madrid shouting 'Down
with the Government!' and posters had appeared in the morning, reading 'We want blood – bring down the ministers!!' In all of Spain, with its
nine million people, there were only six men left who still believed in the
Ofalia government. These were the ministers themselves; and perhaps
not even they. On September 6th, Maria Cristina finally gave in. She
accepted the proffered resignation, and appointed an interim government under the Duke of Frias. The Ofalia cabinet had fallen. It had
fallen not *because* of Benedict Mol, but with his help. Few men can pride
themselves on such a feat; and perhaps in all of history, Mol may be the
only vagrant who ever pulled off such a most remarkable stunt!

21

The Spanish Twilight

I T IS a complete mystery what happened to Benedict Mol once his treasure hunt had failed. As soon as the *Moderado* government had fallen, the opposition newspapers lost all interest in the affair, and never wasted another word on it. The scandal had served their purpose. Now it no longer mattered. The treasure hunt of Santiago was duly forgotten, and so was the treasure hunter himself. Yet there he was, languishing in some wretched Santiago jail, a by-product of politics, greed and his own naive credulity, with only the grimmest prospects to look forward to.

Predictably, Mol was not well loved. He had managed to make himself hateful to a whole country in the few short hours of his dig in San Roque. Common folk readily recognized a foreign impostor, out 'to make fools of the government and the unhappy people of Spain'. He was one of those swindlers from abroad who 'come here to leave us penniless and laugh in our faces,' as the *Eco*'s Betanzos correspondent grumbled. At the same time, he had become a major political liability both to the Galician authorities and to his *Moderado* sponsors, precisely at the time of their worst political crisis. It comes as no surprise that they kept him in jail, partly, perhaps, to protect him from popular fury, but partly also as damage control, to keep him out of the public eye.

Under whose aegis? In what circumstances? We do not know. We only know a little of what happened to Mol afterwards, from the letter which Francisco Rey Romero wrote to Borrow nearly a year later. Borrow had left Spain in mid-September 1838, soon after the scandal of the treasure hunt struck and the Ofalia government fell, to consult with his employers in London. As a matter of fact it is a small miracle that he ever heard of Mol's exploits at all. He had only returned to Madrid from a Bible-peddling tour around Segovia on the 30th of August, and his original plan was to leave immediately for France. But he fell ill with a fever in the first week of September and had to keep to his bed for several days. There, perhaps to kill the time, he must have read the *Eco del Comercio*.

And when he finally did leave Spain for England, he carried with him the copies of the newspaper, for later literary use.

Of course, having read of Mol's Galician adventure, he was curious about the sequel. 'Eager to learn the fate of the Swiss,' he says in *The Bible in Spain*, 'I wrote to my old friend Rey Romero at Compostela'. It sounds most humane, the worries of a caring friend for the well-being of an old acquaintance. But once again the truth is more prosaic. In reality, Borrow was only looking for the tail-piece to his story; and Rey Romero replied mainly for reasons of business, to close his account, now that the prohibition of Borrow's books had become permanent. In June 1839 he wrote Borrow a short and rather dreary letter, rendering accounts of the number of New Testaments sold, how many remained confiscated in the civil governor's office, how much money he still owed and what the British missionary ought to do in the way of permits and licences and dues to recuperate his books. Only at the very end of the page, almost as an afterthought, the old bookseller remembered the treasure hunter, and he wrote the following lines, in a style remarkably clumsy for one who deals in learning and *belles-lettres*:

> The German of the treasure came here last year, backed by the government, to unearth it. However, a few days after his arrival he was thrown in jail, whence he wrote to me, explaining who he was and pointing out that he was the person whom you recommended. For this reason my son went to see him in prison. [The "German"] told [my son] that you had also been arrested, something which I could barely believe. A short while later they took him to Coruña; then they returned him here again, and what happened to him in the end I do not know.

The letter reached Borrow a month later in Seville, and he was glad to have it. He mentioned to his employers that he would 'keep this letter with good care since I attach some importance to it'. And so he did. He took it home with him to England when the Bible Society recalled him at long last. This was the time he decided, after many years of travel and hesitation, to marry his fiancée, Mary Clarke. His new wife owned some small property at Oulton on England's east coast, and there he settled down to a bourgeois life and set out to write. In the early 1840s, in the garden house of his own grounds, he wrote down the adventures of Benedict Mol, the many marvellous episodes repeated throughout this book. But as he came to the very last paragraph, the spot where he described the Rey Romero letter, he discovered that he had no choice but to paraphrase the original text and to change its contents thoroughly. Having just, a few chapters before, described Mol and Rey Romero in animated conversation, he could not very well reproduce this paragraph *verbatim*, for then his readers would immediately understand – from Rey Romero's remarks on Mol 'explaining who he was' – that the bookseller and the treasure hunter had never set eyes on one another. And so he turned the paragraph in question into the following, fantastic version with which to end the adventures of Benedict Mol:

> Eager to learn the fate of the Swiss, I wrote to my old friend Rey Romero, at Compostella. In his answer he states: 'I saw the Swiss in prison, to which place he sent for me, craving my assistance, for the sake of the friendship which I bore to you. But how could I help him? He was speedily after removed from Saint James, I know not whither. It is said that he disappeared on the road.'

In less than a hundred words Borrow had rid himself, not only of the inconsistencies in his story, but also of the treasure hunter himself. If the truth be told, he was no more sentimental about his Swiss Zahori than the Progresista press. Mol had served his purpose; the climax of the treasure hunt had been attained; and a convenient disappearance into the Spanish twilight was as good a dramatic finale as any.

Mol did not 'disappear on the road' at all. We merely lose track of him in jail, in August 1838. That is mainly because we do not really know where to look. There were too many jails in Santiago at this time, and what records of those jails survive today are few, scattered, and mostly incomplete. In five years of civil war, the martial justice system had produced its own abundant harvest of inmates: guerrilla fighters caught in the hills and awaiting execution; urban 'conspirators' who had assisted the Carlist bands with supplies, intelligence, and cash; family members of known rebels, locked up in preventive custody or as hostages; people caught with suspicious materials, even such innocent stuff as horseshoes or rope-ladders; and on top of that the many common criminals of the Galician countryside, always a lavish species, but more so now than ever in the atmosphere of anarchy brought on by civil war. All of these needed to be incarcerated; so soon every major building – especially the recently closed monasteries and convents – was turned into a makeshift jail.

When Rey Romero writes that the authorities '*le pusieron en la Carcel*', it may either mean that they put him 'in *some* jail' or 'in *the* jail'. In the latter case he would have meant the *Cárcel Pública*, the Municipal Jail of Santiago. One can only hope that he was spared that lot. The *Cárcel Pública* was an infamous place, a true little hell on earth. Pascual Madoz, a later geographer, typically called it 'as secure as it is bad', and added that 'its cells are incompatible with all notions of humanity'. Antonio Perez, its warden, himself described the cells he ran as 'inquisitorial dungeons'. And even the City Council, who supervised the place and therefore were primarily responsible for initiating improvements, observed quite blatantly in one of its reports that imprisonment during investigation was already a punishment in itself, since the jail was 'a sepulchre for living beings, where the inmates' health is wrecked and they often lose their lives'.

Wedged in between the palace-style town hall built above and a rocky slope that slanted down from the great main square, the *Cárcel* was a damp, dark, airless cluster of dungeons. Neither daylight nor fresh air ever reached it. In winter, freezing rainwater oozed through the walls from the granite heights behind. In summer, when the weather turned hot, the stench of the graveyard of San Fructuoso chapel, just fifteen yards across the road, invaded the cells. Its eight rooms, with an average size of thirty square meters, had been designed to hold a total of thirty people. In Mol's days, there were 180: men and women, convicted criminals and those awaiting trial or transport, political prisoners, prostitutes and bankrupt debtors. Occasionally even the dangerously insane were locked up here, people that nobody knew what else to do with. A single small fountain built by public charity five years earlier served for all laundry and washing; a lavatory was not built until the 1860s. Inevitably, deadly epidemics of fever and cholera broke out here, the most recent one in April 1837. Since this constituted a health risk for the city as a whole, the new Liberal authorities had started a programme of improvements. Some prisoners were removed to the Convents; others to Coruña; blankets donated by charity were handed out, and a soup-kitchen of sorts was set up in the Great Hospital just across the alley, to feed those inmates whose family did not bring them food and who had no money to buy it, such as, for instance, Antonio do Soto, a prisoner who in May 1837 went without food *for fifteen days* and, having neither clothes nor a blanket, went almost naked both in the daytime and at night.

Of course, even good intentions must be financed. Santiago, cut off from trade and transport by the *guerrilla* bands, was a poor town now. Tax money was scarce, and only the very worst cases could be helped. This left all the others, that nondescript, easily overlooked troupe of victims not miserable enough to arouse official pity, but neither sufficiently rich to eat regular meals, hungry, jealous and rebellious. On the morning of August 31st 1838, this resulted in a riot. As the kettle with grub for those who received official sustenance was carried in from the Hospital's kitchens, thirty four of the unassisted inmates threw themselves upon it in a concerted effort, and divided the contents among themselves. The warden had to call in soldiers to restore order, salvage the kettle, and return the rebels to their cells. As they walked away, the uppity prisoners announced that unless there were food for everyone the next day, they would start a serious mutiny.

The Swiss may have been in the jail at this time, and may have witnessed the riot, but he does not figure in the list of thirty-four prisoners involved. Nor do we find him – or any kind of Swiss or German sounding name – in the few surviving inventories and admittance lists which chance, rather than archivists' care, has preserved for posterity. So we are at a loss about his further adventures, and can only fall back upon conjecture.

One good, educated guess would be that he was kept quite close to Captain-General Valdés. As viceroy, Valdés was not only the highest legal authority in Galicia, but also politically responsible to Madrid for everything which happened in the province. The failure of the treasure hunt – and the wide publicity it received – had turned the Swiss into a political bombshell of the first order. Before the Ofalia government fell, this star of the last great *Moderado* scandal had to be kept well out of sight. Once it had fallen, he might still prove useful to the new *Progresista* kingmakers, to dole out a thrashing to their political foes. In short, there could be no question of cutting him loose, or even letting him out of sight.

As noted above, Rey Romero wrote in 1839 that 'a short while later they took [Mol] to Coruña'. This makes good sense if Valdés had decided to keep the vagrant swindler close. Little more than a month after the dig in San Roque, Valdés had finished his business in Santiago. Mateo Guillade had been cornered and killed; a stroke of luck during a side-show offensive against the local band of Ramón Ramos had delivered into Valdés's hands the *cabecillo*'s eighteen year old son Andrés; and a large number of the Carlist fellow-travellers whom the boy denounced under interrogation, had been arrested, processed, and in some cases shot. Finally, the reorganisation of the army and supplies seems to have been wound up successfully. Therefore, by mid-September, Valdés moved himself, his court and his army back to Coruña, the official seat of the provincial government, and he probably took the Swiss along, to keep him under lock and key until an order came through, or until a decision was reached on what to do with the former Minister's protégé.

There has perhaps never been a country so thoroughly addicted to the pleasures of bureaucratic paperwork as 19th century Spain; no country where the *escribanos*, the courtroom scribes, have filled so many folios with bombastic legal balderdash to satisfy the system's craving for formality. Therefore it is nearly inconceivable that no legal brief would have been drawn up about the case of the Swiss treasure hunter by Valdés's small army of clerks in the *Capitania-General*. But, sadly, there has also rarely been a country given so little to the preservation of its heritage, and if such a brief existed, it has fallen victim to the tooth of time and the thoughtless hand of man. The great archive of the Captain-Generalcy, where such a file would have been kept, did not survive till modern times. It piled up for centuries in the basement of the Captain-General's palace on the waterfront of Coruña's harbour, until, one day in early 1892, the garrison, needing more living space, removed all those 'old and useless' papers of the *Cárcel Real*, the *Audiencia* and the viceroy's personal archive, stacked them up into a huge pile in the square in front, and set the lot alight. It burned for more than three days; and centuries' worth of Galician history went up in whirling smoke.

The legal brief on Benedict Mol may have vanished in this bonfire; and in its absence it is impossible to discover why the man would have been returned to Santiago at a later date, as Rey Romero wrote. It makes no sense at all in any conceivable scenario. Had the authorities wanted to send him to Madrid, or to a labour camp in Castile – such as the one at Palencia or at Valladolid where inmates dug the canal through Spain's most arid province – he would not have been returned to Santiago, since the Apostle's city lay effectively *away* from the heartland by the only true traffic artery in Galicia, the Royal Highway. If, on the other hand, his destination were Lisbon, where the allied Portuguese government interned Spanish political prisoners on the floating *pontones* of the Tagus estuary, or one of the labour camps on the North-African coast, Mol would have been packed into a ship and dispatched from Coruña harbour.

So something else must have been at work, something of which we know nothing, and see nothing, and about which it is vain to speculate. All we can tell is that here, in Santiago, the source falls dry. There are no more clues; and there is no more foundation for an educated, or even an uneducated, guess. But one thing does seem certain in the light of later events: namely that Alejandro Mon, still a man of immense influence in Madrid despite his recent political disgrace, managed to have his protégé set free in the long run. That he summoned him back to Madrid, or perhaps packed him off to France, and laid him up for later use, when the weather cleared and a new attempt to find treasure might be made. To understand what happened, we shall have to turn to the end of the civil war.

22

The Treasure of Ney

THE CARLIST Civil War raged on madly for another twelve months after Benedict Mol's treasure hunt. Then, after nearly six years of marching, countermarching and petty battle; after death, maiming, arbitrary executions and a near endless ritual of small slaughter; after pillaged provinces, verbose proclamations in unreadable prose, and victorious battles which sloth and corruption turned into lost opportunities, both sides discovered that the fodder bags were empty and the land lay scorched and barren at their feet. So the armies at last grew tired of killing and bleeding; and much as the politicians on both sides insisted on obstinate continuation, the soldiers decided that enough was enough, that it was better to accommodate than to exterminate, that more dead peasants and razed villages would carry neither monarch closer to the throne. What is more: the soldiers concluded that the civilian leaders, by their factional infighting, their faulty running of the war effort, and their heartless egotism, had disqualified themselves and forfeited the right to decide the further course of things.

In the summer of 1839, the supreme commanders of both armies, Rafael Maroto for the Carlists and Baldomero Espartero for the Liberals, opened secret negotiations and within a few weeks reached a compromise. The Carlist army was to lay down its arms with honour. Those rebel soldiers who wished to do so, could incorporate themselves in the Spanish army, keeping their titles, ranks, medals and pensions, once they had recognized young Isabel as lawful queen of Spain. The Basque *foros* – the traditional statutes of local rights and privileges which had become the most important bone of contention in the conflict – would be maintained, and both people and property of the rebellious provinces would be respected. In August of 1839, Maroto and Espartero met on a meadow outside the village of Vergara, signed the armistice, and sealed the peace with a symbolic embrace. A tiny spark of Wisdom had finally managed to kindle a torch of Reason. It came too late for many thousands of people and burned too feebly to salvage the country from additional future catastrophe at the hands of its soldiers. But it brought at least a short respite to a land that had nearly bled to death.

As plague follows famine with the iron certainty of a natural law, so military dictatorship necessarily succeeds a civil war. Spain in the 1840s was no exception. Having risen to unassailable prominence for his daredevil bravery and unequalled martial success, General Espartero held in his hand all the strings that controlled the destiny of Spain. In the final months of 1839, he ran his armies into the last pockets of resistance and mopped up what unrelenting Carlists still remained. Don Carlos was driven out of the country into France. The formidable guerrilla leader Ramon Cabrera, dug in in his stronghold around Teruel, held out for half a year longer, but overwhelmed by the flood of Liberal soldiers freed from the Basque Countries, had to call it a day by mid 1840. That done, Espartero, a man of ultra-radical convictions, turned upon the political clique of Madrid lawyers, bankers and merchants. He forced a crisis, swept the tottering government aside, and had himself proclaimed regent of the realm and warden of the child-queen Isabel in place of Queen Mother Maria Cristina. A large tribe of *Moderados*, with Maria Cristina leading the pack, followed the Carlists into French exile.

No one who knows the history of Spain in the 1830s will say that the venal, corrupt, self-serving politicians of the time did not merit a thrashing of sorts. Yet this was not the kind of peacemaking of which Spain now stood in need. Despite his best efforts, Espartero could not control a country in which people had learned to hate one another, provinces had seen independence within reach and officers had tasted the sweet fruits of revolt. Rebellion followed upon rebellion; conspiracy upon conspiracy, killing upon killing. Espartero, who for all his genius regarded all political problems merely in terms of military conflict, knew no better than to answer violence with violence. Barcelona rose; Espartero bombarded her back into obedience. The Basque Countries rose, and Espartero sent the army. In one particularly nasty incident, a rebel band of former Carlists and discontented *Moderados* penetrated as far as the courtyard of the Royal Palace in a nocturnal attempt to kidnap the child-queen. They were only stopped by a small battalion of *Alarbarderos* who stood firm and blocked their way. Furious, Espartero had the leader of the *coup* – a war hero and high aristocrat – shot by firing-squad. Every nobleman, noblewoman and upper class dandy in the land cried out in horrified indignation at one of their peers being treated like a common villain by this Spanish Robespierre.

At long last, Espartero's *Progresista* autocracy came to an end. Too much bloodshed, too many troubles, too much division gradually eroded the loyalties of his backers. After three years he found himself without support when another *coup* struck in the summer of 1843, a *coup* staged by a weird amalgam of *Moderados*, recycled Carlists and frustrated *Progresistas* under the leadership of Maria Cristina and that bizarre, power-obsessed General Ramón Narvaez. Espartero fled to England; Maria Cristina returned to Madrid; Narvaez's sabre reigned supreme.

Until someone has the unlikely idea of writing a true biography of Alejandro Mon we will not know his precise whereabouts throughout these troubled years. Espartero himself hated his guts, so much is certain, and he condemned him to political ostracism as soon as he reached power in 1840. Twice Mon stood for parliament, and twice he was defeated. The *Progresista* era simply had no use for him, the Queen Mother's partisan, the *Moderado avant la lettre*, the scandal-ridden minister of yesteryear. But no sooner had Conservative power been restored to palace and parliament by Narvaez's muskets, than Mon put in a renewed appearance. With his past and his proven talents, he was now one of the Grand Old Men of the *Moderado* party, and he regained, through ballot-less administrative order, his seat in parliament by the autumn of 1843. After a pair of short interim governments of weak and inept civilians – put in, one feels, to avoid the correct impression that Ramón Narvaez had only kicked out the previous dictator to become one himself – a new government was formed in May 1844 under, unsurprisingly, Ramón Narvaez. Its Minister of Finance was Alejandro Mon, who was to embark upon the immense and badly needed overhaul of the fiscal system.

It was, however, during his nine months of forced unemployment, as he was waiting in the wings to be recalled to office, that Mon seems to have undertaken yet another attempt to get his hands on the Santiago treasure. In contrast to 1838, it is impossible to prove that he was the real puppeteer behind the show; but it certainly has his signature written largely over it. A Coruña newspaper printed the following short article in late November of 1843:

The Treasure of Ney

It seems that Mr Sandino, chief tax inspector and interim
civil governor, is involved in a project to discover a treasure, with an estimated value of some sixty million [reales],
which was supposedly buried by the French General Ney
during his presence here at the time of the Peninsular
War. Apparently the hiding place is close to the church of
Laraño, at half or three-quarters of a league from [Santiago].
Rumour has it that Mr Sandino is accompanied by the
French consul and another French person of advanced age,
who probably witnessed the hiding of the carts which are
believed to contain the jewels of gold and silver, and the
bags of money which are the object of the search.

Laraño is a tiny hamlet some three miles west of Santiago, set in the
middle of dark, inaccessible forests of oak and pine trees, among hills
which undulate all the way to the horizon on every side. It isn't much of
a place. The best one can say about it, is that it makes a perfectly peaceful,
pastoral village: a dozen stone houses at the outside, drawn up like a
wagon circle around the grassy little *plaza* with its obligatory bandstand,
its gurgling fountain and its rough-hewn granite *cruceiro*. In spite of its
diminutive size, in the 1840s it was the dozing administrative nucleus
of another eight petty hamlets, which all together totalled a hundred
houses if one includes the isolated farmsteads. It had a school which
boasted sixty pupils; and it had the resident priest and parish church.

That church, San Martin de Laraño, is like any other village chapel
in Galicia. Like its kin, it sports one nave and two small side-chapels
constructed from huge grey granite blocks pock-marked abundantly
with lichen. It has its sacristy tucked snugly under one armpit, and an
ornamental bell tower in the shape of a papal tiara on top, built in that
vague Italian style popular during the wealthy period of New World
commerce. A stone fence closes off a graveyard overgrown with weeds.
A path of crunchy pebbles leads to the front porch, and the cast-iron
entrance gate, last painted in colonial days, squeals like a raven when
pushed open. There is, in short, nothing to distinguish it from any other
small Galician church a hundred miles around; nor anything particular

to attract the attention of that 'Frenchman of advanced age' and his impressive diplomatic retinue – were it not that the road which runs right in front of San Martin just happens to be called the *calle San Roque de Laraño*, after a disappeared chapel. And it was here that the old explorer came prospecting for a major hoard, 'which the French concealed before retreating from this province at the time of the Peninsular War…'

There is no way to tell with certainty if this old Frenchman really was old 'Benedict Mol', released in 1838, put on the shelf and kept around in some unknown place all through the Espartero era, now returned to Compostela for a second try to discover his hoard. But one certainly begins to suspect so, seeing that two quite similar treasure hunters came looking for two identical treasures, in the space of a mere five years, at a spot with an explicit San Roque context, and under the aegis of men from the Treasury. Some very close connection must have existed between the two events. And the most logical link between the two is that both got started by one and the same informer.

This assumption would also clarify a murky point about the treasure hunt of 1838. If this was really the same *Zahori*, who nevertheless went looking for his treasure at a completely different spot, then it shows that Mol only had the vaguest notion of its burial place. In *The Bible in Spain*, it will be remembered, Mol pretends that his dying comrade '*was so exact in his description of the place where it lies, that were I once at Compostella, I should have no difficulty in putting my hand upon it.*' But that was clearly not the case. By the look of it, our good *Zahori* only possessed some rudimentary clues which spoke of a small Galician chapel, roughly associated with San Roque, somewhere in the Santiago neighbourhood. Small wonder, then, that his earlier search failed so dismally. His dig in the cesspool of San Roque hospital was never more than an arbitrary guess; and he was not even sure if his hoard lay buried in a hospital just outside the Santiago city limits, or miles away in the untamed Galician countryside.

Yet none of that lessened his zeal and his dedication; nor did it discourage his sponsors in the Treasury, men such as Sandino who, as the highest fiscal authority in the province, must have been loosely or closely associated with Alejandro Mon himself. Everybody seems to have been quite convinced of the existence of Ney's treasure. They were confident enough, not only to risk another scandal, but even to bring in the French consul from Coruña, with all the possible diplomatic backlash which such a thing might cause. And they were willing to launch yet one more public 'exhibition of avarice and credulity', marching still further down that old, familiar road of folly, which leads ever downhill from a starting point of fabled buried gold...

Unfortunately, we only have the vaguest notion of what happened next. It seems that some time after the Coruña newspaper reported on the visit to Laraño, the old Frenchman found what he was looking for: a place in the woods not too far away from the church, on the slopes of the *Monte de Boa Vista*, the 'Mountain of the Good View', so called – as many a spot around the Apostle's city – for the sight it commands of the venerable cathedral in the distance[12]. In early December, under the aegis of the new civil governor and the chief tax inspector, a trial dig was made halfway up the wooded mountain. A number of men were employed to excavate a trench and remove the dirt. No treasure was found; but the authorities refused to give up hope. The French, after all, would have made sure that their precious hoard could not be discovered too easily. Whole wagons were said to be sunk into the soil – and a wagon can only be buried really deep. It was mid-winter, and the rain and the cold made digging difficult. So the excavated site was filled in again and covered up, with the intention of returning for further prospecting in spring, when the ground would be softer and the hours of daylight longer.

Blessed be those of simple faith... The good officials had counted without the fatal pull of treasure. They forgot how quickly gold fever infects men's minds if it drifts only a fleeting moment in the air. Barely had the earth been shovelled back into the governmental hole, than rumours came through of obscure nocturnal goings-on up on the *Monte de Boa Vista*. On December 8th, Domingo Coreyro, the *Mayordomo* or official village elder of Laraño, was tipped off by a villager called Ramón Parga, that the neighbourhood peasants were making excavations of their own in the dead of night, 'at the very same spot where this had been done by order of the *Intendente*.' Somewhat reluctantly, Coreyro gave notice of the emergency

---

12 The cognomen has many variations, such as *Vista Alegre* (Happy View) and of course the most famous of all: the *Monte del Gozo*, Mountain of Joy, an elevated spot on the road from Lugo where the medieval pilgrims could first make out the spires of the cathedral after months of walking.

to the mayor of Conxo, the nearby Santiago suburb from where Laraño was administered. In reply he was told that he had better be careful. The document does not specify whom he ought to be careful about: the higher authorities in Compostela and Coruña, or the gold-digging *campesinos* of the village. But conceivably the mayor of Conxo meant both. In these decades of easy violence and arbitrary justice, the petty officials of Galicia always stood in fear of one as well as of the other. Their superiors expected them to maintain strict law and order and enforce most unwelcome government policies in their villages. Yet the peasants had a notorious reputation for blind and uncontrolled violence whenever quarrels broke out. And the local officials, who lived among them, were perfectly aware of this attitude, not to say that they regarded their plebeian compatriots with an awe that bordered on terror. In this particular instance, it was whispered that the nightly prospectors came armed with pikes and lances, and set guards around the area to make short work of nosey intruders.

In spite of such apprehensions, Coreyro understood that he had to do *something*. So on two occasions he climbed the *Monte de Boa Vista* at night to see the excavation for himself. The first time he found the site abandoned, everybody having disappeared before he arrived. The following night he did find them working, and was stunned at the number of men and the size of the dig. He tried to reason with the prospectors, and summoned them to stop their illicit quarrying. But they refused to obey, and told him plainly to go to hell, even threatening his person. And in spite of the fact that he saw no weapons among them at all, only spades, shovels and pickaxes, Coreyro thought the better of it and left before things turned ugly.

Now what else could he do? He stood powerless. Coreyro informed the mayor of Conxo, don Domingo Matuto, of his failure to stop the gold-diggers from working. On December 26th, Matuto – just as loath to call in higher powers as the village elder – made one more attempt to end this business without informing Santiago. He published an official proclamation explicitly forbidding nightly digs, and ordered the heads of households of Laraño to patrol the area during the hours of darkness and stop transgressors from going up the mountain. It was a most feeble and impotent order, since it called upon the lawbreakers to maintain the law. Unsurprisingly, it came to nothing. The excavations continued on the following nights, as if no proclamation had ever been issued.

Now even the mayor of Conxo could no longer escape informing the superior authorities in Santiago. On one of the final days of the year, he sent a message to the *Intendente*, who in turn notified the civil governor – and all the government officials went into an instant frenzy. What, one can hear them think, if these peasants find the gold that is rightfully ours? What if they dig it out and take it home? What will Madrid say? How will she *react*?? Whom will she *sack*?? The new governor, don Enrique de Vedia, not yet a month in office, must have had quite a different political *debut* in mind. He ordered immediate action. He requested soldiers from the local military commander, and told the mayor of Conxo to get his act together and put a stop to the digs with extreme prejudice.

At nine in the evening of January 2nd, 1844, Matuto repaired to the San Martin barracks in Santiago and put himself at the head of twenty soldiers, two corporals, a sergeant and an officer. In spite of the fact that Coreyro had assured him there were no weapons at the site, the mayor did not trust himself to go unarmed; so he ordered the soldiers to carry their muskets loaded and with bayonets fixed. It was a good precaution. The first group of peasants they caught once they arrived in the area, a handful of stragglers whom they met near the hamlet of Ponte Viejo, still went unarmed. But these men assured the mayor, after admitting they had come from the 'mine' and were on the way home, that there were still other men up on the mountain and that many of these did indeed carry weapons. It proved no hollow warning, for a second group which the patrol intercepted consisted of nine men armed with pikes and knives and other tools of violence. The mayor had the lot of them marched back to the rear and guarded in a safe place. That done, he put sentinels at the bridges and the crossroads of the area, blocking all escape routes. And then he set out, together with twelve hand-picked soldiers, to climb *Boa Vista* mountain from the opposite side and fall upon the excavators from above.

The atmosphere was now extremely tense. The night was pitch dark, especially on this densely wooded hillside. An eerie, ominous silence reigned throughout the valley; and Matuto was well aware that once Galician peasants took weapons along on illegal outings, they would be perfectly willing to use them. The accuracy of his premonitions was brought home to him before half an hour was out. As, panting and struggling, he reached the top of the ridge, he suddenly saw himself confronted by a sentry, who attacked him with a pike without any warning. It might have been fatal, had he not been saved at the very last moment from being badly hurt by one of the soldiers who quickly interposed himself and wrestled the peasant to the ground. The episode spelled little good for the remainder of the night.

Just before midnight the patrol swept down onto the dig site. As they burst into the clearing, there was nobody left. Somehow an alarm had been given, and on the soldiers' approach everyone had fled down the mountainside, towards the valley. All they found was the excavation itself: a stunning hole of 1,763 square *varas* (some 30 x 40 meters), dug out to the depth of a meter and a half. The major probably felt greatly relieved at the ease with which the peasants had been scattered, but the night was not yet over. Hardly five minutes after he had sat down to take a breath, the cracks of two musket shots were heard in the distance. Then a lot of shouting echoed through the night, and cries for help; and then there was a loud third shot.

Matuto immediately hurried down the mountain towards the place from where the sounds had come. In the hamlet of Rial, where he had posted two guards together with the local *Mayordomo*, he found a soldier perched over two bleeding bodies lying prostrate in the street. One of these, a young man called José Ferreiro, was already dead. The other, José San Martin, was severely wounded and looked like he would not live another hour. It seems they had been shot on sight, at point-blank range, by the sentry stationed in the middle of the village, as they tried to escape. Yet the soldier, Juan de Vila, denied that version vehemently. He claimed that he had arrested the two men as they came down from the mountain, and to keep them under control, had made them lay down on the ground. A little later, he saw a large group of peasants come running at him, and had given them the '*Alto!*'. At that, they had opened fire and hit both prisoners fatally. It was precisely the sort of event that the mayor of Conxo must have dreaded all along: two men shot, endless inquiries to answer, the prospect of a scapegoat being sought…

Matuto did the best he could. He sent someone to fetch the nearest priest, don José Maimo, who tried to confess José San Martin on the spot where he lay in agony. While that was going on, Matuto organised a thorough search of all the surrounding houses. Surely much to his relief, a hoard of weapons was discovered in one Laraño house; which meant he could prove that the local peasants were potential rebels, disposed to disobedience and violence; a fact which would vindicate his actions. Finally, at 3.30 a.m. he ordered the soldiers back to the barracks, dispatched the fourteen prisoners to the *Cárcel Pública*, and had the two victims carried to the *Hospital Real*, one to go to the morgue for autopsy, the other to the sickbay.

As soon as this party arrived, José San Martin was interrogated. There was no time to waste, for he was obviously dying. He declared that he had gone to the *Boa Vista* mountain with José Ferreiro, a slight acquaintance, at 8 p.m. the previous night. They had dug, and then decided to return home, round about midnight. On the way, they met the sentry, who shouted an *Alto*, and then opened fire without more ado. There was no more to it. A few hours later San Martin died. Both corpses were scrupulously dissected by the medics of Santiago, who after much chopping and cutting concluded that the two men had died of gunshots. José Ferreiro was only twenty-one years old. Nobody was ever charged with their murder. Nor was it ever discovered who had fired the third shot which Matuto heard.

Gold fever is indeed a most lethal disease.

23

The Grim Reaper

THE LARAÑO killings are the last we ever hear about the treasure hunter of Santiago and his phantom hoard. There are no more adventures to tell, and there is probably nothing else to discover in the papers of the times or the archives of today. That comes as no surprise. If the 'Frenchman of advanced age' who appeared in Compostela in late 1843 really was George Borrow's 'Benedict Mol', then he must have been seventy years old at least. No matter how ardent his desire to find treasure, no matter how many other attempts the *Moderado* politicians were still willing to undertake, the Swiss must have run out of steam with the wear and tear of age. We do not know where he went. We do not know when he died. Nor does it matter; for he had added his grain of madness to the heap of human folly. He had caused nationwide scandals; helped to topple a government; caused the death of two harmless peasants. If men's lives be measured, not by their accomplishments or their benevolent deeds, but by the impact of their acts upon their equals, then this vagabond veteran of the Peninsular War did not do too badly.

Alejandro Mon, great patron of the silly farce, the inveterate bureaucrat turned would-be adventurer, lived on until 1882. The treasure hunt did not hurt his career at all. From May 1844 until deep into 1846 he was Minister of Finance under the sway of the inevitable Narvaez. In the following decades he would occupy that post time and time again in countless short-lived cabinets, never for longer than a year. He also served as Speaker of the House; as ambassador to Paris; and various times as special envoy to the Vatican. From March to mid-September of 1864 Narvaez even stool-pigeoned him briefly as Prime Minister, and in 1876 he was elevated to senator-for-life. Today Don Alejandro is best remembered for his sensible reforms of the fiscal system and as the Minister who shaved the sharpest edges off the wholesale expropriation of Church lands, thus opening the way for a badly needed reconciliation with Rome. His was a career of paper battles and bureaucratic triumphs, happily devoid of all further heroism or ambitious schemes; the kind that looks marvellous on an official *curriculum vitae* which nobody wants to read. And so much the better. As it is, Spain always had more than its share of passionate, visionary superheroes and the awful damage they do. Yet collective memory often only absorbs the bloodshed and the evil deeds; and men who do not excel in such wickedness tend to be forgotten. Barely anybody today knows Alejandro Mon. Only a handful of fiscal historians look up eagerly at the mention of his name. In February of 2001, the bicentennial of his birth, he was awarded a pedestal of the size and height appropriate to his fame: a commemorative postal stamp of his own, twelve square centimetres of flat paper, with a value of 25 €urocents.

George Borrow died a year earlier than Mon, in 1881. He *was* by nature an adventurer – restless, bohemian and spirited – and he really ought to have kept travelling in order to remain sane, for only a constant change of scenery and an unending, heroic struggle for some Grand Ideal against an implacable Foe, in which he could style himself a fearless martyr, might have saved his mind from whirling into the neurotic. But man is often his own worst counsellor. As it was, Borrow – deep in his heart far more British and bourgeois than he would ever have cared to admit – had settled in a golden cage, in order to write.

His literary career was a bizarre slalom which, over four decades, would take him from the highest pinnacle of sales figures and critical acclaim, to the deepest, most frustrating dell of oblivion. He first wrote *The Zincali*, a romantic account of his beloved Spanish gypsies, which appeared in 1841. It sold a few hundred copies; and even though it gained him a reputation among fellow gyptologists, it did not catch the eye of the general public. Then, the following year, he published his masterpiece, *The Bible in Spain*, which catapulted him to instant fame and fortune. Thousands of copies were sold over the counter. Pirate editions in America alone ran into 20,000 copies or more. All of Britain read the book; politicians referred to it in the House of Commons; every literary salon of London wanted to take a peep at the author.

Perhaps it would have been better had success arrived a little later, a little harder. The public, enchanted with *The Bible*, wanted more Spanish adventure. But Borrow, having run out of Spanish material, turned to his vagabond childhood instead. At the same time mega-success inflamed his dormant egotism. Vindicated by sales and critical approval, he took to the opinion that the public ought to love whatever he deemed to give it. His new books – *Lavengro, The Romany Rye, Wild Wales* – grew ever more eccentric, ever more rambling, ever more uncompromising with the desires of the common reader. For the *gourmet* with the acquired taste, these were still choice, delicious books; but the swine at large refused the proffered pearls. Charles Darwin, an eloquent voice of the age, typically dubbed *Lavengro* 'rubbish, but amusing'. The larger public was less amused. Over time, they turned away from the wayward author, and Borrow was never again to equal his earlier triumphs.

He took it hard. He grew testy, unpredictable, frustrated. He began to affront people at the first suspicion of censure and the first mildly critical remark. He threw temper tantrums, and suffered sudden bouts of madness, which made him jump up in the middle of a conversation, run from the house, and disappear for days on end as he walked frantically through the countryside. Towards the end of his life, after his wife died, he was a sour, grumpy, vengeful old man, sadly overtaken by his own legend; one who bullied his neighbours, wrote interminable postscripts full of raging denunciation, and loved only his dogs and passing bands of gypsies. He died as he had lived – alone – on July 27th, 1881, in his Oulton home. Settled life had not agreed with him.

Epilogue

So was there ever such a treasure, put together from stolen church plate or '*gold moidores and diamonds from the Brazils*', looted in Portugal or pillaged in Galicia, buried in Santiago and forgotten by all except 'Benedict Mol'?

It is impossible to say…

Tales of French treasures, hidden by panicky Napoleonic soldiers on the run, were not rare at all in the mid 19th century. Richard Ford noted in his *Gatherings from Spain* how many such hoards were still being searched for with keen dedication in his day. And he records a strikingly similar case from 1846, in which the municipal authorities of San Sebastian were closely watching the excavations of an elderly French lady, to whom a certain veteran, on his deathbed, had revealed the secret of yet another kettle full of gold…

Yet, as we have seen, the Santiago treasure stands a wee bit apart from all such cheap fairy tales of swindlers, frauds and con men, because there seems to be some logic to the case, and because it fits in well with historical fact. Although we may fairly discard any Portuguese origin, it is far from impossible that part of the church plate confiscated by Ney would have been hidden, either by the French themselves or by their local henchmen, with an eye to a later return of Napoleon's armies. In any case this scenario looked plausible enough for Alejandro Mon and the *Moderado* government to make an attempt at recovery, not just once, but twice within half a decade, in spite of the massive risk of ridicule and political damage.

The treasure was, in any case, not found. Not in 1838 and not in 1843. That may be because there never was one. Or because the treasure hunter looked in the wrong spot. Or – let us not overlook the possibility – because it was found at an earlier date.

Found at an earlier date…? If so: *by whom?*

Why, by lodgers of San Roque Hospital perhaps, or those who had dealings with the spot where it was buried, or – ultimately – by construction workers, the people most likely to run into things hidden in buildings. As it happens, in 1819, two decades before Benedict Mol ever set a foot in Santiago, the San Roque hospital was renovated on the initiative of a merchant – Don Francisco Rial from Villagarcia – perhaps in gratitude for a successful cure. The building was, in fact, so thoroughly rebuilt inside and out, that the only original part which remains today is the hospital's ornate baroque entrance.

In that same year 1819, don Rafael Muzquiz, archbishop of Santiago, made an important donation to the treasury of his cathedral. With lots of pomp and formality, he donated a gorgeous chalice made of *gold and diamonds*, which, according to the great canon-historian Lopez Ferreiro, is still being used during grand solemnities. 'On the 3rd of September of the Holy Year 1819,' Ferreiro writes in his history of the diocese, 'a letter was received [by the cathedral] dated the 18th of August, in which [bishop Muzquiz] communicated that *in recognition of the great benefits which the powerful hand of the Highest has granted him through the intercession of the Holy Apostle (…), he humbly offers a chalice of solid gold inlaid with diamonds, plus its paten, dish and cruets of the same metal.*'

Now from where, one may ask, would Muzquiz suddenly have acquired so much gold and diamonds? Of course, the Santiago diocese was a rich one, and Muzquiz was no poverty-stricken prelate. But even so, gold and diamonds were rare in these days. There is almost no mention of gold in the endless inventories of church plate and jewels made during the French confiscations; and we never ever hear of diamonds; only of the occasional emerald. Had the treasure, Mol´s treasure, that hoard of '*gold moidores and huge diamonds from the Brazils*' perhaps been found during the restoration works of the Hospital? Was it handed over to His Eminence – only slightly against the Royal Prerogative in such cases – by that pious merchant from Villagarcia? Did the bishop then decide not to keep it for himself, but to bestow it on his Church and his beloved Apostle? Once again we shall never know – but if we look at the date on which Muzquiz wrote his letter, all sorts of wild speculations and suspicions of weird cryptic messages suddenly press themselves upon us. That date is the 18th of August, i.e. the day following on the traditional festivities of San Roque. Why in the world would Muzquiz have put that date to his letter? Why did he antedate it by two weeks, if he lived in the bishop's palace next door to the cathedral? And what precisely were those mysterious *great benefits* which God had granted him through the intercession of Saint James?

But, as said before: it is unlikely that the treasure consisted of gold and diamonds; so perhaps no chance find in San Roque hospital was involved in this donation, and bishop Muzquiz simply paid for the chalice out of his own pocket. In that case it is possible that no treasure was found in the 1830s and 40s because the Treasure Hunter of Santiago was simply looking in the wrong spot. It will be obvious, from the pages above, that 'Benedict Mol' had only the vaguest notion where the hoard might be buried. In 1838 he seems to have been looking for 'a church' with some major outbuilding attached. In 1843, he scanned the vicinity of Laraño, and more particularly the *Monte de Boa Vista*, just outside Santiago.

Monte de Boa Vista, that name that occurs so often around Compostela…

And here now for those who still delight in dreaming of hidden hoards.

Just outside the old walls of Compostela, in front of the Puerta Fajera, lies the Alameda, the 19th century municipal park, where Mol supposedly met Borrow on that moonlit night in 1837. In its middle rises the *Monte de Santa Susana*, a green hillock planted with venerable oak trees, topped, ever since the 10th century, with the little church of Santa Susana, which has a graveyard and some outbuildings attached. It was here that Maucune's French troopers made their final stand against the approaching *Alarmas* in May 1809, during that ferocious day-long Battle of the Campo de Estrella described above, which at long last forced the French to flee the city, leaving their baggage behind.

One of the old names of the hill just happens to be… the *Monte de Boa Vista*.

That fabulous treasure of Benedict Mol, oh ye hopeful, may still be waiting…

Appendices

Appendix 1
From George Borrow's The Bible in Spain, *chapter 42*

I N THE above pages, I quoted many of the Benedict Mol episodes from Borrow's *The Bible in Spain* at length, but left out his actual description of the Santiago treasure hunt. There was good reason for this. As mentioned in the text: Borrow's book only gives heavily dramatised versions of events, which often depart considerably from the truth. I therefore decided only to use such parts of his writings which are – for better or for worse – the only available source on the adventures of the Swiss. For the treasure hunt itself, however, we have other, and slightly more reliable, documents, most notably the articles from the *Eco del Comercio*. Consequently there was no need to use Borrow's fanciful version of the tale for my own creative reconstruction.

Even so readers may be curious to know what Borrow made of it. Therefore the text below – from the final pages of chapter 42 of *The Bible in Spain* – reproduces Borrow's distorted, 'rehashed' and embellished description of the great affair.

> It appeared that the government [of Spain] had listened to [Mol's] tale, and had been so struck with Bennet's exaggerated description of the buried treasure, that they imagined that, by a little trouble and outlay, gold and diamonds might be dug up at Saint James sufficient to enrich themselves and to pay off the national debt of Spain. The Swiss returned to Compostella 'like a duke,' to use his own words. The affair, which had at first been kept a profound secret, was speedily divulged. It was, indeed, resolved that the investigation, which involved consequences of so much importance, should take place in a manner the most public and imposing. A solemn festival was drawing nigh, and it was deemed expedient that the search should

185

take place on that day. The day arrived. All the bells in Compostella pealed. The whole populace thronged from their houses, a thousand troops were drawn up in the square, the expectation of all was wound up to the highest pitch. A procession directed its course to the church of San Roque; at its head was the captain-general and the Swiss, brandishing in his hand the magic rattan, close behind walked the *meiga*, the Gallegan witch-wife, by whom the treasure-seeker had been originally guided in the search; numerous masons brought up the rear, bearing implements to break up the ground. The procession enters the church, they pass through it in solemn march, they find themselves in a vaulted passage. The Swiss looks around. 'Dig here,' said he suddenly. 'Yes, dig here,' said the meiga. The masons labour, the floor is broken up, – a horrible and fetid odour arises. . . .

Enough; no treasure was found, and my warning to the unfortunate Swiss turned out but too prophetic. He was forthwith seized and flung into the horrid prison of Saint James, amidst the execrations of thousands, who would have gladly torn him limb from limb.

The affair did not terminate here. The political opponents of the government did not allow so favourable an opportunity to escape for launching the shafts of ridicule. The Moderados were taunted in the cortes for their avarice and credulity, whilst the liberal press wafted on its wings through Spain the story of the treasure-hunt at Saint James.

'After all, it was a *trampa* of Don Jorge's,' said one of my enemies. 'That fellow is at the bottom of half the picardias which happen in Spain.'

Eager to learn the fate of the Swiss, I wrote to my old friend Rey Romero, at Compostella. In his answer he states: 'I saw the Swiss in prison, to which place he sent for me, craving my assistance, for the sake of the friendship which I bore to you. But how could I help him? He was speedily after removed from Saint James, I know not whither. It is said that he disappeared on the road.'

Truth is sometimes stranger than fiction. Where in the whole cycle of romance shall we find anything more wild, grotesque, and sad, than the easily-authenticated history of Benedict Mol, the treasure-digger of Saint James?

Readers interested in the philological niceties of Borrow's creative process as he churned out this marvellous piece of semi-fiction, may consult the five rather scholarly articles I published on the matter between 1999 and 2003 in the *George Borrow Bulletin*, nos. 17, 21, 22, 23 and 27. Here, I merely wish to point out a few of the wilder fancies in the piece.

The first thing to stress is that the treasure hunt did not occur on 'a solemn festival', by which Borrow obviously meant the feast day of San Roque. As explained in chapter 19 above, the authorities deemed it expressly *not* expedient that the search should take place on that day. Church-bashing as ever, Borrow – who probably remembered the celebrations from his own visit to Santiago a year previously – must have put this little innuendo in so as to calumniate the Church once again. For the same reason – and some good Victorian prudishness about latrines – Borrow maintained throughout that the search took place in the church of San Roque, even though he was aware that the Swiss dug in the Hospital next door.

As for the various participants, the '*meiga*' whom Borrow here re-introduces, naturally never walked in the treasure hunt procession, since she was no more than a continuation of the 'woman who laid the cards for (Mol) in Paris', mentioned in the *Eco del Comercio* nº 1,589 of 6 September 1838 (see chapter 13 above). Also, there is no reliable indication anywhere that either the Captain-General or those 'thousand troops' participated in the real-life affair. Although a certain concentration of troops would in theory be possible, since Captain-General Valdés was at this time using Santiago as his military base (see chapter 19), the number is improbably high. For all the war-time tasks and duties in Galicia, Valdés only had some 6,000 active soldiers available *on paper*, and the true number was probably much lower. Rather than to stand by idly in Compostela, these troops would, furthermore, be urgently needed for the military operations against Mateo Guillade in the south of the province, operations which were led by the Marqués de Astaríz, Captain-General of Santiago city. Astaríz's absence in August 1838 proves, furthermore, that the 'Captain-General' who supposedly walked in the treasure hunt procession (chapter 19) could not possibly have been the 'Captain-General' whom Mol supposedly went to see a year before (see chapters 13 and 14), since the latter must have been the city commander instead of the provincial Vice-Roy who resided in Coruña.

Although both Antonio Giménez Cruz and myself have independently worked our way through the densely printed pages of the '*Diario de las Sesiones del Congreso de los Diputados*' for the year 1838, neither of us found any trace of the *Moderados* being 'taunted in the Cortes for their avarice and credulity' as Borrow claims. It may be that such 'taunts' were not included in the transcript of the parliamentary debates; but note that the first session of the Madrid Cortes closed on 20 June 1838, and that the next session only opened in November, months after the Ofalia government fell.

Appendix 2
Press reports and other primary sources

B ELOW, THE orthography, punctuation and accents of the originals are maintained throughout.

Eco del Comercio nº 1,581, 29 August 1838, p. 4

Nos escriben de Betanzos con fecha 18 lo siguiente:

Es muy curiosa la noticia que ahora nos ocupa. Parece que un suizo se presentó hace poco tiempo à los señores ministros, y les manifestó que en Santiago en la iglesia de San Roque se hallaba enterrado un gran tesoro en oro portugués, nada menos que desde el año 1809. El gobierno mandó que el tal suizo bajara á Santiago, y en efecto al presentarse en dicha ciudad ha prestado solemnemente la misma declaracion. En su virtud, van á hacerse las escavaciones que el suizo diga, y ayer era el dia fijado para ocuparse de estos trabajos. Veremos lo que producen.

Por de pronto el suizo está mantenido y ha viajado con comodidad : si nada se encuentra, él dirá que vió enterrar el tesoro, y que despues lo sacarian. Vean vds. un modo de vivir en el mundo. Y no quiero hacer ahora otras reflexiones, no sea que el suizo encuentre lo que busca, y despues sea yo el burlado. En esas nos viéramos.

Tal vez creerán vds. que es broma lo que les digo, pero se engañarian en ese caso : el correo próximo les diré los resultados de las escavaciones ya empezadas, y tal vez concluidas.

Como el suizo dice que el tesoro es inmenso, los ministros se han apresurado á buscarle, porque en la crisis en que se hallan (perdóneme el *Correo Nacional*) vendria como pedrara en ojo de boticario : entonces sí que se aferraban en sus poltronas, que seria otro nuevo tesoro suizo.

[...]

P.D. Es ciertísimo lo de Santiago : tengo carta de personas muy respetables, que oficialmente deben concurrir à las escavaciones.

Eco del Comercio nº 1,584, 1 September 1838, p. 1

EL TESORO DEL SUIZO
Betanzos, 22 de agosto de 1838.

En su oportunidad dijé á vds. que un suizo se habia presentado al ministerio, declarando que en la iglesia de San Roque en la ciudad de Santiago se hallaba enterrado desde 1809 un gran tesoro en oro portugues , y que el suizo habia venido de esa capital con la orden de que se hicieran escavaciones en el sitio que él designara para encontrar el gran caudal que nos regalaba la providencia. Tambien espresé que el 17 del que rije era el dia señalado para hacer las escavaciones ; y en efecto, se practicaron estas á la vista de muchos testigos, dando por resultado lo que sin duda publicará la Gaceta de esa corte, luego que sus redactores estén *debidamente autorizados* para publicar tan fausta noticia.

Pero tal vez, ocupados con la interesante y perentoria cuestion del diezmo , no lo hagan tan pronto como el público quisiera , y yo voy à suplir su falta, *autorizado debidamente* no por el *suizo del tesoro*, ni por sus favorecedores, sino por dos testigos presenciales; advirtiendo que mis dos amigos no me envian ningun *documento oficial* por donde conste que sus ojos y sus narices vieron y olieron lo que ellos aseguran que han visto y han olido. Me importa que hagan vds. esta advertencia, porque el diablo las carga, y yo no quiero cuentas con serranos, que pagan en chorizos.

Pues como iba diciendo de mi cuento, el bueno, del suizo (cuidado que esto no es *oficial* ni yo se quien lo ha visto) se presentó al ministro de las pesetas, y despues de los cumplimientos de *ene* y demas zarandajas , le aseguró, bajo palabra de suizo , que aunque ya no hubiera empréstito ni anticipacion de cien milliones, ni carta siquiera del *amigo* Toreno , no tenia porque afligirse, contando como cosa muy segura con el gran tesoro que él habia visto enterrar ahora la friolera de unos viente y nueve años en un parage que tenia muy bien marcado ; tesoro con el que se podia, no solo salir de apuros, sino hasta echar el bodegon por la ventana. Como el que se ahoga se agarra aunque sea de un celaje, el ministro le apretó la mano, le dió dos ó tres palmaditas en el hombro, le ofreció el oro y el moro si no lo engañaba , y estendiéndole una orden muy ejecutiva y terminante , le mandó enfilase el camino que Tirabeque no pudo andar porque Manso lo dejó lleno de facciosos. Rabiando estaràn vds. porque lleguemos al fin de la historia; pero tengan un poco de paciencia que hay otras cosas que referir, y el tesoro no se va de donde lo enterraron.

Terminó el suizo su viage, que por supuesto lo pagaria el que todo lo *sufre y paga* como dijo el otro: descansó como un patriarca, y cuando le pareció entregó sus papeles: segun estos se designó el dia 17 para la gran maniobra, y se nombraron los individuos que debian contar las onzas portuguesas, limpiarlas si estaban mohosas y entalegarlas con su cuenta y razon para remitirlas al ministro que habia encontrado este gran recurso con que concluir la guerra sin intervencion gringa, sin transacion [sic] con traidores, y sin tragar el encantado emprestito Saffont , ni admitir el muy ventajoso por *muy manoseado* del liberalismo marques de las Marismas.

Amaneció el dia tan ansiado, el suizo almorzó muy bien por cuenta del pueblo español, se surtió de algunos pomos de agua de Colonia, y con una procesion de albañiles y otras personas que por su desgracia no llevaban olores como él, se constituyó (¿no es asi como se dice?) en el hospital de San Roque, donde pensó y repensó cuanto le dió la gana , hasta que de repente se dirigió con toda la comitiva al *cuarto escusado* , que las gentes ordinarias llaman el *comun*. Alli estaba el tesoro, y alli mandó el suizo que los albañiles trabajasen duro y parejo para abrir un boquete que debia tener diez varas de ancho y qué se yo cuantas de profundidad.

¡Vaya una pintura para un abanico…! Los albañiles echaban la gota tan gorda, y de cuando en cuando vomitaban un poco de bilis ; el suizo empapaba un pañuelo y otro en agua de colonia y los olia sin cesar , hasta que se le puso la geta de un palmo de largo; los espectadores, apretándose con los dedos las narices querían evitarse exhalaciones algo mas fuertes que las que olfateó Don Quijote cuando Sancho *se desgració* oyendo la música de los batanes ; y sin embargo, estos, aquel y los otros todos estaban con tanto ojo abierto y sin pestañear , aguardando que pariese la Pepa.

Pero amigos mios, el parto venia de entuertos, y desde las diez de la mañana hasta las cuatro de la tarde que duró el zahumerio, los albañiles no cesaron de trabajar ni de estornudar; los otros pobres, *debidamente autorizados* para dar fe de todo, tenian ya las narices mas rojas y mas gordas que una remolacha; el suizo apuró su provision de agua de colouia [sic], y el *boquete* por su profundidad tocaba en las paredes del infierno, que sin duda se tragó el tesoro, y asi se tragara al suizo y á quien le dió papilla para que no viniera á poner en ridículo al gobierno y á los infelices españoles, siempre el juguete de cierta clase de sugetos que vienen à dejarnos sin blanca y á reirse de nosotros.

Enhorabuena que el señor ministro hubiera oido al suizo y hecho examiuar [sic] si efectivamente existia ese tesoro en el parage que señalara; ¿pero debió darse tanta publicidad á esa revelacion ó delacion que llevaba en sí todos los signos de un engaño? ¿No hubiera sido suficiente comisionar á un corto número de personas de fidelidad y secreto para que presenciasen las escavaciones, evitando asi que en el caso presente el público de Santiago murmurase, como murmura, contra los que han sido el escarnio de un desconocido que para hacer mas sabrosa la burla ordenó las escavaciones en un lugar pestifero, de un personage que para evitar su escarmiento le bastará decir que él vió enterrar el tesoro y que despues le habrán estraido cuándo y cómo hayan teni-lo por conveniente…?

Aqui dejo la pluma; no soy devoto de los ministros actuales, porque en mi entender llevan la patria à su ruina; pero soy español, y quisiera que los gobernantes de mi patria supieran conservar el prestigio que necesitan para llenar su grave encargo ; y ciertamente que *el tesoro del suizo* no contribuye a ese fin. Ustedes harán los comentarios que gusten : yo lamento este estraño suceso, que nos perjudica mas de lo que puede calcularse á primera vista.

Eco del Comercio nº 1,585, 2 September 1838, p. 4

Parece que algunos han dudado de la verdad de los hechos que contenia nuestro folletin de ayer del *tesoro del suizo*, fundàndose en lo ridiculo de aquel suceso.

Nuestro corresponsal de Betanzos, que es persona entendida y veraz, nos dice en dos cartas que sentiria dudasemos de la certeza del articulo en cualquiera de los puntos que abraza, pues puede afirsmar [sic] que son hechos positivos los relatados.

Eco del Comercio nº 1,589, 6 September 1838, p. 3–4

Disculpa y premio del Suizo que buscaba el tesoro

De Betanzos con fecha 29 nos escriben lo siguiente: El suizo que vino a Santiago á descubrir el tesoro que debia afianzar en su poltrona al ministro de Hacienda sin hacienda, parece que llevó unas cuantas mojicones por la pesada burla que nos ha hecho: estrechando por las preguntas que le hacian los chasqueados, dicen repondió que la culpa de todo tenia *la muger que en Paris le echó las cartas y lo habia engañado*. ¿Que tal, señores redactores? ¿Que dicen vds. del suizo y del ministro que lo envió á revolver el *cuarto escusado de un hospital*…? ¡Peor es meneallo…!

Nosotros, n° 180, 2 September 1838, p. 2

El señor MON buscando recursos en la Y.

La equivocacion de un cartero nos ha proporcionado un curioso documento que vamos á copiar para recreo del lector.

Es el caso que como los ministriales han dado en la flor de decir que hacemos oposicion al ministerio porque queremos ser ministros (tanta salud les dé Dios como dicen verdad) un cartero se encontró con una carta cuyo sobre decia: "*Pur el minesttro mais nuevo di los minestrows*", y creyendo que el nuevo ministro, resuelta la nueva crisis que anuncia el *Castellano*, debia de estar entre Nosotros nos embocó la carta. Abrimosla sin reparar y nos encontramos que decia de esta suerte:

Saint Jago el 18 aujosto.

Capaliero minestro.

Mi vengo de jaser el cosa aquello que tu escilencia mandar mí, ensima este tesoro que mi te jablar tu eseliensia. La camino por que mi á fenido, capaliero minestro, estar futre mala, que la borrico grande que ja fenido mi ensima ella, no podia menear el pierna. Esto borrico andar una lejua por tres horas, y por quatro lejuas cansado asi, y jabria el boca como tu eseliensia jabria el suyo cuando mi contar que mi sabia un tesoro en la Jalisia, santo Roco ijlesia, en el vila de saint Jago. A la fin mi estar llejado en este demonio tierra jallega, y mi estar dicho, que ja fenido por partes di capaliero ministro Mon il mas nuefo des ministros del rey muger Cristino. Es á mi deber desir que en entrando su nombre Mon in oregas, esas jallegos metieron risas grandes en los bocas suyos; uno miraba á la otro, y mas risaban, come ellos disian que el Mon estar Coruña intendenta, é estar un futro intendenta que no safia intendentar. Mi no jaser á ellas el caso, é mi desir que ja fenido puscar tesoro per ti minestro, é fenir ellos con mi in saint Roco ijlesia. La, es un puerta, é in costilla de esto puerta es un asiento, é ensima esto asiento es un pujero rondo pur poner el nalgas cuando el fientre sale el cosa aquello. Estar fenidos con mi muchas hombres jallegos é estar ajarrando el naris con el mano suya porque lá juele mucho mal; é metian el risa en sus bocas, é disian: "esto minestro Mon juscar el oro y jallar el merda." Mi la metia en mi boca el silensio é mandar trapajar, trapajar, trapajar: é en trapajando con el asadonas; mis hompres jan sacado mucho tierra é mucho escrementa: mi no saper cual cosa comen las jallegos pur que juele tanto mal el escrementa:. E trapajando se jacia un ajujero tanto jrande pur estar dentro tu esielensia, é todos otros ministros sus companieros; mi creer ser esto ferdad. E come mi ha fisto ajujero tanto jrande é ningun cosa encontrar é todos mucho reir mi ja dicho de non trapajar mas.

Esto carta escripo tí, capaliero minestro, pur saper que mi come suiso jouriado podeis crer, ningun cosa es de tesoro, sino el escrementa; y mi mandar ti un poco de escrementa con una marajato pur ver ser ferdaz esto cosa que mi dise.

Mi andar en Suisa pronto: porque non hay en esto tierra bon vino: esto vino es malo como los minestros, é los minestros estar como las tesoros.

Soy fuestro, capaliero minestro – Frederic Switzemerd.

Esta es la carta y en verdad que nos hubiera costado gran trabajo entenderla á no haber sabido que al señor Mon se habia presentado un suizo en dias pasados diciéndole que él sabia de un tesoro en Santiago de Galicia: el señor Mon crédulo, como todo el que sabe poco, parece que se la coló, y autorizó al suizo para ir á Santiago y hacer escavaciones. Cuentan que el suizo eligió el lugar mas sucio de la iglesia de san Roque, y que la asquerosa operacion se verificó el dia 17. Lo demas lo dice la carta, y basta y sobra para conocer los puntos que alcanza el señor Mon, y admirar los talentos de un ministro que a falta de empréstitos y arbitrios se va á buscar recusos á donde fué el P. Padilla.

[NB this same 'letter' was reprinted in the *Eco del Comercio* nº 1,585, of Sunday 2 September 1838, p. 4, column 2, with a short introduction. The 'Padre Padilla' mentioned at the end, and left out of the translation as incomprehensible to English readers, is the protagonist of an old anecdote which tells how a priest one day angrily addressed his congregation from the pulpit, saying: 'I am sick and tired of preaching against you people's sins, and therefore I've decided *que me voy para la mismísima mierda*'. After which he mounted his mule and rode off. The story gave rise to various popular expressions such as *'vete a donde se fue el padre Padilla'*, roughly translated: 'Go to hell!']

Modesto Lafuente

[From: Modesto Lafuente, *Fray Gerundio*, episode 'El Botanico y el Prado' of 4 September 1838]

'En seguida me acordé del Suizo *zahorí* que fué de acuerdo y con órden del Sr. Mon á extraer un tesoro que decía estar enterrado en el lugar comun del hospital de San Roque de Santiago, y solté una carcajada.'

Letter of Rey Romero to George Borrow, June 1839

[From: Angus Fraser, *Benedict Mol, treasure-hunter of Saint James*, George Borrow Bulletin 12, p. 69–82.]

'El Alemán del tesoro vino aquí el año pasado recomendado del Govierno para descubrirlo. Pero, á pocos dias de su llegada lo metieron en la cárcel, desde donde me ha escrito dándose a conocer, indicando que era el recomendado de vm., en virtud de lo cual fué mi hijo á visitarlo á la prision. Le dijo que vm. tambien había estado arrestado, lo que no quise creer. A poco tiempo lo llevaron á la Coruña; luego lo bolvieron [sic] a traer aquí, y por fin no sé lo que ha sido de él.'

Javier de Burgos

[From: Javier de Burgos, *Anales del Reinado de Isabel II*, Madrid 1851, Tomo 5, libro 15, p. 428.]

'El arrojado Mon, después de pasar sucesivamente por las manos de cuantos quisieron esplotar la miseria publica, llegó hasta entregarse a las de un suizo, que le anunció la existencia de un tesoro, enterrado en Santiago en 1809, en oro portugués. El suizo empezó por hacerse habilitar con fondos y recomendaciones; y, como si quisiese rodear el chasco que meditaba de todo el aparato de un ultrage calificado, se presentó (el 17 de agosto) con gran séquito de operarios en el Hospital de San Roque de aquella ciudad, y mandó hacer, durante seis horas, escavaciones en sus letrinas. Cuando sus pestilentes exhalaciones hubieron infestado la ciudad, declaró que sin duda el pretendido tesoro había sido sacado antes; y bien que la indignación del publico chasqueado castigase al impostor descargando sobre el algunos golpes, no pudo esta satisfacción volver al ministro el decoro que comprometiera, entregándose a tan ridículas esperanzas.'

Antonio Pirala

[From: Antonio Pirala, *Historia de la guerra civil y de los partidos liberal y carlista*, 3rd edition, volume 3, Madrid 1891, p. 171]

'Mon (desgraciado) por un suizo que anunció la existencia de un tesoro enterrado en Santiago en 1809, y provisto de fondos y recomendaciones fui a excavar las letrinas del Hospital de San Roque y a apestar la ciudad, que fue lo que consiguió.'

Bibliography

Bibliography
Main sources

S URELY EVERY historian feels that the tooth of time has been particularly harsh on him, and has deliberately destroyed documents
crucial to his investigation. In the case of *The Treasure Hunter of Santiago*,
however, I believe that feeling to be justified. Simply every archive which
might have contained official papers about the affair has been wantonly
damaged at some point over the last 150 years. Alejandro Mon's papers
– which in accordance with accepted practice of the day he took home
with him after his tenure in office – were burned after his death on his
express wishes. The archive of the Ministry of Finance – where a number
of Mon's documents may have survived for a century – fell victim to
another act of mindless destruction. During the Spanish Civil War of
1936–39 the Republican Commander-in-Chief General Miaja set up his
headquarters here. The weather was cold; fire-wood was scarce; a general
could not be expected to lose a war directing it with frozen fingers. So
the archive was burned in portable stoves to heat the offices. Finally, as
is described in chapter 21, the great archive of the Coruña Captaincy-
General was burned to create space in the 1890s; this after many cartloads
of its papers had been used, in the course of various conflicts, for the
folding of cartridges. With things in such a state, I had to make do with
the little that survived, and turn my poverty into some sort of tinselled,
churrigueresque grandeur.

George Borrow's story of 'Benedict Mol' is told in his travelogue *The
Bible in Spain*, first published in 1843 by Murray in London. Mol appears
in chapters 13, 27, 33, 41 and 42. As noted in chapters 4 and 11 above, *The
Bible* was based on Borrow's more realistic letters home, most of which are
published in T.H. Darlow, *Letters of George Borrow to the British & Foreign
Bible Society*, London: Hodder & Stoughton, 1911 (available on Internet).
Below, these letters will merely be referred to by their date, place and
addressee; which should be sufficient to locate them in Darlow.

In the summer of 1838, the opposition press reported extensively on
the Santiago treasure hunt. The articles in question were published in

the *Eco del Comercio*, nº 1,581 (29 August); 1,584 (1 September); 1,585 (2 September); and 1,589 (6 September). The even more radical newspaper *Nosotros* published the fictional letter of 'Frederick Switzemerd' – reproduced in translation in chapter 20 – in its issue nº 180 of 1 September. On 4 September 1838, Modesto Lafuente referred to the Swiss *Zahori* in the episode 'El Botánico y el Prado' of his highly amusing weekly *Fray Gerundio* (see Lafuente, *Obras Escogidas*, Madrid 1874, part II, Capillas de Madrid, 1 de Julio – Diciembre 1838, 205–213). The original Spanish texts of these sources are reproduced in Appendix 2.

Two contemporary 19th century Spanish historians also told the tale of the treasure hunt, but it seems that neither knew more than what the *Eco* articles contained. The first of these is Javier de Burgos in his *Anales del Reinado de Isabel II* (Madrid 1851, volume 5, 428). The other one is Antonio Pirala, who mentions the episode briefly in his monumental *Historia de la guerra civil y de los partidos liberal y carlista escrita con presencia de memorias y documentos ineditos* (3rd edition, Madrid 1891, volume 3, 171). The closeness of the wording suggests, however, that Pirala merely summarized what he had found in Burgos's *Anales*. See Appendix 2 for both quotes.

Abbreviations and catchwords

FREQUENTLY USED archives, books, series and articles will be referred to by the following abbreviations or catchwords.

Archives and collections

AHD: Archivo Histórico Diocesano, Santiago de Compostela
AHN: Archivo Histórico Nacional, Madrid
AHU: Archivo Histórico de la Universidad de Santiago de Compostela
AM: Archivo Municipal de Santiago, kept by AHU
ARG: Archivo del Reino de Galicia, Coruña
BX: Biblioteca Xeral de Santiago de Compostela
HR: Archivo del Hospital Real de Santiago, kept by AHU

So as not to confuse researchers who are following my leads, I have maintained such standard Spanish catalogue terminology as '*legajo*', '*mazo*', '*caja*' and '*carpeta*' in the references to documents kept by these archives.

Books, periodicals and articles

Andrade: Pardo de Andrade, Manuel, *Los guerrilleros gallegos de 1809*, re-edition by Andrés Martínez Salazár, Coruña 1892, vol. 1.

Artola: Artola Gallego, Miguel, *La España de Fernando VII*, Madrid 1999.

Atkinson: Atkinson, W.C., *A History of Spain and Portugal*, Penguin books 1961.

Barreiro: Barreiro Fernández, José Ramón, *El Carlismo Gallego*, Santiago 1976.

BiS: Borrow, George, *The Bible in Spain*, first published by John Murray, London 1843.

Burgos: Burgos, Javier de, *Anales del Reinado de Isabel II*, 5th volume, Madrid 1851.

Collie: Collie, Michael, *George Borrow: Eccentric*, Cambridge 1982.

Costanti: Pérez Costanti, Pablo, *Notas viejas gallicianas*, 3 volumes, Vigo 1925–1927.

Cronin: Cronin, Vincent, *Napoleon, Stratege und Staatsmann*, München 1983.

Eco: the *Eco del Comercio*, Madrid daily of the 1830s (see above, Main Sources).

Fernández & Freire: Fernández Sánchez, José and Freire Barreiro, Francisco, *Guia de Santiago y sus alrededores*, Santiago 1885.

Ferreiro: López Ferreiro, Antonio, *Historia de la S.A.M. Iglesia Cathedral de Santiago de Compostela*, 11th volume, Santiago 1909.

Ford, *Gatherings*: Ford, Richard, *Gatherings from Spain*, London 1851.

Ford, *HB*: Ford, Richard, *A Hand-Book for Travellers in Spain*, 1845 edition, Centaur press re-edition by Ian Robertson, 3 volumes, London 1966.

Fraser, *Mol*: Fraser, Angus, 'Benedict Mol, Treasure hunter of Saint James', in *GBB* 12, 69–82.

Fraser, *Sleeping*: Fraser, Angus, 'Sleeping under the Angel's Wings', in: *Proceedings of the George Borrow Conference*, Toronto 1991.

García del Barrio: García del Barrio, Manuel, *Succesos militares de Galicia en 1809*, re-edition by Andrés Martínez Salazár, Coruña 1891.

García Barros: García Barros, *Medio Siglo de Vida Coruñesa (1834–1886)*, Sada/Coruña 1970.

GBB: *George Borrow Bulletin*, published twice yearly in Warborough, England.

González López, *Guerra*: González López, Emilio, 'A guerra da independencia en Galicia', in: *Grial* nº 33 (1971), 257–262.

González López, *Reinado*: González López, Emilio, *El Reinado de Isabel II en Galicia*, Sada/Coruña 1984.

González López, *1846*: González López, Emilio, *De Espartero a la Revolución Gallega de 1846*, Sada/Coruña 1985.

Granja: Fernández de la Granja, Joaquín, 'La Ciudad de Tuy durante la invasión Francesa', in: *La Ilustración Gallega y Asturiana*, Madrid, 18 September 1880.

Jenkins: Jenkins, Herbert, *The Life of George Borrow*, London 1912.

Knapp: Knapp, William Ireland, *The Life, Writings and Correspondence of George Borrow*, 1st volume, London 1899.

Longford: Longford, Elizabeth, *Wellington, the years of the Sword*, London 1969.

Madoz: Madoz, Pascual, *Diccionario geográfico-estadístico-histórico de España y sus posesiones de ultramar*, 16 volumes, Madrid 1846–1850.

Mangado: Mangado i Artigas, Josep Maria, *Un impreso desconocido de Frederico Moretti en la Biblioteca de Catalunya* (posted on the website of the *Centro de investigación y documentación de la guitarra clásica en Catalunya* in October 2004).

Marbot: *Mémoires du Général Baron de Marbot*, 3rd volume, Paris 1891.

Mora: Fernández de la Mora, Gonzalo, *'Mon en su siglo'*, in: *La Razón Española* nº 110, 2001 (a speech first read in La Granda, Asturias, on 31 July 2001, and republished on the website of *La Razón Española*).

Ochoa: Ochoa Brun, Miguel-Angel, *Alejandro Mon, embajador de España (conferencia pronunciada en CAJASTUR, el 29 de octobre de 2001)*, Real Instituto de Estudios Asturianos, Oviedo 2002.

Padin: Martínez de Padin, Leopoldo, *Historia politica, religiosa y descriptiva de Galicia*, 1st volume, Madrid 1849.

Portela: Portela Pazos, Sebastiano, *Guerra de Independencia*, Santiago 1964.

Risco: Risco, Vicente, *Manual de Historia de Galicia*, Vigo 1971.

Robertson: Robertson, Ian, *A Commanding Presence*, Chalford 2008.

Stokes: Stokes, Dr. John H., *The Third Great Plague*, Philadelphia/London 1920.

Toreno: Conde de Toreno, *Historia del levantamiento, guerra y revolucion de España*, 1st volume, Madrid 1872.

Yzquierdo: Yzquierdo Perrín, Ramón (et. al), *Os Templos Parroquiais*, Coruña 1993.

References and notes per chapter

THE MORE prominent or controversial statements will be anchored here, per chapter and mainly in order of appearance, in sources referred to by the catchwords above, followed by the number of the volume or issue (where applicable), the chapter (if necessary) and the page number. Occasionally an extra observation will be added to qualify a statement or justify my interpretation of facts.

1 The Carlist Civil War

THE BEST study of the reign of Fernando VII is Artola, *La España de Fernando VII*. The most complete description of the First Carlist Civil War is still Antonio Pirala's *Historia de la guerra civil y de los partidos liberal y carlista escrita con presencia de memorias y documentos inéditos*, first published Madrid 1853. I used the 3rd edition in three volumes, Madrid 1889–1891.

2 George Borrow: the Genius in a Nutshell

THE MOST innovative modern biography of George Borrow is Collie, *George Borrow: Eccentric*. Knapp's *Life, Writings and Correspondence* of 1899 remains, however, the source for most factual material. For Borrow's amazing linguistic skills: see Ridler, Ann, *George Borrow as a Linguist*, Warborough 1996. 'Finest grammar schools': so Borrow himself in his manuscript autobiographies, see *GBB* 14, 35. 'Jargon of Witches': *BiS* chapter 45. Borrow's sale of vernacular scripture and the ensuing religious-political conflict: Missler, Peter, *A Daring Game*, Norwich 2009.

3 Benedict Mol

'FLAMING VAPOURS', 'gasping and naked': Borrow, letter to Brandram of 30 June 1836 from Madrid. The lengthy quote of Borrow's meeting with Mol comes from *BiS* chapter 13. Spring of 1836: note that there is reason to believe that Borrow changed the chronology here, and that he did not meet Mol until the spring of 1837, or possibly even a full year later. As explained in chapter 11, he may have wedged this scene into the early part of *BiS* so as to distribute the Mol episodes evenly throughout the book.

4 Of Truth, Mistrust and Treasure Hunts

For some stunning examples of treasure hunting dupes in Spain, see the many real-life cases described in Suárez López, Jesús, *Tesoros, Ayalgas y Chalgueiros; la fiebre del oro en Asturias*, Gijón 2001.

'Remarkably communicative': *BiS* chapter 41. 'Few delights': Michael Freer in *GBB* 10, 56. Household account book: Phyllis Stanley in *GBB* 16, 45ff and 23, 88f. Pugilists: see the thorough articles by Richard Shepheard in *GBB* 22, 23, 24 and 25. Welsh settle: C. Halliday in *GBB* 21, 49ff. 'Never let the facts': Fraser, *Sleeping*, 30. 'Written against Rome': from the Appendix to Borrow's 1857 *The Romany Rye*.

The more reliable version of Borrow's Finisterre arrest is found in his letter to John Hasfeld of 20 November 1838 (Borrow, *Letters to John Hasfeld 1835–1839*, ed. Angus Fraser, Edinburgh 1982, 29). The 'dramatized' version is found in *BiS* chapter 30. On Traba see De las Casas, Alvaro, *Mr. Borrow por Finisterra*, Santiago 1935, and the article 'Antonio da Traba, el valiente de Finisterre', by Juan Campos Calvo-Sotelo and myself in *GBB* 20, 8–20. Campos Calvo-Sotelo, Juan, *Naufragos de Antaño*, Barcelona 2002, 27ff reproduces the same material in Spanish. The very first time Borrow claimed that he had been arrested *for being Don Carlos* is in a manuscript press-release which he drew up while in jail in May 1838 for the benefit of British journalists. As a result the story found its way into an article in the *Morning Herald* of 21 May 1838 (Fraser, *Sleeping*, Annex 2 and 3).

'Too earnest to dabble in outright fiction': note that this technique of embellished reality was also born from simple need, since Borrow was not a *creative* writer. He definitely lacked the imagination to come up with original plots As a matter of fact, in his entire literary career he only wrote one fictional story, a two-bit novella called '*The Life and Adventures of Joseph Sell*', which, incidentally, nobody has seen since and the existence of which is still a matter of dispute (see Collie, 39ff & 216; Jenkins, 55ff). So very impressed was he with the effort, that he dedicated the better part of two chapters in his pseudo-autobiography *Lavengro* to the onerous ups and downs of the creative process, and – as he put it in chapter 12 of *The Romany Rye* – 'the grisley sufferings which I had undergone whilst engaged in writing (it).'

Moidores: Ventura, António, *George Borrow em Portugal*, Lisbon 2006, 85 note 98. Ventura, a well-informed Portuguese scholar, states specifically that 'moidore' is 'the English name for the old gold coin of 4,800 *reis*'. Robinson Crusoe: see Borrow, *Lavengro*, chapter 3. Note that the 'moidore' returns again as late as Borrow's 1857 *Romany Rye*, chapter 41.

5 The Storm of Andoche Junot

'SPANISH ULCER': Thomson, David, *Europe since Napoleon*, Penguin books 1990, 71 & 121; Longford, 266. 'Shield of the Navy': Trevelyan, G.M., *A Shortened History of England*, Pelican books 1965, 418. Godoy's correspondence: Atkinson, 252ff; Cronin, 334. 28,000 French troops allowed to enter Spain: Toreno, 7, specifies that these consisted of 25,000 infantry, 3,000 cavalry, with another 40,000 French in reserve at Bayonne. Junot's invasion of Portugal: Longford 180f; Toreno, 6ff. Portuguese fleet and escape of royals: Cronin, 357f, Longford, 181.

Spanish troops at Junot's disposal: Mangado, chapter 2, lists these as 14,172 infantry, 3,300 cavalry and 30 canon under Carrafa; 7,780 infantry, 550 cavalry and 30 canon under Solano, and 6,556 infantry plus 25 canon under Taranco. Note, however, that these were probably only the numbers demanded, agreed and promised. Given the hurry and the perpetual Spanish problems with organisation, the forces never materialised in full. Solano invasion: Mangado, chapter 2 and 4; Toreno, 13. Plundering by Carrafa's soldiers and their march to Oporto: Toreno, 12f. Invasion by Taranco: Atkinson, 259; Ferreiro, 215; Portela, 38; Toreno, 13.

Chateau Marrac: Ford, *HB*, 1,395. Taranco dies: Mangado, chapter 2; Toreno, 19. Quesnel in command: Mangado, chapter 5. Carrafa ordered to Lisbon: Mangado, chapter 4. Rebellion of the Spanish Oporto troops: Andrade, 36; González López, *Guerra*, 261; Granja, 332f; Portela, 39. Imprisonment of Carrafa's troops: Mangado, chapter 5; Toreno, 19. Withdrawal of Solano: Mangado, chapter 2 and 4. Mondego bay landing and battle: Longford, 185–200. Sintra Convention: Longford, 201ff. For reasons of clarity I use 'Wellington' throughout the text even though Arthur Wellesley was only raised to a peerage of that name in 1809.

6 Lies and Looters

'FAVOURITE SINS': Longford, 190. Officers against looting: Robertson, 267 credits the French General Phillipon with this. Ney stops looting: Longford, 289. Soult's tremendous participation in pillage: Giménez Cruz, Antonio, *La España pintoresca de David Roberts*, Malaga 2002, 296f. Wellington's Mondego Bay order: Longford, 190. Sack of allied cities: for some examples see Longford, 252, 288f, 336f and 405; Robertson, 256ff.. Wellington on pillage by his own soldiers: Longford 233f; Robertson, 316.

The origin of the Spanish Walloon Guards is a matter of great obscurity and confusion. Some authors maintain that there were already Spanish Walloon regiments in the days of Philip III, roughly in 1600 (so, for instance, Pabón y Suárez de Urbina, Jesús, *Narvaez y su epoca*, Madrid 1983, 130–146). Most others hold that the regiment was set up by the Bourbon king Philip V by a Royal Decree of 10 April 1702, at the start of the War of Spanish Succession. The otherwise knowledgeable Atkinson, 237, however, says that the *Valonas* came to Spain from the Kingdom of Naples with Carlos III in mid 18th century. Since this subject has little direct bearing on the present narrative, I have kept my description conveniently vague. The basic story may be read in the *Espasa Encyclopedia Universal Ilustrada*, vol. 66, Madrid 1929, 786, lemma 'Guardias Valonas'.

The same scholarly laxness may not, of course, be allowed when it comes to the precise whereabouts of the different Walloon regiments in the early days of the Peninsular War, since this reflects immediately on the credibility of Mol's tale. Yet in the absence of a serious study that matter is hardly clearer. The 1807–1808 location of some of the Walloon units and their officers is given – haphazardly – in Toreno on pages 16, 21, 22, 29, 33, 43 and 55, and some additional data may be gleaned from Ford, *HB*, 456 and Albert Rocca's 1815 *Memoirs of the War of the French in Spain*, chapter 5. The most helpful source of all, however, was the fine article by Josep Maria Mangado on Frederico Moretti, which I found on the internet in October 2004. That one needs to consult a site for classical guitar music for the best information concerning military units is perhaps illustrative of the present state of research. By the looks of it Mangado himself took most of his information from the 14-volume study by Gomez de Arteche, *Guerra de Independencia 1808–1814*, of which, however, I only know one copy in a distant archive, so that I have not been able to consult it.

Other websites offered some help, but unfortunately also increased the confusion by freely mixing up the *Guardias Reales*, *Guardias Españolas* and *Guardias Valonas*. This may be the reason why different sources give different numbers for the strength of the Walloon units. The number of 4,300 in 6 battalions, as cited in the text, is the maximum number of men and regiments I ever found listed, and is probably too high. It has merely been maintained to err on the safe side. Mangado, chapter 4, footnote 18, gives the strength and number of the Walloon Guards as three battallions with a total of 2,583 men plus 98 officers, and their whereabouts in early 1808 as in Madrid (1º battallion), Barcelona (2º), in Portuguese Extramadura under Solano (3º).

If George Borrow added the Walloon Guard past to Mol's story, he may have found his inspiration in Jean Potocki's *Manuscrit trouvé à Saragosse*, a bizarre gothic novel whose protagonist is an officer in this regiment. See Missler, Peter, *Manusscrit trouvé a Petersbourg*, GBB 33, 23–34 and GBB 34, 6–15.

Accursio das Neves: so mentioned in Toreno, 13 (unable to locate the book, I have not been able to verify the precise words of das Neves myself). Praise of Oporto town-council: Mangado, chapter 2.

7 The French Connection

REINHARDT SEARCH: Fraser, *Mol,* 74. Borrow hoards papers: Fraser, *Sleeping,* 32. Molo and Helvetian Diet: *Eco* nº 1,584, Saturday 1 September 1838, front page.

There are some other, and no less possible, theories on the origin of the name 'Benedict Mol'. Ms Phyllis Stanley, an investigator from Borrow's native Norwich, points out that a number of Dutch immigrant families named Moll used to live in St Benedict street, at a stone's throw from the Willow Lane home of the Borrow family. Yet another option is that the name contains some warped riddle which winks at the recurrent phrase 'Blessed Mary Flanders' (Defoe's heroine) in chapters 31, 40 and 77 of Borrow's *Lavengro.* 'Blessed' would then correspond to 'Benedict', 'Mary' would stand in the place of 'Mol', while 'Flanders' would echo the equally Belgian Walloons. But why Borrow would introduce such a clumsy riddle here remains to be explained.

French POWs from stranded British vessels in Vigo: AHN, Seccion Estado, legajo 73A, 73B and 73C. Quesnel and his dragoons: Portela, 39.

8 Soult in Oporto

'GREATER PICTURE of the war': Napoleon in a letter to Clarke from Schönbrunn on 15 August 1809 (from the Internet). Admittedly Napoleon wrote this down nearly a year later, but there can be no doubt that his feelings in the autumn of 1808 were identical.

Chase of Moore: Artola, 182; Ford, *HB,* 881ff; García del Barrio, 31f; Tettamancy, F., 'Sir John Moore', in: *Buletin de la Real Academia de Galicia,* vol. 2, año 1907–1909, 261ff. Churchill on 'Corunna': Moorehead, Allen, *Gallipoli,* Ware 1997, 262 note 1. War chest tossed into ravine: Ford, *HB,* 891; Robertson, 82 and 94 note 42 ('Corcul' is probably today's Cruzul on the NVI). Quote Neale: Neale, Adam, *Letters from Portugal and Spain,* 1809.

There is not yet an adequate study of the Napoleonic war in Santiago. To reconstruct events I mainly used the file of random municipal papers in AHU, AM 309, *Libro Consistorios 1809, 1º Trimestre (Dominación Francesa),* and López Ferreiro's excellent – if unfinished – 11th volume (see notes to chapter 9 below). Occupation of Santiago: Ferreiro, 155–169 and appendix 15; Risco, 230. Inquisition palace: Costanti, vol. 1, 287; Ferreiro, 169.

Soult's advance on Oporto: Andrade, 109–149; Artola, 182ff; Ferreiro, 168; García del Barrio 48ff; González López, *Guerra,* 257f; Granja, 322f; Longford, 226. Soult before Tuy: Ford, *HB,* 1,020. Alarmas: Artola 183; García del Barrio, 159–169; González López, *Guerra,* 257f. Taking and sack of Oporto: Marbot, chapter 31, 356ff; Headley, J.T., *Napoleon and his marshals,* vol. 1, New York, circa 1850 (from internet), chapter 10. Vigo siege: González López, *Guerra*, 258; Risco, 231. British frigates (the *Lively* and *Venus*) in Vigo harbour: Ford, *HB*, 1,019. Soult's isolation and columns of relief: Artola, 183f. Huedelet evacuates Tuy: Artola, 184; García del Barrio, 67ff & 163ff; González López, *Guerra*, 259; Granja, 322f.

Wellington takes Oporto and Soult's retreat: Artola, 184f; García del Barrio, 102 & 105; Longford, 227–230; Marbot, chapter 32, 368ff; Robertson, 102–107. 'Red-coated Swiss': Longford, 229. Squeeling pigs: Robertson, 167. 'Unequalled in horrors': Ford, *HB*, 1,022. 'Route of their column': Longford, 230. French soldiers 'smell' hidden food: Longford, 306. Buried alive: Robertson, 211 footnote 24 (but from 1811). Emasculated: Robertson, 107. Soult's losses: according to García del Barrio, 102 & 105, Soult only brought back 9,000 infantry and 2,000 cavalry from Oporto into Galicia; Marbot, chapter 32, 373, says Soult lost 6,000 men and 57 of of the 58 cannon he set out with; Robertson, 107 puts the number of losses during the retreat at 4,000. Additional pillage in Galicia: Andrade, 148; Ford, *HB*, 894. 'Famished wolves': Ford, *HB*, 970.

Cortes's *conquistadores* discard treasure: Prescott, J.F., *History of the Conquest of Mexico*, London 1893, book 5, chapter 4, 378. Money belts on Soult's soldiers: Robertson, 106.

The only way one of Soult's men could have made it to Santiago after the Oporto retreat was by joining Ney's corps when the two marshals seperated again after meeting in Lugo. This is however most unlikely since, according to García del Barrio, 108, Ney reinforced Soult, not the other way around.

9 The Silver of Saint James

'A TREASURE WHICH the French concealed': folio 11 of the ARG file '*Sobre las muertes de José Ferreiro y Jose San Martin*' (for full reference see notes to chapter 22 below). Coruña newspaper: García Barros, 219f. 'Forcible requisitioning': Longford, 235. Marching speeds: Artola, 110; Ford, *HB*, 815. 'La guerre doit nourrir': Ford, *HB*, 1,001. Frederick and French marauding: Duffy, Christopher, *The Military Experience in the Age of Reason*, Ware 1998, 166f.

Ney's confiscations: Ferreiro, 155–189, plus appendices 15 and 22; Ford, *HB*, 1,016 (following Toreno) mentions that the French collected '10 cwt.', or 10 hundredweight of 50.8 kilos each, which would make some 500 kilos. Mint in Coruña: Ferreiro, 187. Bory on church plate: Bory de Saint-Vincent, Jean-Baptiste, *Guide du Voyageur en Espagne*, Paris 1823, 257 and 259. 'The chapter thus took in': Ford, *HB*, 1,000.

Ney to Asturias: García del Barrio, 96. Battle of Campo de Estrella: Artola 186ff; Costanti, vol. 2, 305–308; García del Barrio, 106; Ferreiro, 206–209; Fulgosio, Fernando Alfonso, *Cronica de la Provincia de Coruña*, 93, in Cayetano Rosell (ed.):

Cronica General de España, Madrid 1865. Note that García del Barrio, who was in Vigo at the time, lowers the numbers of soldiers involved to some 9,000 Spanish irregulars and 2,600 French. 41 *arrobas* of silver: Costanti, vol. 2, 306; Ferreiro, 220; Otero Pedrayo, Ramón, *Guia de Santiago de Compostela*, Santiago 1945, 19; Santiago Gadea, A. C. de, *El General Don Pablo Morillo*, Madrid, 1911, III note 8.

Lugo meeting Ney and Soult: Artola, 187; Ferreiro, 213f. Evacuation Santiago: Ferreiro, 209–216. French return on 3 June: Costanti, vol. 3, 239; Ferreiro, 215ff. Battle Sampayo bridge: Artola, 187; Ferreiro, 216f; Ford, *HB*, 1,016; González López, *Guerra*, 259. Gunboats on the river: García del Barrio, III. 'War of the peasantry': Longford, 225. Soult's letter to Joseph: Ferreiro, 217f. 18,000 French soldiers marched out of Galicia: García del Barrio, 114

Further adventures of church plate: Ferreiro, 209–220. 'Only a muddled story': note that the 11th volume of Ferreiro's Santiago church history, from which most of the information on the confiscated silver is taken, remained unfinished at the author's death. Hence it is not always easy to decide what silver was found where at what time from its loosely collected and disorderly documents. Restitutions to San Payo and San Francisco: Ferreiro, 218f. For lack of a liturgical dictionary or a bi-lingual priest, I had to use 'monstrance' where Ferreiro writes 'viril', even though he may have meant only the small moon-shaped component known in English as a 'lunula'. Remnants to be seen in cathedral treasury: Ford, *HB*, 1,009.

10 Red Herring, *Rara Avis*

THE SLIGHTLY adapted quote from the *Eco* comes from its issues nº 1,581 of 29 August 1838 and nº 1,584 of 1 September 1838. 'Richest in Portugal': González López, *Reinado*, 28.

11 Narrative Fraud

GENESIS OF *Bible in Spain*: Collie, 174; Knapp, chapters 36 and 37. Addition of 389 new manuscript pages: Knapp, 385.

12 The City of Santiago

MY DESCRIPTION of Santiago in the late 1830s is based on extensive research for another book, which is too voluminous to reproduce here. The economical data are mainly derived from specific (but at the time unnumbered) files of the Archivo Municipal of Santiago, kept by AHU, mainly the folders: *Estadistica: Precios Medios 1839–60; Estadistica: Fabricas e Industria 1835–1894; Estadisticas especiales 1821–1842; Estadistica: Fabricas e Industrias, Montes e Planteos 1836–1895; Industria, Matriculas altas y bajas 1824–1844, clasificacion de patentes* (i.e. list of business-licences) for the years 1834–1844.

Falling number of pilgrims: Padin, 115; AHU, HR, mazo 1,308 *Enfermos Peregrinos 1827–1884*; also the anonymous manuscript in BX *Manifiesto sobre gastos del Hospital de Santiago*, Santiago 1841. According to these sources, between 1831 and 1840 the pilgrims in the Royal Hospital numbered: 522 (1831), 254 (1832), 215 (1833), 118 (1834), 80 (1835), 37 (1836), 23 (1837), 33 (1838), 20 (1840).

'The carcass remains': Ford, *HB* (1855 edition), 601.

Barreiro Fernández's *El Carlismo Gallego* gives a good enough impression of the political history of Santiago in the 1830s.

Starving lepers: *BiS* ch 27; Gil Rey, J.M. and R.A., *Recuerdos de viaje por Galicia*, Pontevedra 1946, 118f. The two Santiago leper houses, one at San Lazaro and the other at Santa Marta, were stripped of their endowments by the Liberal disentailment, but never given a penny in promised compensation. Their inmates, who previously were not allowed to come closer to town than a certain crucifix outside the walls, were now forced to beg their bread at the side of the road, and in the streets and shops of the town itself. Behold the pleasures of socio-economical modernization!

13 The Pauper from the Machine

THE WHOLE chapter is based on *BiS* chapter 27. Full moon: according to the *Winterthur Pascal Calendar*, the 1837 Pascal Full Moon fell on March 27th; taking the lunar cycle as 29,5 days, the August full moon occurred roughly on August 16th. Rey Romero letter: see below, notes to chapter 21. Paris cartomancer: *Eco* n° 1,589 of 6 September 1838. Canon Ramón Boán: AHD, mazo 426, *Hospitales*.

14 Canon and blunderbuss

THE QUOTED texts come from *BiS* chapter 33. Castellana bridge: *BiS* chapter 26; Missler, Peter, 'The bandit of Castellana', in *GBB* 18, 46–49. 'Seven Bellotas': although Borrow's description of the area corresponds beautifully with the lay-out of the area, this name is unknown, nor is there any indication that it was ever in use (see Missler, Peter, 'A partial judgement', in *GBB* 30, 30–42). Bishop of Mondoñedo: Barreiro, 143 and 162–163.

'Cross water': Gomez Tabanera, J.M., 'La Asturias que conoció George Borrow', in: *Archiveru* XXV, Oviedo 1975, 485 points out that this expression, which in English seems to suggest the crossing of rivers or oceans, in fact goes back on the set phrase '*pasar el agua*', an Asturian magic ritual to ward off the evil eye. The bewitched person mixed water and oil in a glass, poured it into a bull's horn and drank it.

15 A *Zahori* in the *Cárcel de Corte*

ORIGINS AND meanings of Zahori: Dozy, R., *Supplément aux Dictionares Arabes*, 2nd edition, Leiden 1927, 609, lemma 'Zuhoriyya'. Zahori birth: Feijoo, B., *Teatro Critico Universal*, vol. 3, discurso 5, 'Vara divinatoria y zahoris', §§ 21–24; Ford, *HB*, 12; Lafuente, M., *Fray Gerundio*, episode 'La Mujer Zahori' of February 1838. 'Swiss Zahori': Lafuente, *Fray Gerundio*, episode 'El Botanico y el Prado' of 4 September 1838.

'Books and pamphlets' ('libros y folletas contra la religion y moral Cristiana'): AHD, mazo 473, legajo 1º, *Ramo de Imprenta 1777–1894*, letter of 7 July 1868 to the Archbishop of Santiago by an official of the Ferrol Capitania-General; see also Missler, Peter, 'Rey Romero's Testaments', in: *GBB* 28, 32. Borrow and Ofalia: *BiS* chapter 42. Borrow's imprisonment: *BiS* chapter 41; Fraser, *Sleeping*, the whole article.

Lucas in Egypt: Bey Kamal, Ahmed, *Livre des perles enfouies et du mystère précieux au sujet des indications des cachettes, des trouvailles et des trésors*, Service des Antiquités de l'Egypte, Imprimerie de IFAO, Cairo 1907, introduction, page v, footnote 4.

'Depends not on his crimes': John Bowring quoted in Fraser, *Sleeping*, 27. A good description of the Madrid *Cárcel de Corte* may be found in Ayguals de Izco, Wenceslau, *Maria, hija de un jornalero*, Madrid 1845–1846, part 2, chapter 5.

16 His Excellency Alejandro Mon

'SABRE OF Narvaez': Fabian Estapé quoted in Gracia Noriega, José Ignacio, 'Aniversario de Alejandro Mon', in: *La Nueva España*, 5 August 2001. Narvaez's executions: López Garrido, Diego, '¿Como debe ser la Guardia Civil?', in: *El Pais*, 22 February 2004, 16.

For all his importance, Alejandro Mon is still a perfectly undocumented figure. Until Fernández de la Mora's articles appeared in the late 1990s his biography consisted of ten lines and half a dozen dates (some of them wrong). The lamentable state of research is shown best by the fact that the sources *cannot even agree on his last name*. Encyclopedias and historians generally stick to 'Mon y Menéndez', but the Archive of the Madrid Treasury Department graciously corrected my use of the matronym to 'Mon y Pidal', which is also the form maintained by the Internet site of the Moncloa Palace (Spain's Downing Street nº 10). Next to nothing is known of his life before 1836, when he was first elected to parliament. The few data I here offer, have mostly been gathered from short articles in marginal magazines, republished on the internet. Foremost among these is the excellent article by Mora, *Mon en su siglo*, which at last offers some details of Mon's early personal life, such as his siring of an illegitimate child, and explains what happened to Mon's papers. See also: Rull Sabater, Alberto, *Diccionario sucinto de Ministros de Hacienda (s. XIX-XX)*, Instituto de Estudios Fiscales, Madrid 1991, document 16, 168.

Mon's attempts to fix financial troubles: Burgos, 410–421. 'Ridiculous': Burgos, 428. Note that Burgos was himself a prominent former Minister of the Interior, who wrote at a time that Mon was in office and extremely influential. Yet he felt neither scruples nor fright to ascribe the initiative of the scandal to the formidable Chancellor.

Mon's post as Coruña *Intendente* is mentioned in the satyrical letter in *Nosotros* (see chapter 20 and Appendix 2) and there seems to be one letter signed by him in that office on 13 July 1836 in AHU, AM 709, *Sucesos Politicos 1821–1836*, folio 208ff. Galicia as powerbase: González López, *1846*, 134 and 139; also Mora § 6.

17 A Farewell in Madrid

MON'S INVOLVEMENT in the prohibition of Borrow's books: AHN, Seccion Estado, legajo 5.502, nº 59 *Ingleses, Borrow y Graydon*, letter of 25 May 1838 from Mon to Minister of the Interior. 'His spirit chafed': Jenkins, 268. The farewell scene comes from *BiS* chapter 42.

18 The chapel of San Roque

SAINTS COSME and Damian were 3rd century Syria-born twin brothers, and miracle healers who took no payment for help. Hence they were known in Greek as *anargyroi*, i.e. 'the Silverless'. Martyred during the Diocletian persecution, they became patrons saints of physicians, surgeons and apothecaries.

Foundation of San Roque and yearly celebrations: Costanti, vol. 2, 126 and vol. 3, 71ff; Fernández & Freire, 336ff and 505; Yzquierdo, 490f. Additional data came from AHD, mazo 426, *Hospitales*, and from the 'Fichera de Capilla e Hospital de San Roque', contained in the *Plan Especial de Proteccion e Rehabilitacion da Cidade Historica de Santiago de Compostela*, vol. 3, 1997, a working paper of the Servicio de Rehabilitacion del Concello de Santiago.

The history and characteristics of syphilis are best read about in Dr. John Stokes' *The Third Great Plague*, a work written for the general public at a time when the disease was still a major threat to health. Ships of Columbus: Stokes, 11. Mercury treatment: Stokes, 61–67.

Babies of unwed mothers one in eight: this estimate is the result of my own lengthy, but somewhat furtive, reading of the *Libros de Bautizados* of various Santiago parishes kept in AHD. Foundlings: Padin, 113ff; AHD *Libros de bautizados expositos* of the Royal Hospital of various years; AHU, HR, mazo 2.163, lists of expositos 1825–1837 of 23 November 1838.

The observations I make on illegitimate children and foundlings in the Royal Hospital *Incluso* should not be taken as the last word on the subject. They are based only on a quick scan of a few years' worth of entrees in the sacramental books of the Santiago parishes and the Royal Hospital. I was unable to spend more than a few mornings on the subject, and consequently the data lack the statistical thoroughness necessary for anything but an indication of the state of affairs in the 1830s. The 250 abandoned babies here mentioned are only half of the harvest of 400 to 500 that the Royal Hospital yearly received, the other half being brought in from the surrounding province. This stunning total was in fact a considerable improvement, down from the yearly 800 to 900 babies 50 years before. Due to the lack of hygiene, funds, wet-nurses and substitute baby-food, the death-toll among these children was appalling, often a full 80 %. See the unpublished Ms of Dr. Marcos Marin, *Plan presentado a los señores visitadores de esta Real Casa (…) con el fin de mejorar la suerte de los niños expositos*, Santiago 1796, BX Ms 206; and also Ford, *Gatherings*, chapter 17; Ford, *HB*, 409ff (Seville) and III, 1,077 (Madrid).

Measures against carousing gentlemen and lone women: Costanti, vol. 1, 332, 333 and 344; vol. 2, 347ff. Romarias: Ford, *HB*, 186.

Number of San Roque beds in 1600: anonymous Ms 23 in BX, *Historia del arzobispado de Santiago*, from 1863, 231. Borrow on prostitution: letter to Brandram of 19 August 1837 from Santiago. Eguia's measures and families admitted with children: AHD, mazo 426, *Hospitales*, letter by Eguia of 11 May 1832. Groups of 200: Fernández & Freire, 337. Syphilis in war-time: Stokes, 12. Groups of soldiers admitted to San Roque: AHU, HR, mazo 2.161, *Correspondencia*, reports by Canon Boán of soldiers admitted. Six weeks: it is doubtful that a 6-week treatment would really be effective; Stokes, 88, specifies that in modern times, complete treatment often took 2, 3 and sometimes even 5 years.

Thomas Vazquez and the wife of José Rey: AHU, AM (unnumbered), *Hospitalillo de San Roque 1835–1893*. The description given by Stokes, 34, of the swelling of lymph glands in the neighbourhood of the chancre in the first stages of syphilis are in perfect keeping with the symptoms suffered by both Vazquez and Rey. For some astonishing stories of similar denial and refusal of treatment see Stokes, 151ff.

Note Marchand: AHU, AM 309, *Libro Consistorios 1809 1º Trimestre (Dominación Francesa)*, folio 183.

'The Silverless' see first note to this chapter.

19 The Opulent Cesspool

San Roque celebrations: Fernández & Freire, 338 and personal observations. Fight over finances: AHU, AM (unnumbered), *Procesión de Corpus & San Roque 1834–1900*; AHU, AM 394, *Libro consistorios 1837*, folios 47b-48a. Travelling time stagecoach: *BiS* chapter 27; González López, *Reinado*, 114 and 382; AHU, HR, mazo 2.162, *Correspondencia*; Ford, *HB*, 488 estimates that the slow, unwieldy, 4-wheeled *Galera* travelled no faster than 35 km per day; and 52–59 mentions 25–30 miles a day for the more luxurious *Coche de Colleras* (not the same as the Galera, but possibly what Mol had in mind). Guillade and Ramos: Barreiro, 94 and note 89; *Boletín Oficial de la Coruña*, nº 139 of 30 August 1838; González López, *Reinado*, 258b.

My description of the dig in San Roque is based mainly on the front-page article in the *Eco* nº 1,584 of Saturday 1 September 1838. Seeing that the available documents are simply too few and too unreliable for anything else but an approximate reconstruction of the actual treasure hunt, I had to take licence with the material, filling in gaps and adding my own educated guesses. Thus, the entire procession through town – necessary for dramatic effect – stems entirely from my own imagination. In this I am, however, proud to follow in the footsteps of my dear George Borrow, who made an even bigger operetta of things (compare Appendix 1).

On the earnest side, however, the measure of Jeronimo Valdés's involvement as here suggested is pure conjecture. As viceroy, Valdés was the absolute authority in Galicia. Therefore it is most unlikely that the affair would have taken place without his knowledge and permission. Yet Valdés, a prominent *Progresista*, was a great favourite of the opposition press, on which we wholly depend for our information. And while this opposition press gladly took every possible pot-shot at incumbent *Moderados* like Mon, it was careful not to stress the involvement of any of its own champions. Consequently the documents breath not word about the part which Valdés may have played in the affair. The *Eco* nº 1,581 of 29 August 1838, for instance, states only that the Swiss 'presented himself' in Compostela. It does not say *to whom*. Since that is most untypical of a ferocious opposition newspaper which always called a spade a spade when convenient, one suspects that Mol presented himself to an official of their own political hue.

Whereabouts Valdés: various letters in AHU, Fondo Castroviejo Blanco-Ciceron, *Partes 1838*, and letters published in the *Boletín Oficial de la Coruña* of this period. Valdés solicits private funding: *Eco* nº 1,580 of 28 August 1838; also nº 1,588 of 5 September 1838. Treasury in Inquisition Palace: Madoz, vol. 13, 819.

'When Sancho *disgraced* himself': see part 1, chapter 20 of the Quijote, where the knight of the sad countenance and his paunchy squire wait for dawn in a dark night, while listening to the pounding of some watermills, which scares Sancho so much that he relieves himself in his pants.

20 The Fall of Mon

FRANCOPHILE: OCHOA, 28–31. Mephistopheles' scheme: Goethe, *Faust*, Part II, Akt I, line 4890–5064 and 6038–6155. Slow communications: note however that, while ordinary mail took some 10 days to reach Madrid from Santiago, official government dispatches – transported by a sort of Pony Express – went twice as fast (*BiS* chapter 25). Hence it is likely that Mon knew of the outcome of the search long before the news reached the press.

Nameless Betanzos correspondent: the *Eco* articles are anonymous, but the fluent, sardonic style and the occurrence in the text of Tirabeque, a character from *Fray Gerundio*, makes one wonder if the author was not Modesto Lafuente himself. For the quotes from the *Eco*, from *Nosotros*, and Lafuente's use of the scandal, see above General Remarks and Appendix 2. 'The devil take me': Lafuente, *Fray Gerundio*, episode 'La Mujer Zahori' of February 1838. Widows of Comares and other scandals: Burgos, 410–427. 'Bring down the ministers!': Burgos, 426f.

21 The Spanish Twilight

'MAKE FOOLS of the government' and 'leave us penniless': *Eco* nº 1,584 of 1 September 1838.

The all-important Rey Romero letter of June 1839, nowadays kept in the Hispanic Society in New York, was first published partially in Knapp, 270f; and in its entirety in Fraser, *Mol*, 80f. One can only speculate why the old bookseller never breathes a word on the treasure hunt itself, even though he lived less than a mile from San Roque, in a small town where everybody knew everything that happened.

Cárcel Pública: Costanti, vol. 2, 193; Madoz, vol. 13, 818, writes: 'Estas carceles, de las cuales la primera [i.e. the Cárcel Publica] tiene una fuente en el interior, son de boveda y tan seguras como malas; sus calabozos, especialmente los de lo civil, son contrarios a la humanidad.' Pérez and Town Council: AHU, AM (unnumbered), mazo *Corrección Pública: cuentas, nominas, visitas*, addition to the *Expediente sobre carceles*, 1836. Water and graveyard stench: AHU, AM 394, *Libro Consistorios 1837*, session of 29 October 1837. Food riot: ARG, libro 15 (II), legajo 11, nº 1407.4 *Sobre los desordenes en la Carcel por falta de socorro*.

Burning of Coruña archive: letter of Andrés Martínez Salazár, archivist of the Delegación de Hacienda, to Prime Minister Canovas of 27 April 1892 in ARG, Sección Familias, caja 5.845, carpeta 15, doc 13: '[Tengo] el disgusto de comunicarle que un mes antes de visitar el referido archivo, se habia hecho con sus papeles antiguas e "inutiles", un auto da fé, que duro tres dias y medio. Allá va una buena parte de la historia militar de Galicia y, lo que es mas sensible, la de un Audiencia territorial.'

22 The Treasure of Ney

Peace of Vergara and Espartero's autocracy: Atkinson, 280ff. Espartero's military view of politics: Atkinson, 282. Coup to capture Isabel (7 October 1841): Espoz y Mina, Juana de Vega Condesa de, *Memorias*, Madrid 1977, 236ff; Fernández Santander, Carlos, *Juana de Vega, Condesa de Espoz y Mina*, Coruña 1993, 80–83; Ford, *HB*, 1,166; González López, *1846,* 38. Mon's period out of grace: Mora § 3; Ochoa, 28–31.

Coruña newspaper clipping: García Barros, 219f, there reproduced without newspaper title or date. According to AHU, AM 400, *Libro Consistorios 1843*, however, Sandino was in Santiago on official business on 24 November, and while there handed over the *Jefatura Politica* to his successor on 6 December. Laraño in 1840s: Madoz, vol. 10, 76. 'Exhibition of avarice': Ford, *HB*, 1,016, which shows that Ford knew of the Laraño treasure hunt

The subsequent dig of the local peasantry and the violent reaction of the authorities in January 1844 were distilled from two legal briefs, kept in ARG, Seccion V (Castro Arias), legajo 214–1, *Sobre las muertes de José Ferreiro y José San Martin al tiempo de querer arrestarlos con otros que se ocupaban en la excavacion del Monte de Buena Vista donde se decia enterrado un tesoro*, Santiago, 3 January 1844; and ibid, legajo 215–9: *Ramal separado de la causa sobre las muertes de José Ferreiro y José San Martin, en averiguacion de las medidas tomadas para impedir la escavacion [clandes] tina del Monte de Buena Vista,* Santiago, January 1845.

23 The Grim Reaper

Mon's later career: González López, *1846*, 139f, and all of Ochoa. House of Commons: *GBB* 18, 15. Darwin on Lavengro: quoted in *GBB* 23, 87.

Epilogue

San Sebastian treasure hunt: Ford, *Gatherings,* chapter 9, 103. Restoration San Roque: Fernández & Freire, 337; Yzquierdo, 490f. Gift Muzquiz: Ferreiro, 319. Herradura of the Alameda also known as '*Buena Vista*': *Informe de la Comision Municipal de Contabilidad (sobre las) Robledas de San Lorenzo y Sª Susana*, Santiago 1886, 7f.

Index

THE FOLLOWING index is brief and far from exhaustive. It concentrates exclusively on items of interest, but rare occurrence, which are scattered throughout the text and do not possess a chapter of their own. Hence there is no entry for either 'Borrow' or 'Benedict Mol', since both of these appear on practically every page. Nor will there be an item 'Santiago'. For the other items, I include only such of which it is reasonably certain that some future scholar or student will find something which he does not yet know. For instance: the fact that Goya produced some breathtaking paintings of the *Dos de Mayo* uprising in Madrid will not be included, since any one interested in the great Spanish painter must be aware of this.

References are to page number. Items found in footnotes will be marked as '64n'. Items found both in the body text and in a footnote on that same page will be marked '64+n'. Items also found on the following page will be marked '64f'. Items also found on the two following pages will be marked '64ff'.

Alarmas, see Miño Division

Archives, destruction and preservation of: 158, 160f, 199 216f

Astariz, Jacobo Llorente Marquez de: 188

Bazan y Mendoza, Pedro: 53, 71

Boán, Don Ramón (Santiago canon): 107, 214

Borrovians: 22, 46 (Fraser), 224

Bible in Spain, The (genesis and composition of): 23, 25n, 48, 63, 91f, 95, 100, 103f, 106f, 108, 112f, 116, 118–121, 122, 128, 130, 133, 156ff, 167, 174, 185–188, 199, 205, 208

Bonaparte, Joseph (King of Spain): 8n, 35, 50, 53, 58, 70

Bonaparte, Napoleon (Emperor of France): 8, 29–32, 35, 50f, 64, 208

Bory de Saint-Vicente, Jean-Baptiste: 65n

British and Foreign Bible Society (maybe add missionary activities): 12f, 24, 157

British Navy and Warships: 23, 33, 37, 49, 52, 57, 66, 209

Burgos, Javier de: 126, 195, 200, 213

Campo de Estrella, battle of: 66ff, 71, 181

Cárcel de Corte, Madrid, see Jails and prisons

Cárcel Pública of Santiago, see Jails and prisons

Carlist *guerrilleros*: 9f, 97, 99, 110ff, 138, 158, 160, 164

Carlos IV: 30, 34f, 37

Carlos Isidro, 'Don Carlos': 9, 23, 97, 111, 164, 205

Carrafa, General Juan: 32–36, 44, 206
Coaches and Postal Service:: 3, 10, 99, 126, 137, 143, 215, 216
Coruña: 51f, 65, 69, 79, 93, 108, 110f, 124, 127, 137f, 139, 154, 160ff, 165, 168, 188, 193, 199, 216f
Cosme and Damian, saints: 84, 131, 135, 213
Defoe, Daniel and Robinson Crusoe: 25, 205, 208
Desamortización (1835 Confiscation of Church lands): 96, 99, 125, 211
Eco del Comercio (Radical newspaper): 46f, 73, 86, 106f, 128, 142f, 148–152, 156f, 185, 187, 189–192, 194, 199f, 215, 216
Eguia, Nazario: 133
Espartero, Baldomero: 86, 98, 151, 163ff
Fernando VII: 7ff, 30, 34f, 100, 117, 122ff
Finisterra (and Antonio da Traba): 14, 23, 108, 205
Ford, Richard: 66n, 96, 179
Foundlings and illegitimate children: 132, 214
Fraguio, Manuel: 53, 68
Fray Gerundio, see Lafuente, Modesto
Godoy, Manuel: 30–36, 78
Goethe, Johann Wolfgang: 147, 223
Gomez y Damas, Miguel (Carlist General): 98
Gorostidi, Canon-cardinal Francisco de: 97
Graydon, Lieutenant James: 118, 213
Guardia Valona, see Walloon Guard
Guillade, Mateo (Galician Carlist): 138, 161, 187
Hospital Real of Santiago, see Hospitals, leper-houses, lazarets, etc.
Hospitals, leper-houses, lazarets, etc.: 53, 64, 67, 84, 85, 96, 100, 125, 132f, 135, 137, 141, 143, 160, 172, 180, 211, 214
Jails and prisons: 36, 65, 86, 94, 118f, 134, 141, 151, 158–162, 172, 186, 195, 212, 216

Junot, Andoche: 31–37, 39, 41, 44, 50, 51, 53, 78
Lafuente, Modesto: 115f, 152, 200, 216
Laraño: 87, 166–169, 171
López Borricón, Don Francisco (bishop of Modoñedo): 113
Magic and popular superstitions: 19, 23, 104ff, 115f, 119f, 186, 211
Marchand, French General: 53, 71, 76, 127, 135
Martínez Salazár, Andrés: 216f
Maucune, General: 66f, 181
Maria Cristina, Queen Regent: 9, 117, 128, 150, 152f, 155, 164f
Miño Division, Alarmas: and anti-French guerrilleros: 29, 35, 40, 56, 58, 66, 69f, 56f, 61, 63, 70, 71,138
Moidore: 18, 25n, 61, 63, 179, 205
Mon, Alejandro: 88, 122–127, 128, 138f, 140, 147–155, 162, 165, 167, 173f, 179, 193f, 195, 199, 212f, 215f
Mondoñedo: 111, 113
Moore, Sir John: 51f, 51n, 60, 79
Morillo, Pablo: 57, 70, 99
Murray, John (London Publisher): 92
Muzquiz, Don Rafael (Santiago Archbishop): 180f
Napoleon, see Bonaparte, Napoleon
Narvaez, Ramón: 122, 150, 165, 173
Nelson, Lord: 14, 23
Ney, Michel: 39, 51f, 57, 62, 63–72, 73, 75f, 78, 127, 135, 139, 141, 166f, 179, 209
Nosotros (Radical newspaper): 152–155, 193f, 200
Ofalia, Count (Prime Minister of Spain): 117f, 122, 124, 128, 149–155, 156, 160, 188
Oporto: 32–36, 43f, 49, 54–62, 63, 69f, 80, 209
Padre Padilla: 194
Palarea, General: 151f
Pilgrims and Pilgrimage to Santiago: 66n, 93–100, 109, 111, 131+n, 133f, 168n, 211

Pillage, plunder and looting: 32ff, 37, 39f, 43f, 48f, 50, 53, 56, 60ff, 62n, 63–72, 73–76, 135, 166, 179, 210

Prison ships (*'pontones'*) at Lisbon, see Jails and prisons

Quijote, Don: 216

Rey Romero, Francisco: 25, 100, 104ff, 120, 156–159, 161f, 186, 195 216

Ramos, Ramón and Andrés (Galician Carlists): 138, 161

Sandino (Coruña tax inspector): 166f, 217

San Roque hospital: 53, 82–85, 94, 104f, 106f, 131–135, 136–144, 148, 152, 154, 167, 179f, 186f, 189ff, 194f

Seven Bellotas (Asturian area): 112, 211

Sintra Convention: 37, 51n

Solano, General: 32f, 36, 41, 206, 207

Soult, Nicolas Jean de Dieu: 39, 49, 51–62, 63f, 69f, 78, 135, 209

Swiss troops and mercenaries: 3, 16, 42f, 48, 58

Syphilis: 132ff, 213f

Taranco y Llano, General Francisco: 32ff, 36, 43f, 206

Traba, Antonio da, see Finisterra

Treasure hunting beliefs, see: Magic and popular superstitions

Tuy: 33, 54, 57, 61, 66

Valdés, Jerónimo: 86, 138f, 160f, 187, 215(!)

Vigo: 49, 53, 57, 61, 66, 69, 108, 210

Vivas, José: 65, 68

Voto de Santiago: 99

Walloon Guard: 16, 18, 40–44, 48, 73, 206f, 208

Wellington, Arthur Wellesley, Duke of: 37, 40, 48f, 51n, 58, 70, 206

Widows of Comares: 151f

Zahori: 4, 115f, 119f, 137, 152, 167, 194, 200

Acknowledgements

J OHANN GOETHE was terribly mistaken when he claimed that books are produced '5 % by inspiration and 95 % by transpiration'. In reality, at least half the hard labour is done by friends, who contribute their knowledge, offer their sage advice, and patiently endure the frenzied chatter of the obsessed and frustrated author. It would therefore be unforgivable not to bestow due praise on those who helped so much in the writing of *The Treasure Hunter of Santiago*.

For over a decade now, Ann Ridler from Warborough, England, has been my guide, mentor and friend. She saved me from countless blunders, coached me through the mine-fields of my wilder ambitions, and caught every mistake in logic, length and the English language. Few people have such energy, few such stamina, and none such dedication as this unstoppable, untiring, hurricane editor of the *George Borrow Bulletin*.

Juan Campos Calvo-Sotelo, author of the excellent book of nautical drama *Naufragos de Antaño*, is the sort of friend and colleague every investigator can only dream of. He not only shared my intense curiosity for the case of Benedict Mol, but also my many ventures into obscure, out-of-the-way archives and libraries. It was he who first discovered the files on the Laraño treasure hunt in the *Archivo del Reino de Galicia*; but being the generous man he is, he ceded these finds to me without a second thought, although he might have used them, with full justice, for his own book.

As long ago as the summer of the year 2000, I had the privilege and the pleasure first to show my groundbreaking discovery of the *Eco* articles to Antonio Giménez Cruz. Ever since, this great expert on the era and most prominent Spanish Borrovian, has helped me out in a hundred ways great and small.

Four true friends have sacrificed their precious time to read through the various barbarous drafts of the work. Marco Martens from Amsterdam and Ronald Lamars from Utrecht hacked their way, *machete*-style, through the jungle of the first version, showing me how to straighten the story-line and stick to the narrative in hand. Eagle-eyed and infallible M.B. Mencher from Denton, England, close-read the text twice to weed out the many faults in the English language committed by this Dutch Anglo-phoney. Colin Davies, from Pontevedra, Spain, then went to work on the final draft with his relentless wry humour and unforgiving judgement, forcing me to behave like a responsible author to his honoured readers. If any word is spelled correctly, if any reasoning is valid, and if any chapter ever *ends*, it owes more to their concerted efforts, than to any talent of mine.

Many other friends unselfishly contributed essential bits and pieces to research and writing. Juan-Carlos Otero from Santiago brought in his astronomical knowledge to calculate the date of the full moon in August 1837 when Borrow met Benedict Mol in the Alameda of Santiago. Professor Simon Hopkins of Jerusalem University enlightened me on the origins and development of the Arabic word *Zahori*. The Santiago architect Xosé '*Cheche*' Allegue made available the working paper of Santiago's *Servicio de Rehabilitación* on the San Roque complex, so necessary for a good description of the setting of the treasure hunt.

As always, archivists and librarians proved to be the most helpful subspecies of the human kind. The staffs of the *Archivo Histórico de la Universidad*, of the *Archivo Diocesano*, and of the *Biblioteca Xeral*, all in Santiago, were invariably friendly, willing, obliging and efficient. Among the very many, I owe special thanks to Concha Varela Orol, Manuel Facal, Pancho Valle-Inclán and his good buddy Manuel, the most cheerful magazine manager I ever knew. I also owe gratitude to Xosé Ramón Lema Bendaña for his tip that the *Monte de Santa Susana* outside Compostela also used to be known as *Monte de Boa Vista* in the past. Lastly, the head archivist in the reading room of the *Archivo del Reino de Galicia* in Coruña, whose name I unfortunately never learned, brought to my attention the letter from Andrés Martinez Salazar to Prime Minister Canovas on the destruction of the Captain-General's archive, described in chapter 21.

Special mention must be made of Marcial Gondar Portasany from Souto, near Brión, for his tenacious efforts to get *The Treasure Hunter* published in Gallego. Fruitless as his dogged attempts ultimately proved to be, they nevertheless did strengthen my faltering determination to continue with the challenge of the book.

Many scions of that 'small but fierce tribe of Borrovians' have over the years helped me out with research, tips and support. Although the honour-roll is really too long to reproduce in full, I should not fail to mention Ken Barrett, Tom Bean, Kathleen Cann, David Chandler, Michael Collie, David Fernández de Castro, the late Sir Angus Fraser, Richard Hitchcock, Ian Robertson and Phyllis Stanley; all of whom in one way or another contributed substantially to the book.

The Treasure Hunter would not have been published had I not received, once again, the most valuable and generous support from Andrew Dakyns and Clive Wilkins-Jones, fellow Trustees with Dr. Ridler of the George Borrow Trust. Nor would it have appeared in such a splendid shape, had I not had as my publisher Paul Durrant, a magician of the screen and keyboard, able to squeeze beauty out of the darkest mud.

Franja Shilova from Amsterdam, painter to my writing, yin to my yang when it comes to illustrated texts, once again marshalled her tremendous talent to produce the cover illustration painting which graces this edition.

Finally: I owe more than words can express to Palmyra Martínez Espuig, the best human being I have met in my life-time, whose love, kindness and patience is the best proof known to me that God does indeed exist.

You are the lips of April
That kindly kissed the world awake
From dark and dreamless slumber

Estrar, Brion (Spain), May 2010